Confederate Raider in the North Pacific

Murray Morgan has written 19 books, most of which focus on Pacific Northwest and Alaskan history. *Skid Road*, *The Dam*, and *Puget's Sound* were on the Washington Centennary list of "100 Outstanding Books" about the state. *Over Washington*, his most recent work, has sold more than 60,000 copies.

Born in Tacoma in 1916, Murray earned a BA at the University of Washington (1937) and an MS from Columbia University (1942). He has had a long and distinguished career as a writer, newspaper reporter, and college instructor, and currently is a frequent book reviewer for the *Tacoma News Tribune*. Murray along with Rosa, his wife and collaborator, lives and writes in a remodelled dance hall on Trout Lake between Tacoma and Seattle. His high-seas tale of the C.S.S. *Shenandoah* originally appeared in 1948.

"If you want to go on a long salt water cruise, this is your book . . . The ship and its crew deserve this revealing book about them."—*The Commonweal*

"Murray Morgan's book is a valuable addition to Americana. Based on extensive research, entertainingly written, it resurrects an almost forgotten achievement."—*New York Herald Tribune*

"All this valuable original source material was mined, worked over, and sifted into its present form in a most workmanlike manner and the result is a book that reads like a most entertaining novel."—*San Francisco Chronicle*

Confederate Raider in the North Pacific

The Saga of the C.S.S. *Shenandoah,* 1864-65

Murray Morgan

Washington State University Press
Pullman, Washington

Washington State University Press, Pullman, Washington
99164-5910

WSU Press Reprint Series, first printing 1995

Originally published under the title *Dixie Raider: The Saga of the C.S.S. Shenandoah*, by E.P. Dutton & Co., Inc., New York, 1948.

Printed and bound in the United States of America on pH neutral, acid-free paper.

Library of Congress Cataloging-in-Publication Data
Morgan, Murray Cromwell, 1916-
[Dixie raider]
Confederate raider in the north Pacific : the saga of the C.S.S. Shenandoah, 1864-65 / Murray Morgan.
p. cm.
Originally published: Dixie raider. New York : E.P. Dutton, 1948.
Includes bibliographical references.
ISBN 0-87422-123-4 (alk. paper)
1. Shenandoah (Cruiser) 2. United States—History—Civil War, 1861-1865—Naval operations, Confederate. 3. Privateering—Bering Sea—History—19th century. 4. Bering Sea—History, Naval.
I. Title.
E599.S5M7 1995
973.7'57—dc20 95-622
CIP

Cover illustration: The *Shenandoah* towing prisoners from three burning whaling vessels in Bering Strait, June 25, 1865. *Official Records of the Union and Confederate Navies in the War of the Rebellion* (Series I, Vol. III).

For Rosa
Then and Now

CONTENTS

BERING SEA
GREENLAND
ALASKA
CANADA
ALEUTIAN IS.
Atlantic
Ocean
UNITED STATES
NEW YORK
AZORES
MADEIRA
"LAUREL"
"SEA KING"
SAN FRANCISCO
HAWAIIAN IS.
BARRACOUTA
END OF CRUISE OF
AUG. 2 1865
SPOKEN
WAR
CAPE VERDE IS.
"ALINA"
"CHARTER OAK"
"KATE PRINCE"
"ADELAIDE"
EQUATOR
SOUTH AMERICA
SOCIETY IS.
SAMOA IS.
VALPARAISO
CAPE HORN
Pacific Ocean

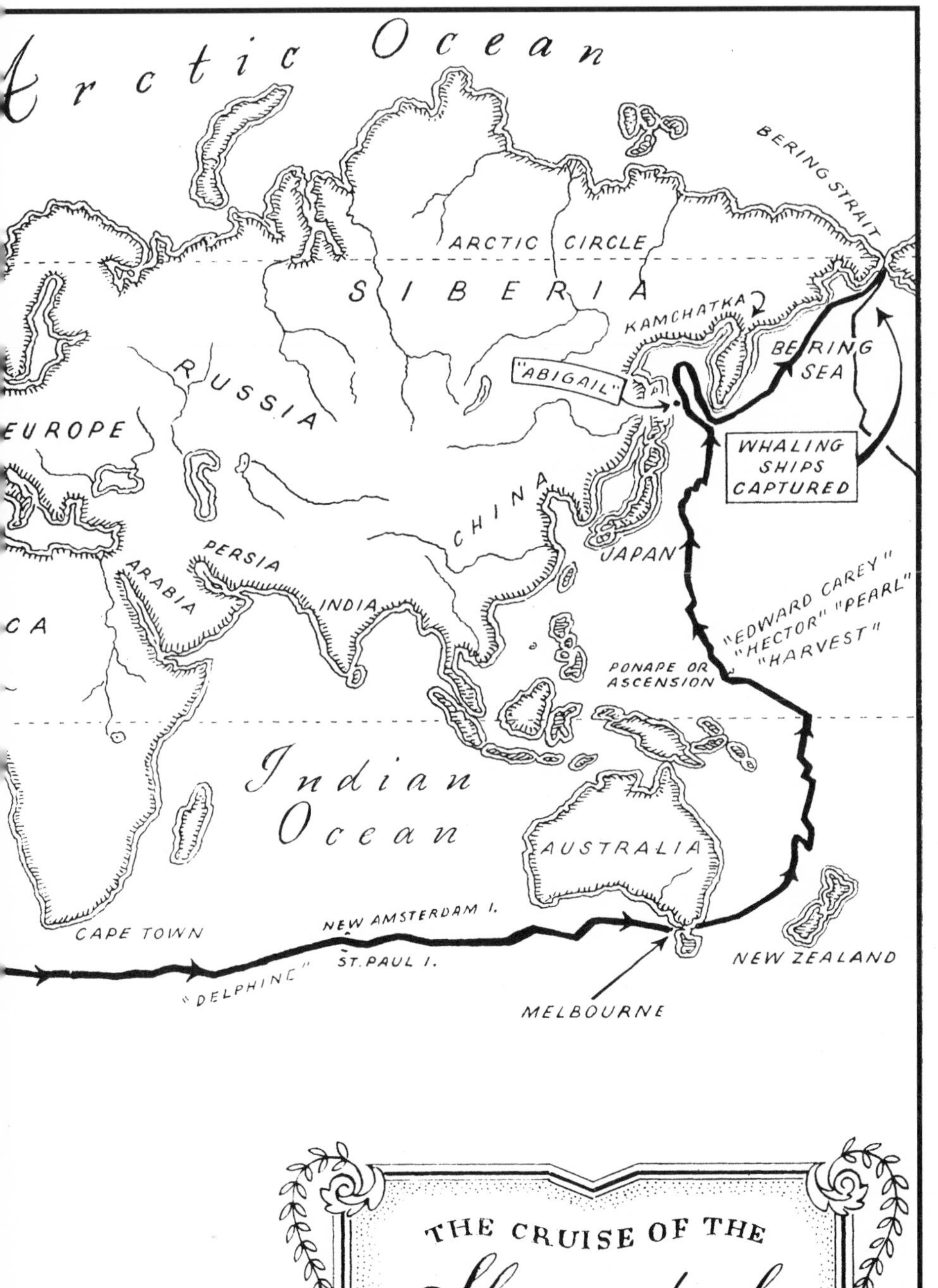
Arctic Ocean
BERING STRAIT
ARCTIC CIRCLE
SIBERIA
KAMCHATKA
BERING SEA
"ABIGAIL"
RUSSIA
EUROPE
WHALING SHIPS CAPTURED
CHINA
JAPAN
PERSIA
ARABIA
"EDWARD CAREY" "HECTOR" "PEARL" "HARVEST"
INDIA
CA
PONAPE OR ASCENSION
Indian Ocean
AUSTRALIA
NEW AMSTERDAM I.
CAPE TOWN
ST. PAUL I.
NEW ZEALAND
"DELPHINE"
MELBOURNE

THE CRUISE OF THE
Shenandoah
BASED ON A CHART DRAWN BY
JACOB WELLS AFTER ONE PLANNED
BY CAPTAIN WADDELL
C.S.S. SHENANDOAH'S
OUTWARD PASSAGE
TO BERING STRAIT
HOMEWARD PASSAGE

Confederate Raider in the North Pacific

ESCAPE

AT ELEVEN o'clock on the morning of Friday, October 7, 1864, a young Virginian in a neat, well-worn suit sat alone at a table in the coffeehouse of Wood's Hotel in the High Holborn district of London. There was little about him that would attract notice, which was well, for he wanted to escape detection.

The Virginian had arrived in London the night before on the train from Liverpool, after a trip that seemed even slower to him than to the other passengers. He hurried to Wood's Hotel and registered as George Brown, which was not his name, then went at once to his room and stayed there until morning when he put in his appearance at the coffeehouse. All this was according to his instructions.

Now, sitting at the table, he nervously played with his handkerchief, pulling a corner of it through the buttonhole of his coat. This accomplished, he opened the copy of the *Times* he had been told to carry. The news under the heading LATEST INTELLIGENCE AMERICA was two weeks old; it was not calculated to encourage a Confederate agent: General Sheridan had galloped to Winchester in time to rally the Union troops, and they were driving Jubal Early's army down the Shenandoah Valley. William Tecumseh Sherman was at Atlanta preparing to move on Charleston. A Confederate plan, daring and elaborate, to capture a Great Lakes steamer and liberate the Southern prisoners of war on Johnstown Island had backfired, and there were some new faces in the island prison. Rumors of peace in America had caused a sharp break in British stocks.

A businessman, carrying a packet of papers, entered the coffeehouse and stood for a moment studying the patrons. His eyes stopped on the young man reading the paper, a handkerchief in his buttonhole. The newcomer crossed to the table. "Is this Mr. Brown?"

The Confederate agent looked up. "Is this Mr. Wright?"

"Yes."

"I am George Brown," the young man said, rising and offering his hand. "Please come with me." He led the way to his room, locked the door, tested it, and, turning to his visitor, handed him a letter. He watched Wright read it. The letter identified the bearer as Lieutenant William C. Whittle, Jr., Confederate States Navy, executive officer on the projected raider *Shenandoah;* it informed the Englishman that he could talk freely before Whittle and give him any information he desired.

Richard Wright was not the type of man usually involved in conspiracy. A Liverpool merchant, prosperous and proud of his family, he had a burgher's respect for safety and six per cent. But he also had investments in cotton, and an American son-in-law who was partner in the Liverpool firm that served as the Confederate bank abroad. Fear for his fortune and love of his family had led this solid citizen down strange paths; for the past month he had eschewed the open dealings of the counting house and gone about his business with the indirectness and caution of a confidence man. The climax of his underground activity had been the purchase of a ship, the *Sea King*, 222 feet long and weighing 1160 tons. A merchantman, built to carry troops and tea, she was one of the fastest ships afloat. Her papers were in his hand.

The plot was simple. Having purchased the *Sea King* with money supplied by his son-in-law's Confederate firm, Mr. Wright would sell her to the Confederates after she was out of British waters. A second British ship, carrying officers, sailors, and armament, would leave Liverpool and meet the *Sea King* off the African coast, and on the high sea the merchantman would change to a man-of-war, from the peaceful *Sea King* into the raider *Shenandoah.* Thus the letter of the British law preventing the sale of armed ships to belligerents would be observed.

Though uncomplicated, the plan called for perfect timing and absolute secrecy. Union warships hovered off the British coast, alert for embryo cruisers. Union spies were thick on the waterfront, ready to relay fact or suspicion about any vessel to the American Embassy.

Except for her captain, no one aboard the *Sea King* knew her mission. None of the Confederate officers had gone near her since she docked in London after her maiden voyage to the Far East. Her preparations were for an ordinary cruise to Bombay with a load of coal. But though the Southerners had stayed away from her until now, one man, young Whittle, had to be smuggled past the Union spies and onto the ship before she sailed for her African rendezvous. As her future executive officer, he needed to make the trip in her to learn what changes were necessary to transform a cargo vessel armed only with two twelve-pound signal guns into a raider destined for duty in the Pacific.

Together the young Virginian and the old Englishman went over the *Sea King's* papers. Built only the year before, she had recently returned from her maiden voyage. On her outward run she had transported British troops to New Zealand, then gone north to pick up a cargo of tea, which she hauled back to London in seventy-nine days. A full-rigged ship, built to outspeed the Yankee Clippers in the Far Eastern trade, she could make sixteen knots under sail, and her 150-horsepower engines would drive her at nine knots in complete calm. Her log showed a one-day cruise of 330 miles. Her propeller could be detached and hoisted out of water so as not to mar her streamline when under sail. Her boilers would condense 500 gallons of fresh water a day. Because she was designed partly as a troop transport, she had ample room for the oversized crew needed on a man-of-war. Her papers were in order, her crew was signed. She stood ready to clear for Bombay with a load of coal.

After examining the papers, Whittle and Wright left the hotel and strolled down Fleet Street to a spot overlooking the East India Dock, where the *Sea King* lay moored. She was a beautiful ship, three-masted, her hull long and narrow and freshly painted a shining black. She looked fast to Whittle — and he was a specialist in fast ships.

As a twenty-year-old junior officer Whittle had been aboard the *Nashville,* first Confederate ship to run the blockade to England. He was still aboard when on the return journey she outraced the Federal cruisers and slipped into dock at Beaufort, North Carolina. With a Union army driving on the port and a Union squadron standing off the harbor, Whittle defied orders of his superior officer to burn the ship. Instead he stole her and, with a quarter of the regular crew, put to sea.

In the dark of night the twenty-year-old boy raced the *Nashville* across the bar at fourteen miles an hour, expecting every moment to tear the bottom off the ship. The enemy cruisers discovered him. He steered between them so they dared not open up with broadsides lest they sink each other. Once clear, he outran pursuit. A day later, in attempting to bring the *Nashville* into Georgetown at night, he ran her on a spit. A squadron of cavalry had sighted her entering the harbor; when she went aground, they surrounded her. Whittle gave orders for his men to rig a hot water hose — the *Nashville* was unarmed — and stand by to repel boarders. But the cavalry was Confederate, the ship was safe, and young Whittle was a hero.

This exploit led to opportunities for others. He had slipped through the blockade with plans for ironclad rams which the South hoped would destroy the Union Navy. Once, near New Orleans, he had been captured; he escaped under gunfire. By 1864, though only twenty-four, he was accustomed to responsibility, to danger, and to conspiratorial secrecy.

Whittle went with Richard Wright to an obscure pub. They were joined by a thickset man in the blue suit of a merchant captain, Peter Corbett, master of the *Sea King*. He reported everything in readiness. The final touches were put on the get-away plan. Mr. Wright was to board the *Sea King* at once; he would stay on her until she reached the Channel port of Deal. Whittle was to come aboard after dark, just before the ship sailed. He would be carried as supercargo; to everyone aboard the ship he would be George Brown, the agent for the owners of the coal that was the ship's only cargo.

The three men shook hands and left the pub separately.

At three o'clock on Saturday morning, "George Brown" checked out of Wood's Hotel and walked along the quiet streets to the waterfront. The *Sea King* stood at the dock gates, ready to go into the river. For a moment the Virginian stood in the shadows of the warehouse and studied the dock, then, his step wobbly as any shellback returning from a last night ashore, he walked over to the ship and crawled over her side at the fore-rigging. No one challenged him, no one raised an alarm. He was just another sailor making his ship at the last moment. Within an hour the *Sea King* pushed out into the Thames and swung downstream.

So far so good.

2

Saturday afternoon a telegram reached Liverpool announcing that the *Sea King* had cleared the Thames Estuary without incident.

As night came, a low fog rolled up the Mersey. It hung wet and chilling over the city and turned the gaslights of Liverpool into golden balls that hung from vanished posts, illuminating only a circle of mist. A messenger hurried through the fog. He called at hotels, at genteel homes that took in boarders, at dives where seamen had rooms. At each stop he gave a man a slip of paper — a receipt for thirty pounds in payment for passage to Nassau on the British steamship *Laurel.* Without other word the messenger hurried on.

The men who received the slips wasted no time. Their rooms were almost bare; they had been without baggage for days. They put on their jackets, said casual good-byes to fellow-roomers, and walked out into the fog as though for a few hours instead of months, or perhaps forever.

They issued singly from the hotels, the rooming houses, the dives. They walked with their collars turned up, the brims of their hats pulled down. If their paths converged, they did not speak; it was forbidden to speak. Wordless and excited, they strode through the fog, down the cobblestoned lanes toward the river. The sound of their heels rang between the houses, and the sound of their heartbeats boomed in their ears. They crossed Bath Street, the railroad tracks, and gathered in a little knot at Prince's Landing Stage.

A tug, the *Storm King,* was waiting. The men flashed their receipts before an attendant and swung down onto the deck. In silence they stood at the rail as the tug nosed through the fog and nuzzled up to the steamship *Laurel.* The tug skipper was puzzled by his uncommunicative passengers. People going on voyages were usually talkative; these men had said not a word.

As each man climbed aboard the *Laurel,* he showed his receipt again and was directed to a cabin. In each cabin was a crate, marked with a diamond and a number corresponding to the one on the man's receipt. Though the markings indicated general merchandise, the boxes contained trunks of clothing. A few of the men opened their boxes and looked at the gray and gold uniforms of officers in the Confederate Navy. Others sat quietly on the bunks and waited. The hours went slowly, but by midnight everyone was on board. Steam was raised. At four o'clock Sunday morning, the *Laurel* pulled her hook from the muddy bottom of Crosby channel. It was daylight when they dropped the pilot off Holyhead. "You've a good bunch of men on this trip," the pilot told Captain J. F. Ramsey of the *Laurel*. "They know their places and they don't ask no questions."

Not until the pilot boat was out of sight against the purple of the shore did the celebration begin. The passengers gathered in the salon. The captain of the *Laurel* came in and received riotous congratulations on getting them safely to sea. The Confederates were fortunate in having Ramsey in their service: not only was he a first lieutenant in the rebel navy but he held a license in the British Merchant Marine — an ideal position for a blockade runner.

Most of the officers who were to take over the *Sea King* were still in their teens or early twenties. Few had seen previous action, and now, whatever doubts they felt they expressed as confidence. But among them were a handful of veterans, men who had been aboard the raider *Alabama* when she sank more enemy vessels than any ship in history, and aboard her, too, when she went down in the English channel under the pounding of the big guns aboard the chain-mailed cruiser *Kearsarge*. These men, tempered by battle and the sea, took their drinks quietly during the celebration aboard the *Laurel*. Most silent of all was James Iredell Waddell, at forty the oldest in the group, their leader, and the only man aboard who knew their destination.

James Waddell was a big, stubborn, hot-tempered man. Standing six feet one, weighing two hundred pounds, he walked with a slight limp. Twenty-three years before, when he was only seventeen, he had challenged another midshipman at Norfolk Naval School to a duel. A bullet was still embedded in his hip.

Huge and handsome and brave, the great-grandson of Hugh Waddell – "the foremost soldier of the colonies" – and the grandson of General Nash, who died on the field at Germantown, he was a natural combat leader. No thinker, though not unintelligent, Waddell was at his best in action. He had first heard cannon fired in anger while aboard the brig-of-war *Somers,* in the Mexican War, while she was supporting General Taylor's forces at Vera Cruz. He was an excellent navigator and, after the Mexican war, had distinguished himself as the acting commander of a fever-wracked crew on the supply ship *Release* off the Panama Isthmus. Describing his exploit long afterward he wrote:

> I was convalescent from the fever. From day to day someone was stricken, until the vessel's complement of men was reduced to one seaman and one boy. I returned to duty. The seaman and myself alternately took the wheel. Our supply of quinine was exhausted; the captain appreciated the danger to which his command was exposed and had prudently close-reefed the topsails; we were favored by fair and stiff winds, a gale might perhaps have been fatal – some of our people were delirious, none able to lend a hand; we fell in with a vessel and secured a small quantity of quinine. The Captain was stricken with the fever and I was the only officer on duty to care for the vessel. Before reaching the port of Matanzas, the Captain directed me to go for that port; I had never been there, I had a chart of the harbor. The vessel entered the harbor when a pilot came alongside; he discovered our condition and left us. The Captain had become delirious from fever and he came on deck in his shirt tail. I feared he would go overboard. He however looked astern and then returned to his cabin. There was nothing left me but to undertake the pilotage, and I succeeded in taking the vessel safely to the anchorage.

Marriage and the wealth of his Maryland bride calmed Waddell. He put in ten quiet years as an instructor of navigation at Annapolis. When the Civil War broke he was with the United States Far Eastern squadron based on China. He resigned his commission while en route home – announcing his decision from the island of St. Helena. In a letter to the Secretary of the Navy he said, "I wish it to be understood that no doctrine of the right of secession, no wish for disunion of the States impel me, but simply because, my home is the home of my people in the South, and I cannot bear arms against it or them."

When the Naval Department refused his back pay unless he signed a promise not to bear arms against the North, he considered it "an attempt on the part of the Hon. Gideon Welles to bribe me. . . . I neglected to make any promises to that debased official." He decided to join the Confederate Navy.

A friend informed me, if I wanted to get South, to visit Marsh Market, Baltimore, and enter said market at the sound end, go to the first beef stall on the right, approach and enquire of a fat man, "the price of beef." I followed the directions, and my fat friend's reply was, "Do you want to go South?" Yes. "I will call for you tomorrow evening about eight o'clock and take you to Carroll Island, a schooner will be there to go to Virginia; where shall I call?" Hoffman Street, No. —.

I had arranged with a friend to meet me in Baltimore if I could find a way to go South. My Baltimore friend telegraphed to a friend in Annapolis, "Send the sample of tobacco," which telegram passed into my friend's hands, and he joined me a short time before I took leave of my wife and child.

We were taken to Carroll Island in a torrent of rain in a two-horse team, and on the journey the driver asked if I was in the vehicle. He said, handing me a small pellet in tinfoil, "Give that to Mr. Benjamin." I took it and wondered who sent it, and who could the driver be.

We reached Carroll Island at midnight, the rain still falling, and we drew up in front of a log cabin half the roof tumbled in, and found ten persons waiting for the schooner. I had paid the butcher one hundred dollars passage money for myself and friend. At daylight a schooner came to anchor and we boarded her, determined to press her into service and sail away for the sacred soil. The schooner was the right one, and her Yankee skipper was for money making, notwithstanding his love for the Union. When we reached the Potomac River, the McClelland fleet of steamboats were on the way for Washington City. I recommended that the people go below, the skipper and myself remaining on deck. We had not yet reached the entrance to the Big Wycomic River, nor did we intend to enter that river while anything warlike was in sight.

Finally things looked clear; we pushed in and were favored with an east wind; we followed the channel by stakes which were driven at intervals along its margin, but we had not pursued our course long, before a boat was seen advancing from the north bank; it had one sitter, and I hailed, "Are you a pilot?" Yes. "Come alongside." We waited for him and he came on board and informed us of a Federal cavalry force in Westmoreland county, and that he would take us to a place where we might safely leave the vessel.

We landed on the north side of a creek into which he had run the schooner, and I was delegated to visit a house near the spot of landing, and learn the news. There was nought about the house or its surroundings to indicate whether anyone was home. I reached the front door and waited for a reply to my rap. An old man, of kind demeanor, opened the door and said, "Friend or foe?" Friends. "Come in friends." I entered. The old man's wife sat at one corner of the fire place, and a lad of sixteen years sat at the other corner, dressed in a Confederate gray uniform, infantry.

I was in the act of stating my mission, when turning to address the old man, he said, "That boy is my grandson, he was in the Battle of Bull Run, and was sent home to die." And a big tear rolled down his furrowed cheeks. "We are old and alone, they can't hurt us, our sons, all of them are gone, some to return no more, others in the army, where they should be," and with that he braced himself up and looked like a man.

I then told him we wanted to get to Richmond, and could he not put us in the way to reach Rappahannock? He furnished us with two vehicles to go as far as a village where we could hire wagons for the journey. We safely reached the village, and there we hired a wagon to take us to the ferry opposite Rappahannock. Our driver was a Yankee and a Union man; we reached the ferry before sunset and found a guard boat, which ferried us to the other side of the Rappahannock River, where we were put in the guard house until the Commanding Officer was appraised of our presence, who ordered the strangers to his quarters. We were accompanied to the hotel by an officer. A private of a Baltimore artillery company recognized us, and we were released and ate supper.

We proceeded in a wagon to a place on the York River railroad, and were fortunate in meeting the train for Richmond. That evening we supped in the Spotswood Hotel, and I delivered the tinfoil pellet to Mr. Benjamin. The following day we visited General Winder, and were recognized, and we visited the Navy Department and entered our applications for commissions in the Navy, similar to those we had relinquished in the Federal Navy. I received my commission as a Lieutenant in the Confederate States Navy, March 27, 1862.

Waddell's Civil War record had not been marked by much success. He saw service at New Orleans but was evacuated when Farragut's fleet was approaching the city. When it was remembered that in the hasty retreat everyone had forgotten to destroy a ram which was being built for the Confederate Navy, Waddell returned in an open boat and blew the ship up just as the Union Navy entered the town. Later he served as an ordnance officer at the battle of Drury's Bluff.

I was then ordered to report to the Navy Department, and with other officers, I was consulted as to the best manner of capturing the enemy's iron vessels, should they enter Charleston Harbor. This was so difficult a conundrum that I gave it up at once, and I answered the Secretary's conundrum by volunteering to attempt the capture, after I had seen the monitors. The senior officers evidently did not relish my volunteering, for one of them said, "We are all ready to volunteer."

I was ordered to Charleston, and ordered by Lieutenant

> Webb, who was in command of what was then called "the forlorn hope" to organize the force, while he looked up steamboats, boats, etc. Colonel Kilt's Infantry regiment, thirteen hundred strong, and all of them voters in Kilt's congressional district, volunteered to fight the monitors *single-handed.* The monitors did not enter the Harbor.

In May, 1863, Waddell slipped through the blockade and went to England. The ship on which he was to serve was held by the British; he had to wait for another. It was a long wait, an eternity of seventeen months. But now the trial was over. He had a command. In his pocket was a letter which began:

> You are about to proceed upon a cruise in the far-distant Pacific, into the seas and among the islands frequented by the great American whaling fleet, a source of abundant wealth to our enemies and a nursery for their seamen. It is hoped that you may be able to greatly damage and disperse that fleet, even if you do not succeed in utterly destroying it. . . .

And ended:

> You have a fine-spirited body of young men under your command, and may reasonably expect to perform good and efficient service. I earnestly wish you Godspeed. I am, sir, your obedient servant,
> *James D. Bulloch*

3

Three men in England knew the full secret behind the departure of the two ships — Whittle on the *Sea King,* Waddell on the *Laurel,* and a half-bald, chop-whiskered gentleman named James D. Bulloch, who stood on a Liverpool hill and watched the running lights of the *Laurel* move down Crosby channel with the outgoing tide.

Bulloch, the naval agent and spy-master of the Confederate Secret Service abroad, was an almost handsome man, with the simple, uncomplicated face of a zealot. An archconservative, reactionary to the point of fanaticism, he was also competent, hardheaded, and capable of transforming the surging flood of his emotions into applied energy. He hated all things Northern, though his sister had married a New Yorker named Roosevelt and had a young son, Theodore, who prayed nightly for God to blast the Southern arms.

Bulloch had a big job. His assignment was to build or buy a navy for an unrecognized nation which had no ships, no shipyards, no ports not under blockade, no naval academy, no easily negotiable source of wealth. He had done well. Studying Britain's Foreign Enlistment Act, which banned recruiting on English soil, he had spotted a loophole through which he slipped a succession of merchant ships – the *Florida,* the *Georgia,* the *Alabama* – to be met and armed on the high seas. He almost succeeded in buying two English-built ironclad rams capable of dispersing the blockading fleets off the Southern ports and – he had dreamed – of steaming up the Potomac to bombard Washington.

But as the war tide turned, as doubts began to grow in England that Jefferson Davis had "made a nation," as high officials began to ponder the precedent Britain was setting in supplying ships with which a minor naval power could destroy the merchant marine of a major power, Bulloch's work became more difficult. Officials failed to blink at the right moments, the laws were interpreted strictly. And Union spies were everywhere.

Though he had personally planned every detail of the *Sea King's* escape, Bulloch had been afraid to go near her. He had seen her the previous year while she lay in the Clyde loading for her first voyage. But so tight was the net of Northern agents that he dared not even go to London when the vessel returned there. So he had arranged for Richard Wright to buy her for £45,000.

Bulloch had inspected the *Laurel.* She was a fast little ship, an iron screw steamer, built for the packet service between

Liverpool and Ireland, and he had crossed the Irish channel in her. Capable of steaming at thirteen knots, she was strong, roomy, a good sea boat. Her draft of water was moderate. After delivering crew and armament to the *Sea King,* she was to become a blockade runner.

Bulloch purchased the *Laurel* and put her in the hands of Henry Lafone, a Liverpool shipping agent, who advertised her for a voyage to Havana carrying freight and a limited number of passengers. Bills of lading were issued in the ordinary way, passage money was paid and tickets written for the Confederates, under assumed names. Not even the clerks in the shipping office saw anything unusual in the preparations for the voyage.

But had there been a slip anywhere? Would a Union ship be waiting off the Mersey? Bulloch could only hope the answers were no. His agents in Europe had reported that the U.S.S. *Niagara* was cruising in the English channel. She might be on a routine voyage, or she might be waiting to pounce. Though the *Sea King* might pass inspection if intercepted, the *Laurel* certainly could not; her hold was full of contraband – shot and shell, gun carriages, powder, small arms, and, in cases stenciled MACHINERY, were enough cannon to arm a cruiser.

Whatever triumph James Bulloch felt as he watched the lights of the *Laurel* fade out down the foggy Channel must have been tempered with anxiety.

Had Charles Francis Adams learned of the two ships?

4

Charles Francis Adams, the American Minister to Great Britain, was more a precision instrument than a human being. A brilliant, polished New Englander, the son and grandson of presidents, compressed to the hardness of a diamond by the accumulated weight of family tradition, he served as the cutting edge of American diplomacy.

Never had America greater need for such a man. Adams's steamer docked in England the same day that Britain recognized the belligerent rights of the South – a shattering diplomatic defeat for the Union. It seemed only a matter of weeks, perhaps of hours, before formal recognition of the Confederacy as a nation. The faintest hint of a *faux pas* might have brought disaster; but Adams went through the diplomatic minuet with the disdainful precision of a ballet master in a ballroom.

When, eventually, the chaotic industrial power of the North was harnessed to the military machine, the power was also felt behind Adams's diplomacy as he cut at the British foreign policy.

In seeking to stop British naval aid to the South, the stern New Englander did not think of himself as enmeshed in a struggle with the conspiratorial James Bulloch. Adams's fight was against the diplomats of England, not the agents of the South. For generations the Adamses had been America's foremost professional enemies of British policy, and if Charles Francis thought himself involved in a personal contest with anyone – which in so cold and aristocratic a man is unlikely – it was with Lord John Russell, the British Secretary for Foreign Affairs, who had spoken most undiplomatically of "the late Union" and who represented the unofficial hope of top British officials that the South would win, thereby "achieving the diminution of a hostile power."

With stiff, precise notes, Adams prodded Russell into awareness of what British-built cruisers of the Confederacy were doing to the Union Merchant Marine. And though British maritime interests rejoiced at the shipping losses suffered by their greatest competitor, Adams kept reminding the British government that the American government held England responsible for every penny of damages.

The first protests bore little fruit. The *Florida* escaped to sea, the *Alabama* followed her. In 1863 two ironclad rams that Bulloch had ordered from Lairds of Liverpool were about to be launched. Though they were nominally intended for a French purchaser, everyone knew they would eventually join the Confederate Navy. When Adams protested, the British replied that they could not stop the ships so long as they were not armed.

The climax had been reached. In his diary Adams wrote, "I clearly see that a collision must now come of it. . . . The prospect is dark for poor America." The next day he dispatched a cold and challenging note to the British Foreign Minister. It ended with the blunt words, "It would be superfluous in me to point out to your Lordship that this is war. . . ."

But it was not war. While Adams was phrasing his final protest, the British Government was reconsidering. The policy was reversed. The rams were halted. The Government, unable to find any legal excuse for detaining them, purchased the pair for Her Majesty's Navy.

After Adams's triumph in the diplomatic duel over the ironclads, James Bulloch's mission became more difficult. No longer able to work openly and rely on a lenient interpretation of the neutrality law, he had to go underground; and his work was hampered by the sympathy of the British working people for the North. The rich and powerful in England were for the Confederates. The House of Lords was estimated at ten to one in hopes of a Southern victory, the House of Commons, five to one. But the poor and disenfranchised – only one man in twenty-three had the vote – were Northern adherents. At a great meeting of trade unionists in London, the Liberal, John Bright, was cheered tumultuously when he said:

> Privilege has shuddered at what might happen to old Europe if this grand experiment (of American democracy) should succeed. But you, the workman, you striving after a better time, you struggling upwards towards the light with slow and painful

> steps, you have no cause to look with jealousy upon a country which, menaced by the great nations of the globe, is that one where labor has met with the highest honor, and where it has reaped its greatest reward. . . . Impartial history will tell that when your press was mainly written to betray, when your statesmen were hostile, when many of your rich men were corrupt, the fate of a continent and its vast population being in peril, you clung to freedom with an unfaltering trust that God in his infinite mercy will yet make it the heritage of all his children.

These Northern sympathizers were quick to carry waterfront rumors about ships to Union officials. There had been such rumors about the *Sea King*. While she was still on the ways, word reached Thomas Dudley, the American Consul at Liverpool, that she looked like a possible raider, and he had gone to inspect her. Another report came in a curiously roundabout manner. The U.S.S. *Wachusett,* patrolling in the South Atlantic, encountered the *Lydia,* an American whaler, off the coast of Brazil. Commander Napoleon Collins gave the whaler some mail to carry north and, after talking to the skipper, he wrote a short note to the Navy Department:

> Captain Babcock, of the American whaler *Lydia,* was informed by an English merchant at Hobart Town, a man of good standing and reliable, whom he feels sure would not attempt to deceive him (although it is possible that the merchant himself might have been deceived), that there was a steam fitting out in England called the *Sea King*. She was to be ready to sail from England by the middle of January. She was to proceed to Australia, calling en route at some place on Van Diemen's Land for coal. Her object was to prey on the whalers in that sea. The merchant received his information from a person who had it from the agent of the vessel. . . .

So American agents had been watching the black-hulled *Sea King*. But they saw nothing unusual. No one heard of her sale to Richard Wright on September 30, or of the power of attorney given her master, Peter Corbett, on October seventh, empowering him to sell her any time within six months for not less than £45,000. Bulloch had put one over.

Only a chance encounter with a Union warship would prevent the *Sea King* and the *Laurel* from reaching their rendezvous.

⸙ 5 ⸙

On the same Saturday morning that the *Sea King* was getting up steam at London, the U.S.S. *Niagara* was cruising off the Dutch port of Flushing, just across the English channel from the mouth of the Thames.

Commodore Thomas Craven planned to go ashore at Flushing and take a packet ship to London; he wanted to talk to the American Minister about the problems of his patrol. But as one of the *Niagara's* small boats was being lowered, the officer of the deck ran up and reported that a large steamer, bark-rigged and flying the Spanish colors, was coming down the Scheldt estuary. While Craven was studying her through his glass, his executive officer repeated a bit of scuttlebutt — he had heard that the acting master had heard a certain Belgian remark a few evenings previously in a Dutch tavern that the Spanish steamer *Cicerone,* then at Antwerp, had taken on board a turret and plating for an ironclad vessel intended for the rebels.

It was a tenuous story, of frayed plausibility, but ironclads were the greatest fear of the Navy. No chances could be taken. Craven ordered his ship to stand in chase of the Spaniard. For eight hours the *Niagara* raced after the *Cicerone.* Before they came within hailing distance, the Spaniard was safe in English waters. Craven decided to keep following her. All day and all night the *Niagara* rode in the wake of the black bark. Sometime during the darkness she passed within a few miles of another black ship, flying the Union Jack. But the *Sea King* and the *Niagara* did not notice each other.

The next morning the *Cicerone* was in neutral waters south of Brighton. The *Niagara* stopped her, boarded her, and sent searching parties into her hold to hunt the turret and iron plating. For three days, seamen scrambled in the Spaniard's holds, seeking contraband but finding nothing. On the twelfth, Commodore Craven went ashore at Dover to wire Adams for instructions. Waiting for him at the Dover Consulate was a message from the Legation at London.

October 11, 1864

Sir: I sent you a telegram about the *Laurel.* The rebels bought her at Liverpool last Tuesday. Captain Semmes (sic) sailed in her on Sunday with eight officers and about 100 men. Forty of them were of the crew of the No. 290, or *Alabama.* She cleared for Matamoras, via Havana and Nassau, which means that she will go anywhere. She took on board in cases six sixty-eight pounders, with the requisite gun carriages, and also small arms. It is doubtless Semmes's purpose to meet and arm some other vessel, as the *Laurel* is not large enough for all the guns, her tonnage being not more than 350. She is new, very strong and very fast, and was built to carry passengers between Liverpool and Sligo, in Ireland. She has one funnel, two masts, is fore-and-aft rigged, has a plain stem, round stern and black hull.

Mr. Dudley, the consul at Liverpool, will take the responsibility of her capture anywhere at sea. I would take her wherever I could find her. I regret I cannot tell where she went from Liverpool.

Benjamin Moran
Secretary of Legation

Commodore Craven released the Cicerone and started for the Channel Islands to look for the *Laurel.* The chase was on.

RENDEZVOUS

FUNCHAL, the main port in the Madeiras island group off northwest Africa, is possibly the most beautiful town in the world. But after forty-eight hours of looking longingly at the curving beach and the whitewashed buildings nestled in the lap of the green-skirted mountains, the crew and passengers on the *Laurel* had had enough of spyglass exploration.

They were not permitted to go ashore. There was only thin pleasure in watching the ox-drawn sleds bounce over the cobblestoned streets, or in seeing other visitors toboggan down the mile-long rock slide from the top of Monte Alto to the center of town. They were not even supposed to speak to the dark-skinned Portuguese boatmen in blue, funnel-shaped caps, cotton shirts, and knee-length linen trousers who paddled out to the *Laurel* in canoes loaded with fish and chickens, tapering bottles of delicate Madeira and jugs of deep red *tinto*, apples and pears, custard-apples and mangoes.

The young men amused themselves with stories of the sea, and by swimming in the warm water of the harbor. At night they watched the fireworks displays staged in honor of the Queen of Portugal's birthday. But for Captain Waddell these were no diversion. He paced the deck, running his hands through his dark hair, stopping from time to time to stare at the shore. He wondered if the American Consul had heard about the suspicious vessel which lay in the harbor and sent no one ashore.

The Portuguese authorities were suspicious. They had come on board after the *Laurel* had taken on some coal and asked pointedly why the ship did not go back to sea. Captain Ramsey had explained that the engine needed repairs. The authorities asked to see the damaged equipment, and Ramsey, a thoughtful man, showed them some broken cogs he had brought along for just such a purpose. The officials took the parts ashore to have new ones made at the government workshop. In another day they would be ready. Waddell wondered what had happened to the *Sea King*. She was not dangerously overdue, but still. . . .

The lookout stationed at the masthead was ordered to report the appearance of any vessels coming in sight of the harbor at night as well as during the day. But hour after hour passed without the expected call. The tension mounted.

Tuesday night, October 18, was a thing of tropic beauty – the weather calm and clear, the moon bright, the air warm. The Confederates on the *Laurel* lolled on the deck, listening to the music floating across the water from the forbidden town. George Harwood, a tough little Englishman who had served aboard the *Alabama*, was repeating the story he told most often – the tale of the fight between the *Alabama* and the *Kearsarge* and how the outcome of the battle turned on a single shell, a shell which lodged in the Union cruiser's sternpost but did not explode.

Suddenly conversation aboard the *Laurel* stopped. The lookout was sliding down from aloft. He ran to Captain Ramsey and reported a ship-rigged vessel in sight. Everyone swarmed into the rigging.

The vessel steamed across the mouth of Funchal anchorage, showing her signal lights. She soon passed out of sight south of the port, but returned within an hour, steaming slowly in the direction she had come from, still burning her lights. Then she was out of sight again.

"That's her," someone said. "That's her."

The few aboard the *Laurel* who had not been let in on the secret of her voyage kept glancing at Waddell, as much as to ask, "Tell us, Captain. It's all out now." The more knowing walked to and fro, turning their quids from cheek to cheek. The tension dissolved in excited laughter and in happy conversations carried on in undertones.

But little could be done before morning. The *Laurel's* papers were in the customhouse ashore, as required by port authorities. They could not be picked up between sundown and sunrise. One by one the men and officers went below until at last only Waddell, of those off duty, was still topside.

As soon as the sun rose, red and hot, from behind the black-crested mountains of Madeira, a man was sent ashore to rout out the customs officials. The fires were kindled in the *Laurel's* furnaces, one anchor was raised, the other hove in to a short stay. While the small boat was still en route to the customs station, the black steamer dipped back into the harbor. She flew the Union Jack, but she also displayed the *Laurel's* signal pennant. The arranged signal. This, without question, was the ship. As she turned to leave the harbor, Waddell could see on her black stern the white lettering, SEA KING — LONDON.

From the bumboats of the Portuguese fruit peddlers rose a shout: "*Otro Alabama! Otro Alabama!*" Another *Alabama!* The cry came as a shock to Waddell. His secret was out already. Everyone in port knew the *Sea King* was to be another Confederate raider. There was no time to lose.

But the port authorities were in no hurry. They did not come aboard with the papers until nearly nine o'clock. "Many were the left-handed blessings bestowed on him for his delay," wrote one of the Confederates. "Five minutes after he had left the ship we were standing out for the *Sea King*."

RENDEZVOUS

↵ 2 ↵

It was a rum voyage, the men on the *Sea King* agreed.

First, the Captain had shipped only unmarried men, the younger the better. Then, he sailed with an almost empty hold – nothing but coal. As soon as the ship was clear of the channel, he ordered her screw raised, the fires banked, and the sails double-reefed. Under easy canvas they had loafed south, as if time weren't money on a sailing ship.

When near Madeira, they had raised steam again, crossed the mouth of Funchal Harbor twice without going in, and spent a night beating back and forth over the silver-flecked sea, killing time until daybreak. When the *Sea King* entered the port the next morning, the supercargo, George Brown, who had acted strangely officious for a coal agent all during the voyage, had suddenly started giving orders, and Captain Corbett had told his men to obey them. He had ordered the quartermaster to hoist the signal pennant for the *Laurel* instead of the *Sea King*. Very strange, that.

Now, back at sea, they were steaming slowly toward the sandy trio of islands known as Las Desertas, a few miles south of Madeira, with the *Laurel* closing in from behind.

The *Laurel,* her engines wide open, churned past, pulling a long wake over the choppy sea. She signaled for the *Sea King* to follow and, after swinging around the little islands, dropped anchor in seventeen fathoms of water in a sheltered cove of Porto Santo, a narrow, scrub-covered island, six miles long and inhabited only by wild goats, seabirds, and a few fishermen.

The crew on the *Sea King* was ordered to prepare for lifting heavy weights. As they erected tackles, rigged purchases to the port main yardarm and readied the preventer braces, the helmsman brought the ship alongside the *Laurel.* The two ships were lashed together. Young Whittle, discarding his role of George Brown, went aboard to meet his fellow officers. Waddell greeted him warmly.

"How is the ship?" he asked.

"A good sailer, but she will take a lot of work."

John Guy, who was to be chief gunner on the raider, went onto the *Sea King* and examined the tackle. "Will it raise three tons?" he asked John Hercus, one of the crewmen.

Hercus whistled. "Three tons! What's your cargo, mate?"

"Cannon."

Hercus whistled again. The men around him looked at each other questioningly. Cannon were queer cargo.

The first box, marked "machinery," was hoisted aboard at three in the afternoon. The heavy case swung in too low and smashed against the bulwark; the rail was ripped loose, the case broken open. A seaman put his hand in and felt the cold metal. "A big 'un."

"Yes," said the gunner, "a sixty-eight pounder."

Everyone worked, the officers with the men. Portuguese fishermen who sailed their small boats alongside were impressed into service. The urgency felt by the Confederate officers transmitted itself to the Englishmen who rode before the mast. Neutral or not, none wanted to be found here by a Union cruiser. By nine at night, the ten tons of guns were aboard. The men knocked off for half an hour's rest – and dinner.

Then back to work in the moonlight. They were handling powder kegs now, and all lights were out. But for those who missed their tobacco there was abundant grog. The cabin boys carried drinks from ship to ship, and the men burned alcohol for energy.

A box slipped from a tackle and burst open on the deck. Twenty-four-pound shot rolled about under foot. Everyone was in too much of a hurry to pick it up. At 2 A.M. the boatswain again ordered a layoff. The men dropped where they were working, too tired even to discuss what was going on. Three hours later they were shaken awake, given more grog, and hustled back to the job. By ten, the decks and holds of the *Sea King* were an untidy arsenal of guns, powder kegs, barrels of shot, tackle, clothing, hard bread, and salt provisions. The last piece of equipment to be swung on board was a large safe. Four men pushed and shoved it aft into the cabin. From its rattling they judged it to be full of silver and gold.

The first mate ordered everyone aft. Uncertain and muttering, the crewmen from the *Sea King* gathered outside the cabin door. If the ship was to be a rebel raider, what of her crew? The door opened. Captain Corbett and Waddell stepped out to face the men. Corbett, stocky and gray-haired, wore the black suit of a merchant captain; he held in his hand the ship's articles. Waddell was in the gray uniform of the Confederacy, two gold bands at the sleeves denoting his rank. The talk hushed.

"Well, men," said Corbett bluntly, "I have sold the ship to the Confederates. She is to belong to their Navy to be a cruiser and burn and destroy merchant vessels and whalers. She is not to fight, men, but only to capture prizes. There will be a first rate chance for any of you young men who will stop by the vessel. All of you men who like to join, I'll give you two months' wages. And this gentleman" – he turned toward Waddell – "is offering good wages. Four pounds a month for able seamen, and ten pounds bounty for joining up. As you are all young men, I advise you to join her, as you will make a fine thing of it. Step forward those who will."

A shuffling of feet, a murmuring – doubt and anxiety, but no volunteers. The angry English voice of Quartermaster John Ellison rose above the uncertain babel. "I agreed with you in London to go to Bombay, Cap'n, which I have my naval certificate to prove. And you, sir, have broken your agreement. Why are we not proceeding to Bombay?"

"Well, men, I cannot help it."

"What of us who do not join?"

"You can come back with me to England," said Corbett.

"No," the quartermaster shouted. "I stop in this ship until I get my money down on the capstan head."

"Well, men, I have no money to pay you."

"You have sold the ship," said Ellison. "What have you done with the money?"

"I have no money to pay you here. You talk too much, Ellison."

"I'll talk a lot more when I get to England. Did you never hear of the Foreign Enlistment Act?"

Waddell was startled by the dissension. A romantic, a believer in the glory of war, he could not understand men who were untempted by adventure. His letter of instructions had predicted he would be able to enlist fifty seamen from the carefully selected crews of the *Sea King* and the *Laurel*. And now — no volunteers.

He had to act before the antagonism smouldering among the men from the *Sea King* burst into open hatred. He raised his hand and stepped forward.

"Men, you are now aboard the Confederate cruiser *Shenandoah*." He read his commission as commander of the ship. Then, trying to keep the impatience and worry out of his voice, he outlined the advantages of shipping aboard the *Shenandoah*. She was to be a raider, not a fighter; her purpose was to destroy Union shipping, not to engage Union men-of-war. There would be little danger (he hated to make a point of that). The pay was good. In addition to being paid for their next two months as sailors on the *Sea King*, they would also be paid as Confederate seamen and receive a bounty for joining. If luck were with them, there would be prize money from the ships they took. The food would be better than aboard any merchantman — the pick of the provisions from the captured Yankee vessels. And there was the adventure of the chase, the thrill of the capture. Who would volunteer?

Two men — a cabin boy and a fireman — stepped forward.

Waddell ordered a bucket of sovereigns brought up from his cabin. He stood before the men, running his hands through the gold coins, letting them clank back into the bucket. He raised the bounty to twelve pounds, to fifteen, to seventeen for a six-month enlistment. He raised the pay for ordinary seamen to five pounds, to six, finally to seven.

He got two more volunteers — an engineer and another cabin boy.

Captain Corbett buttoned his coat. "I'm off, men. Those who won't stop with this ship can follow me." He went over the rail to the *Laurel*. Of the fifty-five men in the *Sea King's* crew, fifty-one went after him. The Confederate officers went along, pleading and arguing; at last cursing.

Whittle approached Ellison, the argumentative quartermaster, and asked, "Why can't you go on the ship? It is good money."

"Sir," said Ellison, rolling his quid and spitting carefully, "I never earned a shilling in my life in America, and I do not wish to fight her battles. England is my country, and I am not ashamed to own it. Under no circumstances could I go."

"Why?"

"You do not know where I belong to. Do you see this on my cap?" He touched the Naval Reserve insignia on his cap. "If I were to desert from this you could not place any confidence in me. No, sir, it is no use. You may try, sir, but I have got the wrong heart in me for this."

They gave up on Ellison. The crew of the *Laurel* had slightly less sales resistance. They had made friends with the Confederates on the voyage south and felt already a part of the conspiracy to get the cruiser to sea. Five joined.

Five seamen from the *Laurel* crew, four from the *Sea King*, and ten who had come as passengers. Nineteen in all. Twenty-three officers. A total of forty-three to man a ship which needed 150 to sail and to fight.

The voyage seemed over before it had begun.

3

James Waddell was a stubborn man. The highest compliment he could pay was to call someone "obstinate." In his letter of resignation from the Navy he had boasted that "opinions (of others) never alter my convictions." But like obdurate characters he went through torture before making up his mind. Though brave, with the braggadocio of those who pride themselves on their fearlessness, he was afraid to assume the responsibility of taking the *Shenandoah* to sea with only half the complement of men he considered minimum.

After every effort at recruiting failed to get more volunteers, he went into conference with Captain Corbett of the *Sea King* and Captain Ramsey of the *Laurel.* They agreed it would be folly to put to sea in a ship which did not have enough men to sail her in a storm, much less to man her guns – if there were time to get her guns mounted. They suggested he sail south with the *Laurel* to the Canaries and try to ship more men there. Waddell wavered. To try to carry on was to risk his ship to the chance of storm, to take cover at Tenerife was to risk blockade and capture by Union cruisers. He turned to young Whittle for advice.

"Don't confer, sir, with parties who are not going with us," exclaimed the Virginian, looking from Corbett to Ramsey. "Call your officers together and learn from their assurances what they can and will do."

The officers were summoned. They filed in, serious and anxious. Waddell studied them, as though seeing them for the first time. They were so very young. Of the commissioned officers, Charles Lining, the ship's surgeon, was the oldest – thirty-one. Whittle, the first lieutenant, was twenty-four, and the other lieutenants, John Grimball, Sidney Smith Lee, Jr., Fred Chew, and Dabney Scales, were all younger. Matthew O'Brien, the chief engineer, was twenty-six. John Mason and Orris Browne were both twenty. Looking at them, Waddell felt very old. He explained the choice that must be made: to run and hide, or to take to the ocean and gamble on getting the ship in shape for a chase, then recruiting seamen from the captured vessels. He said that, speaking for himself, he thought it wiser to go to the Canaries, then asked, "What is your pleasure, gentlemen?"

Every man said, "Take the ocean."

4

There was no dedication ceremony, there wasn't time. While the men worked at clearing the decks, Waddell read the articles commissioning the ship as the Cruiser *Shenandoah*, Confederate States Navy.

Suddenly, across the water from the *Laurel*, came the long-drawn, dreaded words, "Sail ho! Say-ull hooo-oooo." The look-out on the *Shenandoah* spotted her next, "bearing right down on us under topsails, having very much the appearance of a man-of-war."

Waddell gave the order to weigh anchor. The crew raced to the winch – they could not move it. Waddell felt sick. Not even enough manpower to weigh anchor! The officers peeled their gray blouses and added their strength to that of the sailors. "I worked away at the anchor breaks until I thought my arms would break first and the anchor never came away," one of the officers noted in his journal, "but we worked away. At last they came up."

The little *Laurel* had steamed off to investigate the stranger, while the seamen stoked the *Shenandoah's* furnaces, raising steam for flight. But the strange ship sheered away and set English colors. The sigh of relief that went up from the raider almost bellied her sails. The *Laurel* came back and lowered a small boat which came over with three men who had changed their minds and decided to join up.

The ships parted. As the raider and her consort drew apart, the Englishmen who were going home gave three cheers for the ship they hadn't joined. The *Laurel* stood out for Tenerife and was soon only a smudge of smoke on the horizon.

The *Shenandoah* and her tiny crew were on their own.

****

SEA CHANGE

THE GUN tackles were lost. After four days of searching, everyone knew they were not aboard. The gun bolts, which had been lost too, turned up in a beef barrel in the hold, but the tackles were too large to be so easily misplaced. Somehow they had been left behind. Without tackles the guns could not be fired; their recoil would send them through the far side of the ship or down through the deck. There was rope to improvise tackle, but not tackle blocks. Until some were taken from a prize ship, the *Shenandoah* would have to depend on the unbacked bluff of the grim muzzles thrust through the newly sawed ports. The only guns aboard that could be safely fired were the twelve-pounders aft, her civilian side-arms. And for these there was only one shell, plus the usual harmless blanks.

This toothless condition seemed a sorry reward for a hundred hours' work. Except for the hours of the night watch, when the ship was placed under short sail and the crew caught naps, work had been continuous. Waddell took regular turns at the wheel to release a helmsman for roustabout work.

The guns were hoisted onto their mounts and lashed in place near the points in the bulkhead where the ports were to be cut. Only one seaman admitted to wood-working experience; he was assigned to help the Celtic carpenter, John O'Shea, cut out the ports.

There was no powder hold. After a study of the ship's already crowded space, it was decided to build one in the forehold. In the meantime, the powder barrels were stored in the captain's starboard cabin and covered with tarpaulins.

Quarters were not what Annapolis men are led to expect. Some of the officers, including the ship's surgeon, had to sleep on deck. In the steerage quarters, where the junior officers were quartered, there were no furnishings at all except iron tanks full of bread. There were no wash basins. Waddell listed the furniture in the captain's cabin as "one broken plush-velvet bottomed armchair, no berth, no bureau, no lockers for stowing my clothing in, no wash stand, pitcher or basin. The deck covered with a half-worn carpet which smelt of dogs or something worse . . . the most cheerless and offensive spot I had ever occupied."

To Waddell it seemed he was the only worried man aboard. "Responsibility weighed upon my mind, and reflection often created an absence of everything in active movement around me," he noted in his journal. "I was often aroused by some cheerful remarks from an officer, whose responsibility was to the extent of four hours' duty each day, about his experience in the steamer, and it was kind of him to divert my attention even for a few moments; but no sooner would the conversation cease than my mind was again occupied with ship thoughts . . . and I have no doubt I very often appeared to those with me an unsocial and peculiar man. I think that I never reflected until then, and the subject for reflection was full of interest, because national property and an important cruise were trusted to me. It was my first command, and upon the accuracy of all the calculations of my judgment in directing a cruise upon so vast a scale depended success or failure. Success would be shared by every individual under my command, but who would share failure with me. The former has friends; what has the latter? Those who knew me in a subordinate capacity elsewhere found me then changed in position, occupying responsibility to a nation which was struggling for their very existence."

The captain's brooding raised doubts in the minds of a few of his officers. Dr. Lining, the ship's surgeon, was the first to put his doubts in writing. After the council in which it was decided to take the ship to sea, he entered in his diary, "Now it was that the officers came out in their true colors and some that should have been the last to be disheartened flunked, and were only kept up to their work, or rather duty, by the influence of some of the younger officers."

But for most of the Confederates and their crewmen the first days at sea were high adventure – and hard work. They raced bad weather and bad luck. Within a week the portholes were cut; the guns, useless but impressive, were arrayed at midships – held in place by straps run through the scuppers and toggled outside the vessel. The holds were broken out and re-stowed in reasonable order. The decks were clear.

Slowly the excitement wore off. With the worst work out of the way, the remaining tasks turned from sport to day-to-day drudgery. The men were digging into their reserve energy; and at routine jobs they had time for thoughts and doubts.

The bulwarks were so thin they would not stop even a rifle shot. The decks were not reinforced to carry cannon and might collapse if a shot were fired. No plating covered the engine room, and the boilers were above the waterline. If the *Shenandoah* were forced into a fight, it could only end disastrously.

On the first Sunday at sea, Waddell ordered that no work be done on board. But as the men settled down for their first rest, the wind died. Orders were changed, and the five men of the black gang labored all day stoking the fires as the ship steamed south. On Monday the *Shenandoah* ran into her first squall. She weathered it easily but uncomfortably: the decks leaked. The men lying on the berth deck got little sleep as water dripped down on them. With a heavy sea running, spray from the waves puffed in through the seams of the hull.

The gripes grew louder.

On Tuesday the engine broke down. The black gang was shorthanded, only five men knowing machinery, but the damage proved minor. Repairs were made within four hours. Nevertheless a new worry had been added: would the engines hold up?

At the end of the first week, everyone was worn out, the weather was unpleasant, and though the ship looked formidable, she was in no shape to fight.

2

During Wednesday night, the sky cleared and a brisk wind came from the north. Early in the morning the cry sounded from masthead, "Sail ho!"

"Where away?" bawled the officer of the deck.

"About two points on the lee bow, sir, and standing the same as we are."

"Can you make her out?"

"Aye, aye, sir. A square-rigged vessel. We appear to be raising her fast. I see her better now. A bark with long mastheads and the looks of an American."

The news was relayed to Waddell. His was a delicate decision. His instructions had been to take no prizes for a month; this would give Captain Corbett time to return to England and transfer the register of the ship. But to spend three more weeks playing hide and seek would be fatal. More seamen had to be recruited, supplies had to be found, and, above all, something had to take the crew's mind off its troubles. "Give chase," he said. The officer of the deck bawled, "Stand in chase."

Under steam and sail the *Shenandoah* bore down on the stranger. In honor of her first hunt, the raider crossed her royal yards, but even under crowded canvas she gained slowly. The men swarmed into the rigging. Every spyglass on the vessel was brought topside and passed from hand to hand. Caught by the excitement of the chase, the men urged the ship forward, talking to her as though to a race horse.

Two hours after the start of the chase, they could make out the ensign flying from her peak: English. A ripple of disappointment tinged with disbelief ran through the crew. "Damn my eyes but she's an American if Boston ever built one," someone swore. Waddell, studying her through his glasses, agreed. He ordered the chase continued. To allay the stranger's possible suspicions, the *Shenandoah* raised the English flag.

For another hour the race went on. At last the *Shenandoah* was within range. Waddell gave the order to bring her around, and Whittle relayed it to the officer of the deck. The gunner raced aft to the twelve-pounder. A puff of smoke, a drumbeat of sound rolling across the water, and the stranger hove to.

A boarding party was put over the side in one of the ship's boats. Leadership fell to the sailing-master, Irvine Bulloch, a tough-fibered young Georgian, brother to the Confederate naval agent James Bulloch, and a veteran of the *Alabama* cruise. With him went Breedlove Smith, the paymaster, also an old hand from the *Alabama,* and six seamen.

Aboard the raider everyone watched anxiously as the little boat pulled toward the stranger. The ship was still moving with the wind and, according to Lining, "She forged through the water so fast that we thought our boat would never catch her, and we were thinking it time to fire another shot ahead of her when she put her mizzen topsail to the mast and our boat got alongside."

All during the long row the boarding party had debated the

vessel's structure. Everyone agreed her lines were American, but as she swung around they could read the name on her stern: MOGUL — LONDON.

The captain met them at the rail and escorted Bulloch and Smith to his cabin — a snug room with a solid bed, a big table, whale-oil lamps, curtains in the ports, flowers growing in boxes. His wife and children were aboard. He spread his papers on the big table. The ship was British. Built in New England for the Far East trade, she had been sold to an English company the year before. Satisfied that her papers were in order, the boarding party started back to the *Shenandoah.*

"We waited most anxiously on board to see whether her flag would come down or not," Lining noted that night in his journal, "and we were very much disappointed when we saw our boat shove off from her."

Cornelius Hunt, a master's mate from Maryland, felt differently. "The captain and his family seemed so cozey and contented in their little home on the sea," he confessed, "that I was half glad to find that they were really entitled to the protection of the flag they flew, and safe from capture."

The younger officers were able to forget their disappointment with a good laugh. Orris Browne, a twenty-year-old passed midshipman making his first voyage, was ordered to change sail during darkness that night. He shouted back at the officer of the deck, "I can't find the ropes tonight, Mr. Grimball, won't tomorrow do as well?" After the tension of the day, the remark seemed funnier than it really was.

But Waddell did not join in the laugh. In his uncomfortable cabin he was scratching in his journal an entry that reflected his disappointment: ". . . like many other American vessels she had changed owners in consequence of the war. She may have been sold in good faith; so far as her papers were concerned the sale was in form, but that is not necessarily infallible proof."

3

Actually the sale of the *Mogul* to English owners had been a tribute to Confederate raiders rather than a trick to deceive them. By far the greatest part of the damage done to the Union Merchant Marine during the Civil War came by such sales. For every Northern ship sunk by rebel raiders, eight others were sold to foreign owners.

This flight from the flag was unwarranted. Confederate naval officials made a basic strategic mistake. For years they concentrated on trying to buy and build ships abroad capable of driving the Union blockaders away from Southern ports. Their raiders were only incidental and, in all, destroyed only fifty ships. More than 29,000 voyages were made to foreign ports by American vessels during the war. If the advice of some naval officers – including Waddell – to forget about fighting battles and instead to concentrate on commerce raiding had been heeded, the destruction might have been great enough to force the shift of cruisers from blockade to convoy duty.

As it was, the raiders' bag of Northern shipping was no greater than the annual loss to storm and ice – one half of one per cent. But with the headlines reporting the terrible depredations of Southern "sea devils," insurance companies happily jacked their rates to uncalled-for heights, from a prewar average of less than one-half of one per cent to more than eight per cent for voyages passing through the South Atlantic, the favorite haunt of the raiders.

Seven per cent additional cost was enough to discourage shippers. They by-passed the fast American vessels for the slower, cheaper, surer English ships. More and more American bottoms rode empty: their owners were faced with the choice of gambling on an uninsured voyage (an unbusinesslike proceeding) or selling the ship to a foreigner, under whose flag it would be safe.

More than 1600 vessels, totaling nearly 750,000 tons, were sold. British owners took over most of them.

Though the raiders were an effective weapon of economic warfare and grievously damaged enemy businessmen, they were almost completely ineffective as agents for a blockade. More and more cargoes were carried in foreign bottoms, to be sure, but more and more got through. Each month through the war, cargo totals hit a new high at Northern ports, whereas, to the South, each month the strangle hold of the blockade was clamped tighter.

FIRST PRIZE

By Friday, October 29, the *Shenandoah* had reached a point almost due south of the Azores and due west of Dakar. "Another sail ahead," Dr. Lining wrote in his journal that night. "During the day we gained on her very rapidly, but night came on before we came up to her. All the wise ones on board pronounced her to be a Yankee, but we didn't get near enough to raise her hull, so it remains in uncertainty. We will change our course a little during the night to be in good position in the morning."

But the next morning the stranger was still a long way off. They gained on her so slowly, the winds being light, that around noon Waddell ordered steam raised. By one, the ships were close enough so that the *Shenandoah* ran up the English flag. The men watched eagerly for the stranger's answer. It was not long in coming. There was no need for glasses. The flag was large and new: the Stars and Stripes. A cheer went up from the men on the raider.

The raider broke out her royals and topgallant sails and, under this press of canvas, rapidly drew within gunshot. A blank brought the Yankee around. The boarding party, under Bulloch and Midshipman John Mason, set off at once.

As the six seaman rowed him over to the prize, Mason looked at them disapprovingly. They wore their work clothes, shabby, dirty, and conglomerate; the young officer was unhappy that the men under him were not properly dressed for his first warlike engagement. Somewhat to his relief he saw that the men waiting at the rail of the ship were in shirtsleeves. Anyone willing to be captured in improper dress, he felt, would not have enough sensibility to look down on the Confederates for their unmilitary costumes.

Edward Staples, master of the Yankee bark, greeted the rebel officers coolly as they came over the side.

"Sir," Bulloch said to him, "I have the honor to inform you that your craft is a prize to the Confederate States of America. You must get your papers and proceed aboard our ship."

Staples hesitated a moment, then disappeared down the companionway. In a moment he was back, carrying a tin box containing his documents. Bulloch stayed aboard the prize, and Mason escorted the captured captain to the *Shenandoah.* He was taken to the wardroom, where a prize board consisting of Waddell, Dr. Lining, and Breedlove Smith, the paymaster, was waiting. They put him under oath, then examined the ship's papers. They showed her to be the *Alina,* a brand-new bark, from Searsport, Maine, on her first voyage. She had picked up a $50,000 cargo of railroad iron at Newport, Wales, and was en route to Argentina, where British interests were building a railroad. The papers indicated that the cargo belonged to a neutral; this being the case, the Confederate States could be held responsible for its destruction. But Waddell located a loophole – the papers had not be notarized. The cargo was, therefore, presumably American.

"Sir, your ship is condemned and we must sink her. You may return to her for your personal possessions."

Wordlessly, Captain Staples left. He did not speak as he was rowed back, as he made his last trip around the new vessel in which most of his life's savings were invested. He gathered the items he most wished to save and, still unblinking, climbed down the *Alina's* glossy sides to the small boat.

But as he and Master's Mate Hunt were rowed back to the raider, the Yankee said to the Marylander, "I tell you what, maty. I've a daughter at home that that craft yonder was named for, and it goes against me cursedly to see her destroyed."

"Neither myself nor my brother officers have any disposition to do you a personal injury," Hunt said slowly. Of all the Southerners abroad the *Shenandoah,* he was the most appalled by the destruction of war, the least inclined to hate the enemy. "Our orders are to prey upon the commerce of the United States, and in carrying them out, private individuals have to suffer, just as the widows and orphans of the South have done and are doing from the invading armies acting under the instructions of your Government."

"I know it is only the fortune of war and I must take my chances with the rest," Staples said resolutely, and then sighed. "But it's damned hard, and I hope I shall have an opportunity of returning your polite attentions before this muss is over, that's all."

The *Alina* was well equipped, and the officers of the *Shenandoah* picked her cabin clean. For hours the small boats plied between the two ships, bringing back basins, pitchers, mess crockery, knives, forks, books. Waddell got a spring-bottomed mattress. The pick of the provisions were brought aboard for the mess; to everyone's relief, tackle blocks were found that met the requirements for the guns. The next capture would not have to be taken by bluff alone.

"We were all green on the subject of plundering," Lining wrote in his journal that night, "and such a scene of indiscriminate plundering commenced as I never saw before or expect to see again. Everything which could possibly be of any use was seized upon and put into the boats. I was looking out especially for the eatables and got a very good store of canned meats. After all the useful things were disposed of the spirit of plunder still prevailed, and cabin doors were taken down, drawers from under bunks taken out and sent on board."

The twelve-man crew and the three officers of the *Alina* were brought on board the raider. To Waddell, the crewmen seemed "like rats in a strange garret" as they roamed the deck. The *Shenandoah* regulars fell into conversation with their captives, assuring them that they would come to no harm, boasting of what a fine ship the raider was, mentioning the bountiful pay. They wanted recruits.

Seven of the twelve joined the raider. Three were French, three German and one Malay; none owed allegiance to the flag they sailed under. For them the choice was between gold or irons — the men who did not join were herded into the top-gallant forecastle (where the ship's hens and sheep were kept) and put in leg irons. "Seven men!" exclaimed the ship's surgeon on hearing of the recruits, "what a deal of work that will take off the officers' hands."

Captain Staples and his mates were paroled and given the freedom of the ship.

By mid-afternoon all booty was aboard, and the time had come to destroy the prize. Since her cargo was heavy, Waddell decided to scuttle her. They were in well-traveled waters, and a burning ship might frighten away other prizes — or attract Union cruisers.

Five men, under John O'Shea, the carpenter, made the last trip to the *Alina*. O'Shea appreciated the beautiful workmanship of the bark, a prime product of the best shipyards in the world. He felt little triumph as he and his men bored holes in the hull. With the water pouring in, they climbed up, scurried over the side, and rowed away.

On the *Shenandoah*, men and officers lined the rail in a death watch on the doomed ship. There was no cheering. Seamen all, they felt the horror of seeing a ship go down.

Her sails still set, the *Alina* moved slowly before a light breeze and settled as she went. After twenty minutes, her stern dipped, her bow shot up, and thus kneeling, she slid out of sight. The groan and crack as her masts were wrenched loose by the weight of the water made the men on the *Shenandoah* wince, as though they were listening to sounds of torture. After the ship was gone, huge bubbles broke on the mirrored surface of the ocean. Spars and bits of debris bobbed up.

The *Shenandoah,* in solemn triumph, steamed away. In the wardroom, Captain Staples refused the drinks offered him by the celebrant Confederate officers.

2

On the day that the *Shenandoah* took her first prize, Captain Corbett, late of the *Sea King,* was arrested.

The *Laurel,* bearing the refugees from the reconverted raider, arrived at Tenerife on October 21, the day after leaving her consort. No one was allowed ashore until the ship was coaled and her steam was up. Then Captain Ramsey asked permission of the port authorities to land forty-three passengers, the officers and crew of the *Sea King,* "wrecked off the Desertas Islands."

Permission was granted, and the men came ashore. At the British Consulate, Consul Henry Grattan heard of the loss of the steamer. He waited for the skipper to appear with the ship's papers. A week passed and still Corbett did not come around. The delay seemed peculiar to Grattan. He sent word to Corbett that he wanted to see him. Corbett came, bearing the ship's register. He explained that the *Sea King* had been sold, not lost.

Quartermaster John Ellison came too. He was still angry at the trick he felt had been played on him when he signed for a two-year voyage that lasted only two weeks. He brought along John Allen, another member of the Royal Navy Volunteers. Their testimony impressed Consul Grattan. That evening he wrote to Earl Russell, the Secretary of Foreign Affairs:

> These depositions in my opinion contain evidence sufficient to substantiate a charge against the master, P. S. Corbett, of an infringement of the Foreign Enlistment Act; I therefore, pursuant to paragraph 127 of the Consular Instructions, deem it proper to send the offender in safe custody to England.

Another letter, written the same night, would have given the Confederates a counterbalancing bit of pleasure. In Antwerp, Commodore Craven of the U.S.S. *Niagara* penned a report to the Secretary of Navy on the results of his hunt for Confederates. After holding the Spanish steamer *Cicerone* for seventy hours, he had learned it was all a mistake and, releasing her, "proceeded down to the Channel Islands, where I made a thorough but fruitless search for the *Laurel*."

HAPPY HUNTING GROUND

AFTER sinking the *Alina,* the *Shenandoah* cruised south into the 1800-mile gap between the bulge of Africa and the bulge of South America. Through this intercontinental channel coursed a huge volume of marine traffic: every ship to the Orient, to California, to the Russian fur posts in Alaska, to India, to Australia; every clipper that hauled tea, every whaler except the handful of Hudson Bay craft, every trader loaded with trinkets for the South Pacific natives. Here, between the bulges, the *Alabama* had had a field day, and here the *Shenandoah* might make a killing.

For a week the raider went without prey. Two sails were chased, but both were English disappointments. The weather went bad; squall after squall forced the ship to reef its sails, and the short-handed crew loathed the sound of the boatswain's whistle. The persistent rain trickled through the leaky deck into officers' rooms and crew's berth space alike. After a long day's work it was no pleasure to turn into a wet bunk.

The crewmen washed clothes in the rain. A few officers tried their hands at scrubbing but soon gave up and hired washermen from the ranks to complete the job. "Grunt all" was the gag of the week and drew laughs long after the freshness had worn off the phrase.

Work had settled down enough so that the lazy felt safe in gold-bricking. On Friday, November 4, Lining said in his diary that "The Carpenter, O'Shea, being ordered by the first lieutenant to do something rushed into the wardroom where I was sitting and said, 'Doctor, I want you to put me on your list!' I saw that he was in a pet and after a few words of conversation I told him that I couldn't do so, that he hadn't thought his foot bad enough to come on the list before, and that I could not put him on it now without a better reason. I suppose he will never forgive me."

Just before sundown that evening, a schooner was sighted. Waddell ordered a course set that would enable the *Shenandoah* to stand in chase the next morning. Around midnight the wind faded. When daylight came, a flat calm had settled over the sea. The schooner was still in sight, and the raider ran toward her under steam. At 7:30 the signal gun sounded; in reply the schooner raised the American flag. Prize number two.

The *Charter Oak* of Boston was bound around Cape Horn with a mixed cargo, mostly fruits and vegetables, for San Francisco. She was a tiny ship for such a voyage – less than 150 tons burden – but her captain, Samuel Gilman, a happy Californian, had no qualms about making the voyage. Aboard with him were a mate, three Portuguese seamen, and his wife, her widowed sister, and her four-year-old son.

Sam Gilman took the capture of his ship as a fine joke. When Waddell told him she was to be destroyed, he giggled and said, "Well, if you're going to burn her, for God's sake bring the preserved fruit on board."

The fruit was brought, as well as nearly a ton of canned tomatoes. Though tiny, the *Charter Oak* was well furnished. The last boats to return from her were loaded to the water's edge with sofas, chairs, and small tables. Quarters in the *Shenandoah* began to have a prosperous air.

After the fruit was aboard, the easy-going master of the captive remembered there was also a hogshead of ice in the hold. It was soon located and put over the side into a boat, which it almost swamped. The oarsmen, trying to maneuver the overloaded boat back to the *Shenandoah,* got too far astern and ran into the propeller; it stove in the stern and John Grimball, the officer in charge, suffered a badly cut hand. But at last the hogshead was raised to the raider's deck. When it was opened, after the *Shenandoah* was under weigh, all hands gathered for a cool treat. But the ice had melted. The hogshead held only water and sawdust.

Among the other trophies aboard the *Charter Oak* were a sword, which Waddell took, and a double-barreled shotgun, which he wanted but could not have because Whittle, who had been given the task of allotting captured material, put the gun in the ship's arsenal.

Pawing through the Portuguese sailors' belongings, the Confederate seamen made a surprising discovery — three blue army coats, faded but unmistakably Federal. The Portuguese were Union bounty-jumpers, men who enlisted, claimed the big bounties offered volunteers, and at the first opportunity went over the hill. Leery of such loyalty, Waddell made no attempt to recruit the prize's crew. All three were put in irons.

Shortly before sundown, the destruction team went aboard the schooner. The bulkheads were ripped off and piled in the cabin and forecastle. Turpentine found in the hold was sloshed on the decks. The hatches were opened to give a draft, the halyards severed so the sails hung loosely. Then, the sacrifice readied, men took torches from the galley, tossed them in the hold, touched them to the turpentine, and ran for the rail.

The wind was light, and the schooner burned steadily. The flames licked along her decks, ran up the masts as far as the wooden trucks at the top. As darkness fell, the glare of the fire reflected against the sky.

Waddell wanted to be sure the *Charter Oak* burned all the way, that no freak of luck saved her. He ran the *Shenandoah* to leeward of the burning hulk, out of reach of cinders. It was not safe to stay around the beacon of the burning ship, but the captain felt that a Union cruiser, if in the neighborhood, would be under steam and, in all probability, would run to windward to observe the fire; this would give the raider a chance to see her first and slip away in the darkness. No cruiser appeared.

The women prisoners, though both under thirty, broke no hearts aboard the cruiser. Even Lining, a ladies' man who usually gave a girl the benefit of any doubt, pronounced them plain. And young Mason, fresh from a year in France, complained that they "were certainly a bore. . . . The most stupid women I ever saw. They were not pretty in the least and could not talk or say a word. And they came to meals with the most remarkable-looking dressing gowns on."

But to Waddell, a courtly and romantic Carolinian, all girls were pretty, and all women were ladies. A huge man, long married to a tiny woman with whom he was deeply in love, he consciously thought of himself as gallant. The master of the *Charter Oak* had had two hundred dollars in gold in the strongbox of his ship. Waddell confiscated it, but when Mrs. Gilman came aboard he presented it to her on the condition that she promise not to return a cent of it to her husband.

"The promise of course was a mere pretense," he admitted in his journal. "The fact was I felt a compassion for the women. They would be landed I did not know where and the thought of inflicting unnecessary severity on a female made my heart shrink within."

The women, the little boy, and Captain Gilman were assigned the starboard side of the Captain's two-room cabin — the old gunpowder room.

Captain Staples of the *Alina* had refused to watch the chase. He stayed below in the wardroom. When Gilman was brought in, the two masters greeted each other sympathetically.

"What did he do to you?" the Maine man asked after a time.
"He burned her," said the Californian with a giggle.
Staples turned his back and walked away.

2

The next day was Sunday, the first Sunday of the month, and, by naval custom, the correct time for reading the Articles of War. The crew was mustered on the poop deck. Whittle, dressed in full uniform, read the Articles, speaking slowly so that his Virginia accent would not baffle the foreign-born who were accustomed to the basic English of the forecastle.

After the formation, James Oar, an English cabin boy who had joined from the *Laurel,* approached Lining.

"I say, sir," he began, a troubled expression on his fourteen-year-old countenance, "isn't there a great deal of punishment by death in it?"

Lining had a good laugh, and, a short time later, a good scare. Whittle swallowed a piece of glass. The doctor had no remedy to suggest except a strong emetic. Everything came out all right.

3

The bark *De Godfrey,* of Boston, was chased and captured on the afternoon of Monday, November 7. She was an old ship, slow and heavy-laden, valued at only $10,000, but carrying a $26,000 cargo of pork and beef and lumber from Boston around the Horn to Valparaiso, Chile.

Waddell ordered the beef brought for the *Shenandoah's* mess, but the boarding party found 40,000 feet of lumber stowed on top of the food. To jettison the lumber would have taken more than a day, so the *Godfrey,* food and all, was put to the torch. The boarders knocked down the bulkheads in the cabin and pantry and threw them on the cabin deck, then touched them off. No combustibles were needed. An old ship, tinder-dry, the bark made a spectacular fire.

"Darkness had settled when the rigging and sails took fire," according to Hunt, "but every rope could be seen as distinctly as upon a painted canvas, as the flames made their way from the deck and writhed upward like fiery serpents. Soon the yards came thundering down by the run as the lifts and halyards yielded to the devouring element, the standing rigging parted like blazing flax, and the spars simultaneously went by the board and left the hulk wrapped from stem to stern in one fierce blaze, like a floating, fiery furnace."

As the ship burned, her captain, Sam Hallett, walked the quarter-deck, his arms folded across his chest, his face lighted by the glare from his vessel. Mrs. Gilman and the red-headed widow Gage stood at the rail with Whittle, watching the fire. For a time no one spoke.

"That was a vessel which had done her duty well for forty years," said Hallett as the *Godfrey* disintegrated and, with a hiss of steam, a belch of smoke, disappeared. "She faced old Boreas in every part of the world, in the service of her master, and after such a career to be destroyed by man on a calm night, on this tropic sea — too bad, too bad."

There was again silence, until the red-headed widow, whose husband had died a hero's unpleasant death in the fighting at Harper's Ferry, said, "It is but another result of the terrible war at home. Would to God it was over, that the destruction of life and property might cease!"

"War is a bad thing, there's no denying it," resumed the captain, "bad enough on land, where at least you've a solid foundation under you, but infinitely worse at sea, where it destroys the few planks that you have learned to trust to keep you from going to Davy Jones's. There is no sight so awful as a ship on fire, even when, as now, you know there is no human being on board. But there's no use grumbling."

To Waddell, too, the destruction of a ship was an awful thing. He firmly believed that wooden ships were alive:

> What else except the sailor's belief in the life of ships makes the parallel between ships' lives and men's lives so pleasant and constant a fable. As on land, so on sea, you have them of all sorts; there is the national ship, proud, stately, warlike; there is the great merchantman, rich, solid, busy; there is the fat bustling trader, toiling up and down the coast with coals or cattle or produce; there are the graceful, lively, gaily-dressed pleasure crafts, yachts and despatch boats, the ladies of the sea; there are the industrious, disregarded smacks and pungys, working hard for every inch of luck they get and taking the weather pretty much as it comes, which nobody counts and nobody cares for; and the reason why a ship's fate affects one so much is always the sailor's reason. When we see a great vessel rolling lonely at sea, her masts gone, her gear loose and adrift, and sheets of foaming sea pouring in and out of her helpless sides, who wants the fable explained. Many such a craft, once proud and capable, wallows among the screaming sea-birds of destiny upon the waters of life. Practical and unimaginative people may say, what difference does it make to the ship? but no sailor will listen to that.
>
> Imaginative theorists have declared that naval supremacy is due to a pronoun. We call a ship "she" and other tongues call a ship "it." She implies that the ship carries us and is in some manner alive, as a sailor in his heart privately believes, or why does he talk about her foot, her waist, her head, her divinity when the graceful thing floats on the surface of the water? There is life in the craft from the time she leaves the ways into the tide until the hour when her timbers are laid on the sand or rocks, or, the saddest of all, in the ship broker's yard.
>
> The worst of the iron plated vessel is that the black, ugly armor has no such vitality and cannot be christened with the pretty, old-fashioned names which helped the sailors' superstition out. We cannot answer for such hideous monsters; they are created out of dull mineral which came from the bowels of the earth, and should they all come to grief like the *Monitor*, the blacksmith will some day turn them into pots and pans, iron railings and boilers. But the timber of the wooden ship grows

in the sunlight, it waved in the forest and heard the wind sing, before bending to the breeze under topsails.

4

With as many prisoners on board as crewmen, Waddell was worried. The captured mates were refractory. Two, who had refused to help clean up their quarters in steerage, were locked in the forecastle with the livestock and crewmen. The others might be planning to make trouble. Captain Staples was friendly with the Marylander, Cornelius Hunt, but surly with the other Confederate officers. The undermanned ship seemed overcrowded.

So when the *Shenandoah* came up with the Danish brig *Anna Jans* on Thursday morning, Waddell decided, against the advice of his officers, to see if the foreigner would haul some of the prisoners to a neutral port. The master of the *Anna Jans* agreed, "for the slight consideration of a chronometer, a barrel of beef and one of biscuits," to take some of the Yankees to Rio de Janeiro – but no women. Women jinxed a ship; if you didn't believe it, how did they happen to be aboard the *Shenandoah?*

Unloaded on the Dane were Captains Hallet and Staples, their four mates, and two seamen. The chronometer, used to pay for their passage, had been taken from the *Alina.* "Captain Staples," Waddell observed dryly in his journal, "accompanies his instrument."

The departure of the prisoners widened the breech which had opened between Waddell and his officers during the council over putting to sea shorthanded. "We are glad to get them out of the ship," Lining noted in his diary, "though I doubt the policy of letting them go at this time, as it is very important for us to keep our movements unknown for some time and these men may surmise our destination and will certainly describe our ship, her armament, etc. We still keep

JAMES WADDELL

(see p. 19)

Confederate Cruiser *Shenandoah* in Hobson's Bay
From a Melbourne newspaper *(see p. 123)*

Visitors on board the *Shenandoah*
From a Melbourne newspaper *(see p. 128)*

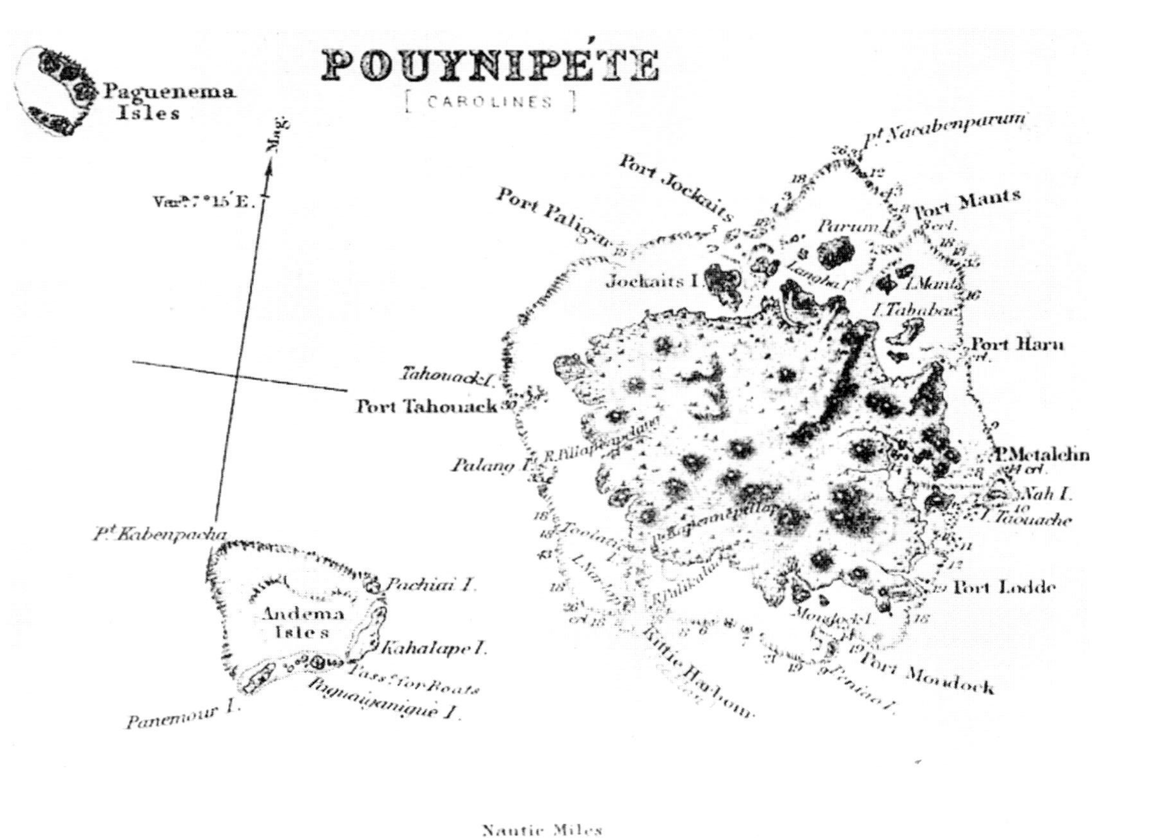

PONAPE

From an old whaling chart, dated 1867, in the Library of Congress collection *(see p. 166)*

The *Shenandoah* Amid the Ice *From The Illustrated London News* *(see p. 201)*

The *Shenandoah* Towing Prisoners from Three Burning Whaling Vessels in Bering Strait, June 25, 1865 *(see p. 233)*

Official Records of the Union and Confederate Navies in the War of the Rebellion (Series I, Vol. III)

The Confederate States Steamer *Shenandoah* in the Mersey

From The Illustrated London News (see p. 297)

EARL RUSSELL
From Harper's Illustrated Weekly, 1865

From a photo. by Brady

HON. CHARLES F. ADAMS
From Harper's Illustrated Weekly

(see p. 306)

Captain Gilman, his party and crew . . . hoping we might get an opportunity to send them to California, where they want to go. But as any ship we meet going to California will in all probability be a Yankee and therefore a prize, I don't see the use of keeping them and letting the rest go."

5

"I think she's a steamer, sir," the deck officers reported to Waddell after studying the quarry through a spyglass.

Waddell examined the ship for himself. She looked like no steamer he had ever seen; in fact, like no ship he had ever seen. She was a hermaphrodite brig — a two-master, square-rigged forward and shooner-rigged aft, and from the port side jutted a large paddle wheel.

The odds were long that a steamer would be a warship, which the *Shenandoah* was in no condition to encounter. But the more the salts studied the stranger, the more they were sure that, whatever else she was, she couldn't be a steamer. The mainsail was broken out and the chase started.

The brig *Susan,* of New York, was perhaps the worst ship afloat. She was so slow, barnacles grew on her bottom, so leaky that the crew could not pump her out as fast as she made water. The puzzling paddle wheel proved to be attached to the pumps, so that the *Susan* pumped herself out as she sailed; but she moved so slowly, even when there was a good breeze, that she was always heavy with water. She was forty-six days out of Cardiff with a load of coal for southern Brazil, and her crew had began to doubt that she would make it. They left her gladly, and three men — two deck hands and a cabin boy — signed on the *Shenandoah* immediately. The raider also adopted the *Susan's* dog. The skipper, a German named Frederich Hansen, asked for appointment as an acting master's mate on the cruiser, but Waddell mistook him for a Jew and, too much a gentleman of his period to let his ship's needs override his racial prejudices, decided "it was impossible to find ship room for his accommodations."

"The novel character of my political position embarrassed me more than the feeble condition of my command, and that was fraught with painful apprehensions enough," Waddell confessed in his notes. "I had the compass to guide me as a sailor, but my instructions made me a magistrate in a new field of duty, and where the law was not very clear to lawyers. Managing a vessel in unsettled, stormy weather and exposure to the dangers of the sea was a thing I had studied from my boyhood; fighting was a profession that I had prepared myself for by the study of the best models; but now I was to sail and fight and to decide questions of international law that lawyers had quarreled over with all their books before them. I was in all matters to act promptly and without counsel. . . ."

On Saturday, November 12, the skipper was presented with two particularly perplexing legal problems.

The *Kate Prince* was sighted at sundown on Friday. She was south and east of the cruiser and standing to south and west. With the sun at their backs, it was difficult for the raiders to determine her size; but she looked fast, even formidable. When Waddell set a course he hoped would bring the ships together about midnight, there were men aboard who muttered that it would be a good thing if they never saw the stranger again.

It was the first night chase. No one went below. The men leaned on the rail or hung in the rigging, looking across the narrow circle of dark water that surrounded them, listening to the hiss of the water as the copper-coated hull slid through it, the slap of the waves against the teak planks, the hum of the rigging, the creaking of the masts. In low voices, as though the stranger might overhear them, they debated her nationality. Some thought she was a Union cruiser.

Just after midnight, she loomed out of the darkness to port, a clipper ship, big, beautiful and, judging by her rakish masts and overhanging bow, New England-built. When only a hundred yards off, the *Shenandoah* sounded her signal gun. The *Kate Prince* cut canvas and heeled around. As the cruiser glided past and turned to cover the stranger with a broadside of four guns, Whittle hailed her, asking her identity. The answer sounded like "Free States."

The gig was lowered and a boarding party under Sidney Smith Lee, Jr., nephew of General Lee, started over for her. Someone aboard the *Shenandoah* could not wait, shouted: "Where hail you from?"

"Portsmouth."

"Portsmouth, England?"

"Portsmouth, New Hampshire."

In half an hour the boarders were back with Captain Henry Libby and First Mate William Corfield, along with the ship's papers. She was American, but the cargo was British – Cardiff coal bound for Bahia. The papers for the coal were properly notarized. To destroy the cargo would be an act unfriendly to England. Deciding to bond her, Waddell set the clipper's value at $40,000. Captain Libby signed a ransom note, agreeing to pay that sum within six months after the end of the war; he also promised to take the *Shenandoah's* prisoners to Brazil.

While the ransom negotiations were in progress, Lieutenant Lee returned in one of the *Kate Prince's* boats and asked to speak to Waddell. His news was interesting. Captain Libby's wife was aboard. She claimed to be a Southern woman and said the crew, Southern sympathizers to a man, would all twenty-one join the *Shenandoah,* and that she wanted to sail aboard the cruiser as well. Waddell said no. Two women on the cruiser were enough of a problem without adding a third, and tempting though twenty-one men might be, there was the problem of the coal. The bond stood.

The raider's prisoners were put aboard the cartel. Mrs. Gilman and Mrs. Gage thanked the captain for his courtesies, while Captain Gilman joked with the officers about not wanting to meet them again. The master of the *Kate Prince* sent over a barrel of potatoes for the Confederate officers' mess. By 3 A.M., the ships were moving apart in the moonlight.

But not everyone was satisfied with the result. "This, I think, was a great mistake," Lining confided to his journal. "A ship worth so much money and ransomed for the sake of a cargo not worth over seventeen thousand dollars at the most. Better to have burned her and let our government settle about the cargo afterwards. However the deed is done, and there is no use talking about it."

Twelve hours later, the *Shenandoah* overhauled the brig *Adelaide,* which hoisted the Argentine flag but looked so American that Waddell sent an officer aboard to check her papers. These looked suspicious, so the prize officer sent the captain and his certificates over to the cruiser for Waddell's scrutiny.

"And now took place the most curious of circumstances, making the greatest mess I have ever known," wrote Lining. "She proved to be the bark *Adelaide,* formerly the *Adelaide Pendergrast,* Captain Williams, bound from New York to Rio with a cargo of flour. It was evident that she had been put under the Buenos Ayres flag for some purpose, the only question was, was it a bona fide transfer. The Captain of her did some tall swearing in order to clear himself and bark, and finally ended by admitting that Mr. Pendergrast was the true owner of the bark, thus perjuring himself.

"It appears that the bark is the property of a Mr. Pendergrast of Baltimore, who is a good Southerner, and who to save his property from the Yankees put the bark under the BA flag, making a fictitious transfer of his vessel.

"The cargo was shipped by Phipps & Co. of New York whose

names only appeared in the invoice. On account of the cargo and the mixture of the transfer and cargo, Captain Waddell determined to burn her, and let the Government settle with Mr. P. I was among those who went off to the prize. She had on board a good many Portuguese who were returning to Brazil, and their blank faces when they were told to take their things and go on board of us was most ludicrous.

"She had a great many nice things as hams, preserved fruits, etc., and we sent them on board. When we had nearly got through we, or rather Bulloch, discovered a whole batch of letters and gave them to me to take care of. Fortunately I had got all I wanted off her, and came on board in one of the cargo boats and gave the letters to Capt. W. On opening some of them what should come out but that Mr. P was not only the owner of the brig but of the cargo also and Phipps' name only appeared to shield them from the Yankee Government. Now as Mr. P was known to be a good Confederate at heart, we did not wish to destroy any of his property. Orders were immediately given to send back to her all that had been taken out of her. This was done, but it was found impossible to restore her to her original state.

"The cabin was much knocked to pieces in making preparations to burn her. Kerosene oil had been thrown over the deck, tar and oil had been poured upon the floor in the forehold to light her quickly, a good many articles taken from her had been lost or destroyed and other injury had been done. But what could we do? We could only write to Mr. P apologizing for our mistake.

"Then arose another question. If we let the vessel go in this way, would not the Yankees come down on Mr. P as one who so sympathized with our cause that our ships would not touch his property. To remedy this we committed an unlawful act – we bonded the cargo, although acknowledging the ship to be under a neutral flag. If this does not produce some complication, and perhaps row, I shall be very much surprised. However it is done, and there is no help for it. Her captain seemed very glad to get off in any way and took the ship back most joyfully. Before we had got through transferring her things back it was nearly dark; when we steamed off on our course, we also saw the *Adelaide* bear away on hers."

6

The *Lizzie M. Stacey,* a small and speedy schooner, made a run for it. Her captain, William Archer, suspected nothing when he saw the white-sailed, black-hulled *Shenandoah* bearing down on him, but he was proud of his ship and hated to be passed. He crowded on the canvas.

The chase lasted four hours. Pushed by light breezes, the two vessels moved across the shining blue seas only one degree north of the equator. The *Shenandoah* had to lower her propeller and add steam to sail-power before she could overhaul the little schooner, but at 3 P.M. on Sunday, November 13, a warning shot from the signal gun brought the runaway around. Grimball boarded her and ordered the captain and his mate to go before Waddell.

Erect and angry, Captain Archer came over the side of the *Shenandoah* a few moments later. The good-natured Hunt complimented him on his nerve in setting out in such a small ship.

"Shiver my timbers if there ain't the most lubberly set of sailors afloat in these latitudes that I ever fell in with," Archer exploded. "Why, day before yesterday, I run across the bows of a big English ship bound to Australia, and all hands made a rush forward when I hove in sight, as though I'd been the Sea Serpent or some other almighty curiosity. They invited me to come on board, but there was a stiff breeze blowing at the time, and I'd no notion of losing a good run for the sake of showing off a little before a lot of chaps who seem to think nothing less than a seventy-four is safe to cross the ocean in."

The *Lizzie's* mate, a huge Irishman with hair as red as his brogue was thick, came cursing aboard in time to hear the last of Archer's blast. "Faith, and the ould man is right," he bellowed. "The dirty blackguards wouldn't have appreciated the compliment of a visit from us, and what's more, my hearty, if we'd had ten guns aboard her, you wouldn't have got us without a bit of a shindy, or if the breeze had been a bit stiffer, we'd given her the square sail, and all hell wouldn't have caught her."

Looking over the *Lizzie,* the Confederates thought the mate might be right. She was a beautiful little ship. Archer told Waddell that she belonged to Brewer & Co.; he was taking her to Honolulu to be sold. Years afterward, Archer described his interview with the Confederate skipper and his experiences aboard the raider:

> I told him (Waddell) I was Master of the *Lizzie M. Stacey* and where we were bound. He asked me if there was any jewelry, gold, silver or other valuables on my vessel. I told him none that I was aware of. I told him that my cargo consisted of half barrels of soft pine, in shooks. Also that there was on board about thirty barrels of salt and thirty tons of iron.
>
> He wanted to know if I thought that would sink her if she was to be scuttled. I thought not as the cargo was rather light, and then he said he would burn the vessel.
>
> He sent the cockswain to tell Mr. Grimball to burn our vessel. I asked him if he was not going to let me go on board again, and he said they had no room for any baggage on their vessel. He said, however, that I might go on board and get a suit of clothes if I wished. I went, and found that they had been over our vessel and taken about everything there was of any value. They had been through my stateroom and taken everything out. I should think there were as many as twenty or thirty men went on board from the Cruiser, tearing everything to pieces and taking whatever they wanted. I took a suit of clothes from the vessel and that was all I could get.

I went on board the *Lizzie M. Stacey* with Mr. Gimball and remained there until she was set on fire. . . . The crew were put forward, in irons, and I was kept among the after guards. I was not put in irons, but was kept in a small space and was not allowed to go about freely. . . .

One of our seamen, James Strong, joined the crew of the *Shenandoah,* and received a bounty of, I think, six pounds (or six dollars). Another seaman, Jacob Hanson, a Swede, also joined the Cruiser. And also Charles Hopkins (cook and steward). He was forced to join. They hung him up by his thumbs from seven in the morning until noon. I do not know that he then agreed to join the *Shenandoah.* We were not allowed to have any conversation with each other. Hopkins was a light mulatto from Baltimore. He was both cook and steward.

I never had any conversation with Hanson (sic) after he was hung up by his thumbs. I suppose he was forced to join the Confederacy. He did not tell me so and I cannot state positively for what he was hung up. An officer of the *Shenandoah* told me that he was hung up to make him join their vessel. This officer had been suspended from duty for talking to me, as he said. Strong joined the vessel as soon as we went on board. I did not see Hopkins hung up. All I know about it was what I learned from the officer Hunt. I do not know that they hung up Hanson. I saw him come aft with a spyglass and I supposed that he joined voluntarily. I saw Hopkins walking about assisting the cook, after he was said to have been hung up.

I said to Hunt, "I see Hopkins seems to be working with the cook." "Yes," said Hunt, "he has joined the vessel. They hung him up in the morning and he stayed there till noon. He was hung so that his toes just touched the floor when the vessel was on an even keel." Hunt said that Hopkins called to the Master-at-arms to tell the mate that his shoulder blades were nearly pulled out, and to come and let him down.

Waddell toyed with the idea of transferring one of his thirty-two-pound rifles to the *Lizzie* and using her as a tender. But he was too shorthanded. Reluctantly, he ordered her burned. Just as the fire began to "take," and the schooner was burning brightly, a breeze sprang up. With all her sail set, the burning ship, unguided, sped toward her destroyer. For a moment, excitement akin to panic caught the cruiser's crew. Then Whittle, relieving the young officer of the deck on instructions from Waddell, began to issue crisp orders. The yards were braced back, the *Shenandoah* slowly turned, and her blazing victim ran harmlessly past.

She was the last prize for three weeks.

7

The *Shenandoah* – *Sea King* secret was out.

The British steamer *Calabar,* docking in Liverpool after a voyage from Tenerife, Canary Islands, had brought Captain Corbett and the angry crew of the former *Sea King.* The story of the metamorphosis of the merchantman spread through town.

While the *Lizzie* was being run down and destroyed just north of the Equator, the American Consul in Liverpool was spreading the alarm to the Union naval forces. In an urgent letter dispatched to Commodore Craven of the U.S.S. *Niagara,* the Consul reported:

> The *Laurel* went to Madeira, where she lay some three days. The steamer *Sea King,* that sailed from London on the 8th of October, went off the island and on the 18th signalled the *Laurel* to come out. She immediately got up steam and both steamers went to a small barren island within sight of Madeira, and the *Laurel* transferred to the *Sea King* the six guns and carriages, a large quantity of shot, shell, powder, etc. . . .
>
> The *Laurel* went to Tenerife and landed the men who would not join the *Shenandoah.* The latter vessel went in another direction and is no doubt burning and destroying vessels.
>
> I, am, sir, etc.
>
> THOMAS H. DUDLEY

More details were soon available. The crewmen from the *Sea King* were paid off at the Sailor's Home. They asked money for the entire voyage but had to settle for an extra three months' wages. Still dissatisfied, two of the men, John Wilson, a seaman, and John Hercus, a carpenter, called on the American Consul and furnished him with a description of the ship and a story of its transfer.

There was good news awaiting Captain Corbett upon his arrival in England. The Law Officers of the Crown, after studying the charges made against him by the British officials at Tenerife, decided that he had not violated the Foreign Enlistment Act. "The criminal act must have been committed within some part of her Majesty's dominions, a word which as here used does not – in our opinion – include a British ship at sea. . . ."

But when the depositions of Wilson and Hercus reached the Crown Officers, after moving slowly through the winding channels of international diplomacy, Corbett was again arrested. Released on bond, he was not brought to trial until weeks after the *Shenandoah's* voyage was ended.

On November 19, the *Index*, a propaganda paper published in London, announced the existence of the raider. After accusing the Northern naval forces of treachery in sinking the cruiser *Florida* while she was in a Brazilian port, that article went on

> . . . at the same time when the *Florida* was treacherously seized in the Bahia harbour, the Confederate flag was hoisted on a new cruiser at least the equal of the *Florida* in armament, speed and general efficiency. The *Shenandoah* starts upon her career with every promise of emulating the fame of her predecessors. She is commanded by Lieutenant Waddell, Confederate States' Navy, and a gallant staff of officers. Having received her crew and armament – everything in fact that constitutes her a belligerent vessel – on the high seas, far beyond any neutral jurisdiction, there can fortunately be no pretense of accusing her of any violation of municipal laws or international obligations. It is evident that Federal commerce is balked of the expected reward of the

murderous outrage in Bahia, for already the telegraph has advised us of the doings of no less than three Confederate cruisers. . . . To this formidable list of ubiquitous enemies, the New York Chamber of Commerce must now add a fourth, and Confederate sympathizers paraphrasing the familiar *Le roi est mort; vive le roi,* may exulting exclaim, the *Florida* is gone, long live the *Shenandoah.*

ROLLING DOWN PAST RIO

"AHOY."

The voice came from below the bows of the *Shenandoah* shortly after eight o'clock on the evening of November 15.

"What's wantin'?" drawled John Grimball, a South Carolinian, the officer of the deck.

"Heave to," said the surly voice. "I want to come on board."

Grimball drawled the orders, and the *Shenandoah* swung around. A few moments later a strange figure came clambering over the side: a large man in an oilskin coat, who wore a wig of Manila yarn repulsively resembling curly yellow hair. He was crowned with a chafing dish. In his right hand he held a harpoon and in his left an enormous speaking trumpet. Behind him were a husky female in a fantastic dress, her crockery breasts awry, and a red-aproned barber who carried a two-foot razor and a bucketful of churned tar and grease.

"What ship is this?" the wigged behemoth demanded.

"The Confederate cruiser *Shenandoah,* Your Majesty," Grimball replied, saluting smartly.

"Bring them before me."

The shellbacks, men who had been admitted to King Neptune's court on previous crossings of the Equator, set out in pursuit of the first-timers. The chase was especially pleasant because nearly all the crewmen were old-timers while all but a handful of the officers were greenhorns. Neptune's subjects were found hiding in the galley, in the holds, under bunks, rolled up in hammocks. One by one they were dragged before His Majesty, who declared them hideous and untidy and sentenced them to be shaved.

The laconic Fred Chew was first captured.

"Where are you from?" thundered Neptune.

"Why, ah'm from Missouri, Your Maj—" Chew began. Before he could complete the sentence he was interrupted by the barber, who scooped up a handful of sludge from his bucket and plopped it in the lieutenant's mouth.

"Where?" said Neptune. "Speak up, man!" But Chew, still spitting, did not attempt to answer. He was quickly pinned, lathered with grease-molasses-and-tar, shaved with the wooden razor, and rinsed with a two-inch stream of salt water – played by a hose powered by a donkey engine – and was then pronounced a confirmed shellback.

Mason and Browne, the young midshipmen, got through the initiation without special incident. When McNulty, the trigger-tempered ship's surgeon, was dragged before the monarch, everyone waited happily for the explosion.

"Where are you from?"

"Ireland to be sure."

Slap went a handful of sludge into McNulty's mouth. Crash went the barber on the deck as McNulty brought up a right from the deck. The Celt started for Neptune, but a dash of water in the face blinded him a moment, and the annointed grabbed him and held him while he was shaved.

Two officers who had not crossed the Line before particularly enjoyed the royal show; for them it was savored by the sweetness of getting away with something. Having given permission for the party, young Whittle, the executive officer felt himself immune. And his Annapolis classmate, John Grimball, who was officer of the deck, could not be touched.

But when the court had considered the cases of everyone else aboard, the attendants grabbed Whittle and led him, passionately protesting, to a wet and slippery fate. No sooner had the executive officer been handled with proper disrespect than Waddell appeared and relieved the reluctant Grimball from duty lest he miss meeting his Majesty.

2

Out of the early chaos aboard the *Shenandoah* had come order — and routine.

The guns were mounted and ready. Two rifled Whitworths, thirty-two-pounders, were at the forward ports. Four smooth bore guns, capable of hurling sixty-eight-pound shot, were midships. Aft were the popguns, the twelve-pound signalers. The deck beneath each gun had been plated with iron, and additional braces were worked 'tween decks. The ports were widened to give the Whitworths a high angle of fire; they had a range of three miles. Though any pair of guns might be fired simultaneously, Gunner John Guy declared it would be impossible to fire a broadside. The *Shenandoah,* he feared, would disintegrate.

Except for the guns, the upper deck was clear. The 'tween decks area was exceptionally lofty for a ship of the Sixties — nearly eight feet. The forward area 'tween decks still held some surplus coal, but the midships section had been cleared for the crew. Iron fittings were built into the hull for the hammocks, which were slung by night and stowed out of sight by day. Tables and sea chests, all taken from prizes, were the only furniture.

The two staterooms aft were used by Waddell for his cabin. The central salon served as the officers' wardroom; opening from the salon were eight small cabins, built for commercial passengers, and now used by the commissioned officers. Two commissioned officers, Mason and Browne, the youngest, slept in steerage with the petty officers.

Captain Waddell's cabin was no longer the gloomy hole he had disconsolately described as "the most cheerless and offensive spot I ever occupied." There was a new carpet now, a fine bed with a deep mattress, a sofa, a mahogany table lined with books, an easy chair. With the routine established, Waddell had some time of his own. He spent it reading – mostly on matters pertaining to international law. Besides the standard books on navigation, he had been furnished with Phillimore's *Law of Nations.* "I had read Wharton and Vattel on International Law," he recalled later, "and had also studied the fundamental principles of law found in Blackstone. Most of my leisure hours were devoted to Phillimore, and I found him a good friend, but requiring brown study."

Books brought by the individual officers, plus those taken from the prize ships, totaled nearly six hundred. Most of them were pooled in a ship's library, cared for by Master's Mate Hunt. Scott and Dickens were the most popular authors, and the absence of four pages from *Martin Chuzzlewit* was a shipboard tragedy. Most of the officers had lived in France while waiting to be assigned to a ship and consequently read some French. *Les Misérables* in an eleven-volume edition was considered a cultural duty. Mason and Browne practiced their French daily with a Burgundian from the crew of the *Alina,* and in the wardroom, French phrases were as much a part of the regular conversation as was sea slang.

Off-duty diversions ran in cycles. One man would start to sew, and for a few days the wardroom would look like a sewing circle. Someone would remember a puzzle, and conundrums would be the order of the day. Cards were forbidden (though occasional undercover games of whist were held), but checkers, backgammon, and cribbage were permitted. Chess was the favorite game, and Whittle the champ.

Up forward the amusements were more physical – dances and wrestling and singing "shanties." The spinning of fabulous forecastle histories took up the usual amount of time. Already a dozen nationalities were represented in the crew—American, English, French, Swedish, Hanoverian, Dutch, Malay, Negro, Danish, Portuguese, Irish, Hindu – and the common denominators were the rhythm of song and dance, the violence of physical contest. Some of the men, handy with knives, spent their time making cribbage boards and canes.

There were three messes – one for commissioned officers, one for petty officers, and one for the crew. Waddell ate alone in his cabin. The food was standard sea fare, and the complaints were equally standard. The basic ingredients were unleavened biscuit, called hard-tack, corned beef with a flavor indicated by its nickname, "salt horse," duff, a combination of flour, lard, and yeast, set in a bag and boiled in equal parts of salt and fresh water until hard, then served with molasses. Both officers' messes had the same food; the crew fared on poorer stuff. Aboard the *Shenandoah,* this standard sea fare was supplemented with delicacies from the prize ships – preserved fruits, canned tomatoes, fresh beef, rum. In the topgallant forecastle were sheep and hogs and fowl, slaughtered on holidays or whenever Dr. Lining decided the antiscorbutic properties of fresh meat were needed to prevent scurvy.

Most of the crew were issued a loose, grayish-brown uniform, but many continued to wear the clothes they had joined in; striped shirts, tams, German whites, British blues, and even Yankee striped pants were as common as the Confederate gray, except on Sundays, when the men stood muster in uniform, then changed to Sunday shore clothes in order to air them.

While the ship was in the tropics, Waddell issued an order that officers, when they went out of the wardroom, must wear their uniforms. Black or blue pants were allowed, but nothing but gray coats or jackets, and no slouch hats. The order was unpopular.

The usual shipboard feuds and friendships sprouted. Mason and Browne, friends ashore, became inseparable. Neither of them liked the sailing master, Irvine Bulloch. Though they were on their first cruise, and Bulloch was a veteran of the *Alabama,* both, in Mason's words, "felt a little put out at being placed on this vessel as his subordinates for he has never been before any board of examiners, having been all the time nearly at sea; at least he was out of the way when the examining boards were appointed. He was made master by Captain Semmes, having been on the *Alabama* during her whole cruise."

Whittle and Lining were close, but Lining greatly admired Smith Lee, while Whittle couldn't stand him. During the days just after crossing the equator, Lining passed judgment on two other officers in his journal:

> Of all the old growls I ever met with, old O'Shea, our carpenter, beats. He has taken a great dislike to me, first when I would not put him upon the list when he wanted to go (being in a pet with the first lieutenant) and then because I would not constantly inquire about his foot. The fact is that he has been a politician in some navy yard in the U.S. and accustomed to have all about him do just as he wanted them to do, and now he can't get that and thinks he must growl. Today I wanted some Litharge and as it comes in his department I asked for some. He first said he had it; then that he did not know what it was, as he was not a painter, and finally I had to go to Whittle to get it. If he knew how little I cared for his growling he would stop it.
>
> Alcott, our sailmaker, is a goodfornothing lazy chap and has now been on the list some time with not much; so I told him today that he seemed not to improve that the best thing I could do was get the captain to let me survey him at the first port we got to and send him home invalided to be discharged from the Navy. This I thought would scare him, but he only said, "Yes, sir," as if he cared not a thing.

Relations between Waddell and his subalterns were correct but cool. No one challenged his authority, but in the wardroom bull sessions, several of the officers questioned the skipper's judgment. Responsibility had rendered him cautious, and, shorthanded, Waddell refused to take chances; at night he kept the canvas shorter than the men felt necessary for safety. The youngsters thought him timid, while the captain, separated by a barrier of age and authority, underestimated the capacities of the twenty-year-olds.

On December 3, Dr. Lining reported in his journal that:

> The Island of Tristan da Cunha is only distant from us today about 160 miles. As around this island is a favorite whaling ground, I and some of the others thought it might be a good thing for us if we were to cruise around it for a week or more. The Captain was going right by it; so I went and had a talk with him, and I think rather persuaded him to do it, although the wind is not very fair for us to get there. At least I hope so, as he put her on the wind, which is all we can do.

3

The *Edward,* of New Bedford, was an old ship, bark-rigged, bluff-bowed, and square-sterned. Built as a merchantman in 1818, she had been unable to match the speed of the streamlined clippers and was soon enrolled in the whaling fleet where speed was less important than thick oak sides.

She had sailed through the great days of New England whaling. Built when Nantucket was still the center of the industry, she was still around when New Bedford, with its deep water harbor, became the oil capital of the world, replacing the island town. She had helped thin out the rich-oiled sperm whales, and when they were too few to be profitable quarry, had gone with the other New Englanders to more distant waters – to the South Pacific, the Antarctic, the Bering Sea, the Arctic – after right whales and bowheads. In her time she entered every ocean in pursuit of leviathan, and though the Federal government had purchased nearly forty ships of her vintage to make up the Great Stone Fleet, sunk outside Southern harbors as part of the blockade, the *Edward* was spared. She was still considered fit for the three-year voyage to the whaling grounds.

Four months out of New Bedford, bound for the Arctic, she was in no hurry. It was early December and the ice would not break up in Bering Strait until spring. Her master, Edward Worth, shaped a course which would take him through the old whaling grounds around Tristan da Cunha.

On Saturday, December 3, the cry "Blows-ows, thar she blows!" sounded from the masthead.

"Where away?"

"Three points astern."

Captain Worth hoped it would be a sperm. The waters around Tristan da Cunha had once been the favorite haunt of the oiliest of all whales, and some were still taken there. But this was a right whale, or a bowhead. Worth could tell by the spout. A sperm has a single nostril, and when it comes to the surface and releases the air from its massive lungs, a single column of warm air is vaporized into steam; the right and the bowhead have two nostrils – and off to the starboard of the *Edward,* twin columns of steam still hung in the cool sea air.

Worth studied the position of the whale. It could be taken. He gave the order to "lower away."

Two boats were put over the side. With practiced precision the crews threw their weight into the long ash oars. The whale was a mile away, cruising slowly along the surface. As the boats approached, the great bulk slid out of sight. The whaleboats changed course; the prey had been in sight for twenty-five minutes and the hunters, knowing the habits of the species, guessed it would stay under water for the same time, swim at the same speed, and keep on course.

When the whale surfaced, the lead boat was almost beside it. "Stand up," ordered the officer of the boat. The helmsman arose and fitted his left knee into the clumsy cleat, a brace, and put his right foot back on the first thwart. He picked up the iron, the long, beautifully balanced, razor-edged throwing harpoon. Delicately he raised the iron and stood, tense and braced, poised to hurl it into the slaty bulk alongside.

The officer said, "Give it to him."

The boat-steerer's arm lashed forward. The iron sank home. The sea churned as the whale shot forward in startled agony; the white hemp harpoon line hummed hotly as it ran out over the rollers at the bow. The whaleboat skimmed over the water as the great beast rushed forward. Quickly the boat-steerer and officer traded places, the helmsman going back to the oar that served as tiller, the officer going to the bow with a forty-pound blunderbuss – a gun with a short barrel and two-inch muzzle that fired a short-fused shell a foot long.

After a two-mile run, the whale sounded. When it came up, the boat was again alongside. The officer raised the shoulder gun, braced himself, and tugged at the massive trigger. The shot went home. The hunters could hear the muffled explosion inside the monster. A twin plume of red puffed into the air, and the men were covered with blood. The faint sound of cheering rolled across the water from the *Edward;* the men left behind had seen the whale show the red flag. A few minutes later the whale rolled onto its side, and the triumphant shout, "Fin out," marked the end of the chase.

Lines were fastened with sharp hooks to the monster's head, and the long row begun back to the *Edward,* the forty-foot carcass in tow. It was evening before the ship was reached and the prize made secure on the starboard side.

The cutting stage was lowered and a blubber hook inserted between the eye and the fin. A mate with a razor-edged spade freed the blubber from the flesh. Power was applied to the falls, and the "blanket piece," unwinding spirally, was peeled from the carcass like the skin of an apple and hoisted to the masthead, then lowered into the hold, where, in the blubber room, it was cut into "horse pieces," chunks about one foot wide and two feet long. These pieces were tossed up on deck and sliced with a mincing knife that produced "bible leaves," small slices of blubber, resembling thick book pages attached to a thin binding.

Fires were built in the try works at midships and the "bible leaves" put into two large iron try pots. When the oil was boiled out, the scraps of blubber were tossed in the fire. They burned brightly. Other scraps in a wire basket, suspended from a yardarm, gave light as the blubber crews aboard the *Edward* worked through the night and on into the morning of December 4.

4

"This has been an eventful day for us," Lining wrote in his journal on the night of December 4. "We had a scare and took a prize. Early this morning a sail was reported in sight on our lee beam. She looked Yankeeish, so we made for her. About 5:15 A.M. we came near enough for her to make out any colors we might hoist. So we ran up the American flag. She immediately hoisted the Italian and hove to. I got on deck about 5:30 A.M., about which time we were preparing to lower a boat to send on board of her. Soon afterwards Mr. Bulloch went on board, when she proved to be the *Dea del Mare* from Genoa bound to Rangoon for a cargo. She had been a Yankee ship but was lawfully transferred to her present owners. Mr. B told her that we were the U.S.S. *De Soto* on a cruise after Confederates. To deceive them, all our men had taken off their caps and gray suits and were dressed as much as possible in blue.

"Before we got through with this two other sail were sighted, one astern, the other on our lee. We made for the latter. Everybody remarked that they could not tell what sail she was under, but when we came near enough to make her hull out, we, or rather some of us, were very well satisfied to draw off. She was a long, low, bark-rigged vessel, carrying a great deal of lower-sails, with her main-royal set, but seemed to have no fore-royal yard at all. Her stem had no sheer in it, being right up and down, her stern round, and something on deck abaft the mainmast had something the appearance of a smokestack lowered. There was a great variety of opinion as to whether she was a gunboat or not. I for one thought she was, although, of course, I knew not of what nation. The only thing against her being a gunboat that I could see was that she had no quarter boats at the davits. However we hauled up and stood off on the wind, while the stranger was going off under studding sails. The wind was fresh, and as we were under all sail except studding sails we went ten knots through the water, so we soon left our friend behind and ran him out of sight.

"At 10:45 A.M. made land on weather beam, only to be seen indistinctly through the clouds. It proved to be Inaccessible Island of the Tristan da Cunha group and soon after we caught a glimpse of the latter high up in the clouds. At noon the Island of Tristan da Cunha bore to the northward and westward distant about forty miles. The captain said that it had been his intention to go there had the wind been fair, but to get there now we would have to lose a good deal of time which he preferred to spend at the port we were going to; or we would have to get up steam which he did not wish to do. Almost 5 P.M. we saw a sail on our lee bow and stood away for it. At 5:35 P.M. we came close enough to hoist our colors, English, when she ran up the Yankee flag. It was of no use to fire a gun, as she was already hove to under topsails, engaged in trying out blubber, as we could see by the fire on board of her. She had taken a whale yesterday afternoon."

Shortly after 6:30, Captain Worth came up over the side of the *Shenandoah.* His face was set against sorrow. "Good afternoon, gentlemen," he said to the officers who had gathered to greet him. "You have a fine ship here for a cruiser."

"Yes, sir," John Grimball replied affably, "and that vessel of yours looks as if she was familiar with traveling salt water."

The New Englander looked from the young South Carolinian to the familiar old hulk of his ship rolling gently in the light swell, her bloody booty still lashed alongside.

"Yes," he said, leaning against the bulwarks, "she was laid on the stocks before you and I were thought of."

The old *Edward* was condemned. The size of her crew presented a problem; there were twenty-five men aboard her, including the captain and three mates, tough and angry seamen, mostly Portuguese – too big a mouthful of prisoners for the raider to digest easily. Only one man, a carpenter, was willing to join the Confederates. "All the rest," said Mason, "were either Yankees who we did not want or Dagos who are not worth having." The men and mates were locked in the forecastle with the prisoners from the *Lizzie M. Stacey.* Captain Worth was paroled.

The *Shenandoah* lay beside her victim for two days, gorging herself on the whaler's fine supplies. The cruiser took on nearly a ton of hardtack, a quantity of rope, some sail, and a large amount of clothing Waddell felt his men would need in the far north.

Though their mission was to destroy the Yankee whaling fleet, less than a half-dozen men aboard the *Shenandoah* had ever seen a whaler. Except for Joshua Minor, a master's mate who had been aboard a whaler taken by the *Alabama* and risen to the rank of an officer after joining the Confederates, none of the raiders had seen a whaleship trying out blubber. All the officers went aboard the prize on an inspection tour. "Blubber," reported Lining, "was much as I imagined it, but not so thick. It had a horrid smell and as the ship was greasy I soon satisfied myself and came off."

On Tuesday morning, the lookout made out a sail a little abaft the port beam, and as the cruiser was already under steam, Waddell decided to find out who the newcomer was. But before the *Shenandoah* could move away from the whaler, a squall of rain hid the stranger. No one had taken her exact bearings, and the officers disagreed as to her whereabouts. Waddell made the decision and steamed off in a direction which Whittle, Grimball and Lining assured him would bring the raider out behind her. When the rain lifted, Waddell found his officers had been right.

"The Captain was much put out to find that he was wrong and told me that he would have given a great deal to have been right, as we seemed so much to rejoice over his mistake," Lining wrote, "but I told him it was not rejoicing to find him wrong but everybody likes to find themselves right."

The ship proved to be English, so the *Shenandoah* returned to the whaler and took off the last of the supplies. The *Edward* had five excellent whaleboats. The raider raised two of them on her davits and took the other three in tow. At five o'clock, the *Edward* was put to the torch. Her oily decks were soon a mass of flame. The *Shenandoah* steamed away at half-speed toward the snow-capped cone of Tristan da Cunha.

At 10:30 the burning prize disappeared in the darkness.

TRISTAN DA CUNHA

THE *Shenandoah* steamed slowly through the thick kelp beds that fringed Tristan da Cunha. The basalt cliffs shot up a sheer five hundred feet from the dull-green water pulsing against the beach. From the lip of the cliff the land folded back into gently rolling hills that slanted up toward the cone of a dead volcano. After six weeks out of sight of land, the scent of grass and wet earth and brush was tantalizingly sweet to the men aboard the raider.

On the northern side of the island the cliffs were dented by a valley which dipped to within a hundred feet of the sea. Well back from the lip of the low cliff were a group of stone houses, roofed with tussock grass. A British flag flew from a pole before the largest house.

The *Shenandoah* hove to in the shallow Falmouth Bay. The *Edward's* three whaleboats were pulled alongside, the prisoners released and told to gather the clothing they had salvaged from their ships and row ashore.

"We all felt sorry for Captain Worth," Lining admitted. "There was a frankness and freedom from all meanness which made us respect him. We gave him everything which we thought it right to do. I gave him as much medicine as he wanted, and as many fish hooks as he would take. Whittle had given to him his quadrant and a book on navigation."[1]

The boats, loaded with twenty-eight men and the provisions, pulled away from the *Shenandoah* shortly after 8 A.M. At the same time a boat was seen to put out from the island, a queer little canvas craft made out of driftwood from South America and canvas from wrecked ships. In a few minutes the boat was rocking alongside, its occupants ready to sell vegetables and fresh meat.

"Who be you?" one of the men called. "I do not know your flag."

"The Confederate cruiser *Shenandoah*. We intend to leave some prisoners with you."

"And where the devil did you get your prisoners?"

"From a whaler not far from here."

"Just so, to be sure. And what became of the whaler?"

"We burned her."

"Whew! Is that the way you dispose of all vessels you fall in with?"

"Only if they belong to the United States. Not otherwise."

"Well, my hearties, you know your own business, but my notion is that these sort of pranks will get you in the devil's own muss before you are through with it. What your quarrel with the United States is I don't know, but I swear I don't believe they'll stand this kind of work."

Waddell told the men he would buy all the food they would sell, and they went ashore with the news. Soon another boat came out. It was rowed by four men and carried as passenger a heavy-set, ruddy-faced Dutchman with a double-spiked beard which reached to his waist. He introduced himself as Peter Green, the spokesman for the island, but added, "I only speak for the others. We are all equal here."

He protested against the *Shenandoah's* landing the prisoners at Tristan. There were only fifty persons on the island, and to raise the population by more than half would seriously endanger food supplies. Though there was livestock, it had to be carefully husbanded. The mice were eating the grain. The vegetables were barely sufficient to feed the natives. Green was convincing, but Waddell was adamant.

At last Green pointed to the flag flying over his house. The island was British territory, he said. To land men here when they were not wanted would be an act unfriendly to Her Majesty and would be reported to authorities in Cape Town. Waddell hesitated. Always worried about the international implications of his voyage, he was reluctant to do anything which might offend Britain.

Finally he asked, "Do you have papers to prove that your island is under British protection?"

2

Peter Green could not prove that Tristan da Cunha was English. No one could, for the nationality of the island was an international question mark.

Discovered by the Portuguese, coveted by the Dutch, once ruled by an American king from Salem, Massachusetts, occupied for a year-and-a-half by British troops guarding Napoleon on St. Helena (a thousand miles away), Tristan and its sister islands – Nightingale and Inaccessible – were the orphans of the Atlantic. Many wanted them but nobody claimed them.

The islands are the tops of volcanoes rising from the submarine elevation which runs down the middle of the Atlantic. They were first sighted by a Portuguese expedition under Admiral Tristao da Cunha in 1506, and the admiral was not bashful in bestowing a name on the group. Lying in the path of the prevailing trade winds, the islands were often seen but seldom visited, during the next three centuries, by ships en route to the Indies. Only at one point, on Tristan, the largest island, was a landing possible, and even there the anchorage was not safe in a north wind.

A party of American hunters under Captain John Patten, of Philadelphia, went ashore on Tristan in 1790 and spent a profitable seven months killing seal. Though they were the first known occupants of the island, they found goats there – presumably the sole survivors from some shipwreck. During the next ten years, the Dutch decided Tristan would make a nice station on the way to Transvaal and the Indies. Two colonizing expeditions were organized; both went broke before they left Holland.

On December 27, 1810, Tristan received not only settlers but a monarch. King Jonathan Lambert, American, and his two subjects, Thomas Currie and a man known only as Williams, came ashore in a small boat from the bark *Baltic*. Lambert raised a white flag, studded with red and blue diamonds, and sent back to Boston with the *Baltic's* skipper a remarkable proclamation:

> Know all men by these presents, that I, Jonathan Lambert, late of Salem, in the State of Massachusetts, United States of America, and citizen thereof, have this 4th day of February in the year of Our Lord Eighteen Hundred and Eleven, taken absolute possession of the Island of Tristan da Cunha, so called, viz., the great island and the others known by the names of Inaccessible and Nightingale Islands, solely for myself and my heirs, for ever, with the rights of conveying the whole or any part thereof, to one or more persons, by deed of sale, free gift or otherwise, as I, or they (my heirs) may herafter think fitting or proper. . . .
>
> And lastly be it known that I hold myself and my people in the course of our traffic and intercourse with any other people to be bound by the principles of hospitality and good fellowship and the laws of nations (if any there are) as established by the best Writers on that subject, and by no other Laws whatever, until time produce particular Contracts or other Engagements.

The reign of King Jonathan lasted eighteen months, during which time the number of his subjects was increased fifty per cent by the arrival of another American, who jumped the

British ship *Queen Charlotte*. On May 17, 1812, the King and his two subject Yankees went fishing and never came back. Presumably they drowned.

The Englishman, Currie, inherited the isle. He was not lonely, for during the War of 1812, American privateers based themselves on Tristan and sailed out to raid British shipping. Currie's diary records a battle in which an unnamed American corvette outfought and captured the British brig *Penguin* five months after the war officially ended.

A year later the British landed a garrison of redcoats on the island to make certain no one used it as a base in attempting the liberation of Bonaparte. Currie was still on the island. He appears to have been quite a character. Every few weeks he would appear with a handful of gold and buy grog. The legend sprang up that he had a hidden treasure, and British troops spent their off-duty hours trailing him through the tall grass, hoping to learn the hiding place. Currie once promised to give the money to the man he liked best on the island, but he fell dead during a drinking bout before making good this pledge. The money was never found.

After eighteen months of incessant complaining by the commander of the garrison, who claimed that the outpost was not only uncomfortable but useless, the troops were withdrawn. They left behind three soldiers who asked permission to colonize. The leader of the group was a Scotch corporal, William Glass, who had with him his wife, a Negress from Cape Town, and two children, the youngest of whom was born on the island. Glass and his companions, Sam Burnell and John Nankivel, set up a communist community.

In return for agreeing to look after some of the military supplies for the next six months, they were given livestock. Five years later, the Government not having come back for its supplies, and Glass's letters on the subject having gone unanswered, Burnell was dispatched aboard a passing whaler with instructions to discover whether the colony could use the goods. Burnell never returned.

The tiny colony prospered. Without benefit of chamber of commerce, it attracted new inhabitants. To the shipwrecked any land looks good, and the rocks around Tristan claimed many victims. Some colored women came from Cape Colony. After a few years the nubile daughters of the founding fathers played Lorelei to men aboard the New England whalers that, during the Thirties, began to cruise after sperm whales in the waters around Tristan. When the old patriarch Glass died in 1853, the population was too big for the island; it numbered nearly a hundred. The problem of *Lebensraum* was solved when Mrs. Glass, her children and grandchildren, twenty-four in all, left to join her sons in America.

With the death of Glass, who had run the community on a basis of patriarchal communism, leadership fell to Peter Green, a solid, middle-aged Dutchman who had come ashore from a wrecked ship in 1836 and promptly anglicized his name. Green was chosen as chief because he spoke three languages – French in addition to English and his native tongue – and also because his fine, two-pronged beard impressed the hirsute Yankee whaling masters.

But not even the Dutchman's fine foliage could keep Waddell from depositing the prisoners on Tristan when he found that Green's only claim to English protection was the fact that the original founders of the settlement had been British. The flag was a gift from a passing merchantman. Waddell did agree, however, to send ashore more supplies – four barrels of salt beef, four of pork and 1680 pounds of bread. Waddell also bought beef at eight cents a pound and paid for it in flour, from the *Edward*, at the rate of seven dollars a barrel.

The islanders horrified the Confederates by towing the barrels of flour through the surf to shore.

At 2 P.M. the supplies had been swapped and the *Shenan-*

doah, not having dropped anchor or sent one of her own men ashore, steamed away from the island. Watching the snow-topped cone fade away to starboard, the Confederates felt a little guilty.

"We had left our captured foes on an island thousands of miles from their homes," Hunt wrote, "and none of us were quite satisfied with the part we were necessitated to play. But I question whether our Yankee acquaintances stood much in need of our sympathy after all. They had the free range of a charming island, where reigned perennial summer; besides, there were a number of the gentler sex in want of mates, I learned, and where there are pretty women so circumstanced, there can sailors be happy."

3

The prisoners settled down to make the best of the dubious delights of Tristan. It was no paradise. Though the islanders were hospitable and took the refugees into the stone cottages, the surplus maidens were still mateless when, on December 28, a steamer was sighted. Signals were set on shore, and the ship hove to in Falmouth Bay. It was the U.S.S. *Iroquois,* C. R. P. Rodgers commanding, bound in pursuit of the *Shenandoah.*

A ship more unlikely to catch the fleet raider would be hard to find. The *Iroquois* was a beat-up old tub with scant canvas and leaky boilers. She could not make over seven knots under sail and she could not carry enough coal to make a voyage of more than a few hundred miles. The enlistments of her crewmen were running out, and none would agree to rejoin the ship. Her commander had just received a letter authorizing him to bring her home when, on December 12, at Montevideo, Uruguay, he saw in a Brazilian newspaper a report that the *Kate Prince* and *Anna Jans* had reached Rio and Bahia with survivors from ships sunk by the *Shenandoah.*

"Believing that the *Shenandoah* would go toward the Cape of Good Hope," Commander Rodgers reported to the Secretary of Navy, "I went with all dispatch to Tristan da Cunha, at which anchorage I arrived on the 28th and found that the *Shenandoah* had touched there just three weeks before to land the officers and crews of the whaling bark *Edward,* of New Bedford, . . . and of the schooner *Lizzie M. Stacey,* of and from Boston. I immediately took all these officers and men on board the *Iroquois,* and sailed the same evening for Cape Town."

But the incident of the island does not end with the departure of the Yankee prisoners. Twenty-two years later, when the whaling industry had died out and Tristan had fallen on bad times, old Dutch Peter Green wrote a letter to a friend:

> I have wrote to the [British] Admiralty about the *Shenandoah* business the U.S. owe to us a little bill for keeping 27 prisoners but as it is rather national i dount like to write to the U. States i would not mention this but we have lately been unfortunate and i think it is a just claim we have kept several ship's crews at Tristan but we had always plenty in former days likewise deserters from American whale ships.

There is no record of the Admiralty forwarding the claim, or of the bill ever having been paid.

HOLIDAY CRUISE

On the night after leaving Tristan da Cunha, Captain Waddell, whose nocturnal worries were a ship's joke, could not sleep. His uneasy ear was disturbed by a new sound, a grating – faint but ominous – in the propeller shaft. He sent for Engineer O'Brien, who heard nothing wrong. All night the fretting captain tossed in his bunk. The next morning the cruiser was put under sail, the propeller triced up, and an inspection made. There was a crack entirely across the brass band on the coupling of the propeller shaft.

The situation was serious. Temporary repairs could be made, but there was no telling how long they would hold. To travel under steam was to risk permanent damage to the bearings and sternpost. This left Waddell with two alternatives, neither enticing. He could take the *Shenandoah* to Cape Town for repairs; it was the nearest port, but by now, he was sure, a Yankee man-of-war must be on his trail, and the Cape was one of the first places where they would look for him. On the other hand, if he tried to make Melbourne, he would have to rely on sailpower for the six thousand mile voyage.

"After turning the subject over in my mind," Waddell wrote, "I decided it best to cross the Indian Ocean under sail, hoping to keep company with good luck, for I had certainly been favored in overcoming difficulties during the seven preceding weeks. The ship was given a more southerly course, that she might be thrown into strong west winds, which belt encircles the earth south of the parallel of forty-three degrees with more violence than the corresponding belt north of the same parallel in north latitude."

Waddell was wrong about the winds; more than just strong, they were violent. The Shenandoah needed all her good luck to survive them.

Five days after dropping the prisoners, the cruiser crossed the meridian of Greenwich. She was six thousand miles south of her starting-point on the Thames. A fresh west gale was blowing, and the sea was running high. "No sail in sight," Lining noted in his journal, "but as yet we are all good friends, have no quarrelling but good jokes are going around all the time and good spirits prevailing. Smith Lee is the life of all and he is all the time getting off some joke or other on Dr. McN, who is now 'a doctor just from Paris, a little deaf, but great on curing diseases of the ear.' "

On December 17, the *Shenandoah* passed the meridian of the Cape of Good Hope. She was a week ahead of the tentative schedule outlined for her in Bulloch's letter to Waddell – but she was in serious trouble.

The wind had reached gale proportions. The *Shenandoah* drove forward under light canvas. Like all sharp and narrow vessels of great length, she rolled deep, and the fact that she was "by the head" – drawing more water forward than aft – made her hard to steer. Sea after sea tumbled in over her bulwarks, and the deck was constantly inches deep in water which splashed into the cabins and poured through the leaks onto the berth deck below.

All guns in the battery were secured with extra tackles. Preventer braces and backstays were run through the eyelets and every rope drawn taut. Hatches were battened, and men stood by the relieving tackles to prevent the ship from swinging into the wind if the wheel ropes parted under the growing strain.

Though the winds remained fierce, the weather was changeable. At times the ship plowed through a glittering blue sea under a summer sun, and then, only minutes later, the sky would be overcast, hail would rattle on the deck, or great blasts of rain would sweep across the ocean, "falling horizontal," and striking hard enough to hurt. Everyone was wet, everyone uncomfortable.

"To get a meal in Christian fashion was the next thing to impossible," Hunt wrote. "The steward, after much devious navigating would succeed at last in placing it on the table, and the next moment a heavy lurch of the ship would scatter dishes and contents in every direction. Once, not satisfied with such a piece of impertinence, old Neptune sent a sea over our starboard quarter which came pouring down upon us like a cataract, and the remnant of our dinner, previously disposed around the cabin floor by the first accident, was by the second submerged under a couple feet of water."

Life for the crew was even rougher, though the shellbacks were more accustomed to it than the young officers. "Little parties of men may be seen congregating on the different parts of the berth deck," Hunt continued, "each listening to some tough yarn, spun by some old shellback of their number. Suddenly the sound of the boatswain's call is heard, sharp and shrill above the howling of the tempest, and for the moment conversation ceases, and every man anxiously awaits to learn the nature of the summons. It is nothing any more serious this time than to call all hands to the agreeable duty of 'splicing the main brace,' and in an instant there is a general rush for the deck, where the grog is served to each in turn.

"To a landsman it may seem the height of recklessness to serve out any intoxicating beverage at such a time to a ship's company, but the omission of such an item in the routine of their lives would probably engender a feeling of dissatisfaction more to be dreaded than any trifling excess in which they would be likely to indulge."

The *Shenandoah* was caught in a revolving gale. Hour by hour, day by day, the storm increased in violence. A huge wave, the highest Waddell had ever seen, came surging down on the rolling ship. It towered over her, hung poised, then smashed down on deck. The boards groaned under the impact. Water stood even with the top of the bulwarks for the length of the deck, and under the great burden the cruiser lost her run, shuddered to a standstill in the wildly tossing ocean. The men thought they could feel her settling. On the next wave she might founder.

Over the howl of the wind came the shouted orders from Whittle: "Clear the ports! Clear the ports!"

The crew grabbed axes and crowbars and half-waded, half-swam to the rail. Waist deep in water, they smashed at the ports, knocking loose the coverings, giving the tons of water held in by the bulwarks a chance to drain off before the next wave broke over.

The captain was convinced. To stay so far south was to invite disaster. He changed the course to north of east, seeking better weather, and finding it.

Though the gale was left behind, tremendous seas were still running. The *Shenandoah* was "buffeted, tossed, and knocked about as an empty bottle might be driven in the wake of a steamship." The squalls kept the ship from drying out, and the seas breaking against her sides sent fine spray through the open seams of the teak hull into the berth deck. All the bedding was wet.

"Our rudder also is making a most terrible row, jarring the whole afterpart of the ship, and making me think, sometimes, that the whole thing will be wrenched off," Lining reported. "It makes such a noise that the Captain cannot sleep and would give $5000 had he never taken command of this ship, so much is he worried and bothered."

Day after dripping day of standing a wet watch, eating in a flooded mess, turning into a damp bed left everyone's nerves frayed. Conversation wore thin. Men went through the motions of their duties mechanically, unthinkingly.

For Waddell it was worst of all. Responsibility weighed heavily on him, and the more he worried the more he tried to shoulder all the details. He did not have confidence in his young officers and especially did he distrust the judgment of Fred Chew.

The likable Missourian was, according to Lining, " a most unfortunate fellow. If anything happens it is sure to be in his room; one day his *chez,* as he calls it, completely capsized and made a perfect wreck of it. I went on deck to tell him of it, and his trunk, which he had up airing, made another capsize and sent some letters which he very much values into the deep. With his trunk still overturned and with the wind blowing his things about, there he stood gazing at his letters to the great danger of everything else going." A few days later, "Another misfortune happened to Chew. The ship was rolling a great deal, and he as officer of the deck made a slide to leeward and nearly went overboard. His cap did go, which made quite a loss."

These little misfortunes, though a source of shipboard humor, did nothing to increase the captain's confidence in Chew. The matter came to a head when,on a particularly rough night, Waddell asked Joshua Minor, a master's mate, to stand Chew's watch.

"This morning," said Lining in his journal, "Chew feels very much hurt about it, and after some time came and asked me about what he should do, as I had been talking to Scales about it. I gave him my opinion very freely, for I thought his dignity and position as an officer would be injured unless he did something. He then went and talked with the Captain, who gave him no redress or satisfaction, saying that he would do it again should circumstances arise to make it advisable, in his opinion. Thereupon Chew requested to be relieved from duty and said that he would apply to leave the ship.

"There, I think he was wrong, as I would allow no man to run me out of his ship under such circumstances. I would refuse duty and let him be the one to send me out if he wanted to. Chew's watch came round and he was not called, neither was anything said to him, but we saw the Captain and Mr. Whittle in most earnest conversation. At about 9 P.M. the Captain sent for Mr. W. on deck and after he had been up there almost three quarters of an hour Mr. Chew was sent for, and in a short time down came old Chew, his face all lit up and said that he was to be called to keep his watch.

"What the exact nature of the conversation was I don't know, but one of the provisos was that in very heavy weather Mr. Whittle was to keep watch with him. I was very glad when everything was finally arranged, as any such row between a Captain and an officer always breeds discord in a ship, and I want nothing like that during this cruise."

The next day Lining learned from Whittle "something of his conversation with the Captain yesterday and how the Captain had said that all his old friends had deserted him, and that everybody had turned against him. How childish and foolish that is, for if he would only act rightly we would all be with him."

2

On Christmas morning another storm blew up. Dabney Scales, the watch officer, entered in the log:

> From 4 to 8 A.M. fresh gales from the southwest; very heavy sea running; shipped several seas; 5:20 wind increasing, close-reefed main topsail; 5:30 battened down hatches.

At exactly six another "buster" crashed down on the deck. "It came nearly up to the rail," according to Lining, "washed one man west over the lee rail into the sea but fortunately the next sea washed him back again. Several men were swimming on deck. Whittle knocked out the lee port aft and hollered for all hands to come on deck. It was not until then that I got up.

"In the meantime the sea had come aft, burst open the wardroom door, and completely flooded the wardroom. It came into my room in such quantities as to make everything on the floor wringing wet and some of it even was washed up in my bunk. It rushed in and out in floods. I got my valise on a chair and intended to take it quietly until Whittle cried out, when I went out in the wardroom in my bare feet, in fact just as I got out of bed.

"There what a scene presented itself! Everyone of the officers up and in their bare feet looking in a hopeless kind of way at the water while some were starting to get it under. Smith stood at his door with a mat, trying to keep the water out; when finding his attempts ineffectual he gracefully resigned the task and returned to his bed. Chew stood up on his trunk and moved between that and his bed in a helpless energy trying as he said to 'stare the water out of his room.'

"The water was bitterly cold, having 42 degrees, and every now and then we had to get up on something to relieve the cold. At last the water in the wardroom was pretty well cleaned out and we began at our individual rooms. I was trying to bail out mine with two pairs of stockings when Williams, the cabin boy, came to my rescue and between us we got it all out. I went back to bed almost seven to try and get warm again, at which I did not succeed before breakfast time.

"What a looking room ours was! Soaking wet, and everything near the floor in the same way one shows not. A great beginning to a happy Christmas."

With the *Shenandoah* buttoned up against a gale, regulations forbade any fires. But Whittle suspended the rules and told Charles Hopkins, the Negro cook, impressed from the *Stacey,* to fix a proper feast for the officers' mess. The steward fought his way over the slippery deck to the topgallant forecastle and brought back to the galley the last goose. He wrung the bird's neck, cleaned it, plucked it, stuffed it with ship's biscuits, canned tomatoes, and dried apples soaked in rum, and put it on to roast.

No attempt had been made at holiday decorations in the wardroom. Instead of a graceful candelabrum on a linen-covered table, smoky lamps, rocking violently as the ship boxed about in the stormy sea, lit the narrow room. There was no tablecloth. No one dressed for dinner – no one had a dry uniform.

The bearded men sat in silence and looked at each other morosely, their thoughts miles away. Most of the officers were young; this was their first Christmas at sea. A few were married. Waddell, who joined his subalterns at the mess, could remember every detail of the Christmases at home. He and his wife, Ann, always went to her parents' Maryland mansion – Christmas was soft voices, carols, "God Rest Ye, Merry Gentlemen," branches of evergreen, little gifts, the look in Ann's eyes, a long table, the shine of silver, turkey.

The Hindu cabin boy staggered in with the goose, barely able to keep his balance in the storm. He brought other dishes: fresh pork, corned beef, fresh potatoes, and mince pies. But the goose was the *pièce de résistance,* and the *pièce de résistance* was tough. Twice while Waddell was carving a sudden pitch of the ship tossed the bird off the table and into the water sloshing about the wardroom floor. Each time it was retrieved, without comment, and eventually all were served.

After his first bite, Hunt proclaimed the goose to be "the identical fowl that Commodore Noah took with him on his first and last cruise." The witticism fell flat. Grimly the officers finished the holiday feast. In silence they went to their cabins or donned their sou'westers and rolled out onto the pitching deck to stand a watch.

Nobody sang of goodwill toward men.

⸙ 3 ⸙

The Government of His Majesty, the Emperor of Brazil, was deeply offended. So, though ordinarily it moved with the slowness of all governments and all imperial bureaucracies, it moved swiftly. Late in November, the *Kate Prince* reached Brazil and reported its seizure and search by the *Shenandoah*. When the imperial authorities found that the boarding officers had broken the seal placed on the cargo records by the Brazilian consul at Cardiff, it took them less than a month to decide this was an affront His Majesty could not suffer in silence. Just before the holidays, the Rio de Janiero *Jornal do Commercio* carried the government office's announcement of its unhappiness:

> The Imperial Government having had information that the Confederate Steamer *Shenandoah* boarded at sea the galley *Kitty Prince,* from Cardiff to the province of Bahia, and that in such act the commander of that steamer (J. I. Waddell) opened the manifest of the said galley, breaking the seal of the Brazilian consulate, have resolved to prohibit the entrance into any port of the Empire of said steamer, or of any other vessel commanded by the said Waddell.

Fighting the storm in the Indian Ocean, four thousand miles away, Waddell probably would not have been worried about this Christmas greeting, even had he known of it.

QUEEN OF THE DELPHINE

THE gale blew itself out. On the morning of December 29, the wind shifted to the south, bringing squalls of fine rain and an ugly cross sea that broke high on the sides of the *Shenandoah*. The raider wallowed through the broken sea under short canvas.

At 9 A.M. a lookout reported a sail far astern, visible only occasionally between squalls. When it could be determined how much canvas the newcomer was carrying, Waddell ordered the *Shenandoah* be made to hold her luff, to prevent the stranger's passing out of gunshot range to windward. By two o'clock she was hull up. Everyone having a telescope watched eagerly as she approached. She looked new; her hull was painted white with green trim, and the white cotton canvas and long sky poles indicated an American.

As usual, the *Shenandoah* was flying the English ensign. When the stranger drew up astern, the raider signaled, asking her nationality. She hoisted a flag so faded that it could not be made out. But the unsuspecting stranger made no effort to draw away and soon was near enough for the red, white, and blue pattern of the colors to be recognizable. A cheer broke out on the *Shenandoah*.

When the ships were not far apart, a seaman on the Yankee held up a blackboard, a familiar way in which one vessel enquired of another her longitude. The *Shenandoah* did not answer. Unable to pass to the windward, the stranger kept away and ran under the *Shenandoah's* stern. As she swept past, the raider ran down the British flag and hoisted her Confederate ensign. The poop-deck popgun let off a blank shot.

But the *Delphine* — her name was now visible on her stern — did not stop. Driving forward before a strong wind, under a cloud of canvas, she looked as though she might make a run for it. The *Shenandoah* was under very short canvas, having taken in sail to let the other ship come up, and the *Delphine* might well be out of range before the raider could clew down more canvas. Again the signal gun popped its warning. The forward Whitworth was cleared for action; its rifled snout swung menacingly toward the fleeing bark. And still the *Delphine* drew away.

The raider crew scrambled aloft to set more sail. The gunners began to cut fuse for the *Shenandoah's* first shot "in anger." Gunner John Guy decided on solid ball rather than explosive shell. If the first shot missed, the *Delphine* would be out of range before a second could be fired.

Then, unexpectedly, the *Delphine* hove to.

2

William Green Nichols, master of the *Delphine,* was a big, cautious, unhappy man, who had married the boss's daughter, a girl of half his age and twice his determination.

In seven years she had pushed him up from second mate on a creaky tub owned by her father to skipper of a fine merchantman on her maiden voyage. But the baptismal trip of the *Delphine* had been one misfortune after another. Reaching London with a load of wheat, Nichols had been unable to find further cargo; British merchants were unwilling to trust their goods to American bottoms while Confederate raiders were still at sea. Finally Nichols agreed to make a run in ballast to the Burmese port of Akyab and there pick up some rice polishing machinery.

For a time all went well. The *Delphine* slipped safely through the dangerous intercontinental channel of the South Atlantic and on fair winds rounded the Cape. One calm day early in December, Nichols' six-year-old son, Phinneas, fell into conversation with one of the crewmen, a German. The boy wanted to know what the man was reading. "A Bible," he was told. Could his papa read it? he asked. No, it was in German, the sailor said, but he had an English Bible the captain could read. He rummaged in his ditty bag and brought out a small Bible, which he gave to the boy. Phinneas took it to his father.

"Papa, this is an English Bible. Can you read it?"

Captain Nichols opened the book at random to the 27th chapter of Acts and began to read aloud to his son. "Paul admonished them, and said unto them, Sirs, I percieve that this voyage will be with hurt and much damage, not only of the lading and ship, but also of our lives. . . ." He stopped, horrified. To him the words were prophetic, an omen of disaster. When a storm blew up a few days later, Nichols resigned himself to death. He expected the bark to founder. When it survived the gale, his surprise was as great as his joy. His chronometer seemed wrong, but soon he saw ahead a black-hulled ship, and he set his course toward her in order to ask the latitude.

When he saw the *Shenandoah's* armament, heard the cannon, recognized the flag, Nichols was too upset to give orders. The first mate looked to him, but he said nothing. His young wife was at his side. Over and over she said, "Rebels. They're rebels."

The cannon sounded again.

"Bring her round," said Nichols, his voice flat with despair.

"No," protested his wife. "We can get away. We will be out of range before they can set their canvas."

"Bring her round," Nichols repeated. "It is the will of God."

And now, aboard the raider, he saw his wife had been right. They could have escaped. The rebel was so shorthanded she could man only one gun; even that one crew had to be drained from the force which should have been aloft. If the *Delphine* had kept going, if the one additional shot the Confederates could have fired before he was out of range had missed, he would have been free. He hated to think what his wife would say.

Standing in the *Shenandoah's* cabin in front of the table at which a bearded, gray-suited Confederate officer was examining the *Delphine's* papers, Nichols tried desperately to think of of some way to save his ship, to redeem himself in his wife's eyes. The rebel officer looked up at him. "Your ship is a Confederate prize, sir. She will be burned."

Nichols felt his knees jell. "My wife," he said. "My wife. She is aboard. Ill. It would kill her to change ships in this weather."

Waddell hesitated. Always there was Ann. . . . What if it were his Ann sick aboard a ship a thousand miles from anywhere? What if she were ordered to leave the ship she knew for quarters aboard an enemy raider? He asked, "What ails her, sir?"

"Her nerves. Her nerves are bad. She is upset and run down. She has a fever."

Waddell looked back over the papers. The *Delphine* was in ballast; there were no stores to ransom. She was a new ship, worth at least $25,000, the best prize since the *Alina.* His reverie was interrupted by the executive officer. "Begging your pardon, sir," said Whittle, "but this may be a Yankee trick. Why not dispatch the ship's surgeon to see if the woman can be moved?"

Dr. Lining soon determined that Mrs. Nichols was far from

the frail creature her husband had described. "She is a woman of some culture," he reported back to Waddell, "in perfect health and very decided."

⸙ 3 ⸙

Lillias Nichols was not a model prisoner. Long accustomed to having her own way, she bossed her captors with the same assurance with which she gave orders to her husband. The tall, well-shaped, temperamental woman of twenty-six was to prove as much of a problem to the raiders as a storm at sea.

Two trips were needed to transport Mrs. Nichols, her son, her maid, and her baggage (trunks, a library, a caged canary) to the *Shenandoah.* The sea, still choppy, threatened to smash the whaleboat against the side of the cruiser. It was necessary to rig a whip to the main yard and hoist the women aboard in a boatswain's chair. Mrs. Nichols gave instructions on how to lower the chair, whom to take first, when to haul away. She overruled the officer of the whaleboat at every turn.

Whittle gravely welcomed the captive aboard. She met his gaze with studied contempt, looked about the storm-battered decks of the raider, and remarked, "If I had been in command, you would never have taken the *Delphine.*"

"I will show you to your cabin, Madam."

The Nichols family had been assigned to the "ladies chamber" – the starboard half of the captain's cabins. Waddell stepped onto the deck as the executive officer showed Mrs. Nichols to the quarters. She noticed the two stripes on Waddell's sleeves and stopped, facing him. "Are you the pirate chief?"

"I have the honor to be captain of the Confederate States steamer *Shenandoah,* Madam," said Waddell, who that night confided to his journal his belief that "a refractory lady can be controlled by a quiet courtesy, but no flattery."

"What do you intend doing with us? I demand that we be put ashore immediately."

"The nearest land is St. Paul's Island. Would you care to be landed there?"

Daughter and wife of ship masters, Lillias Nichols knew of St. Paul – an uninhabited island four thousand miles from a major port, one of the loneliest spots in the world. Once a Frenchman, shipwrecked at St. Paul, had lived three years without sighting a sail. "No," she said abruptly, and, stepping past Waddell, slammed the door.

"As you desire, Madam," said Waddell to the closed door, "and now I must excuse myself."

4

The crew of the *Delphine,* mostly Germans, were brought aboard and locked in irons in the forecastle, along with some sheep and a pig also taken from the prize. The mates, too, were locked up, including Captain Nichols' brother, Irving, who was inclined to be impudent. When Waddell asked him if the *Delphine* had any money aboard, Irving shouted, "Money? Money be damned. What the bloody hell do you think I'd be doing with money at sea?" And when Grimball asked if there were any preserved meats or fruits on the prize, he answered, "Great God almighty, man, are you hungry?" So he was confined like a common sailor.

While a prize crew readied the *Delphine* for destruction, little Phinny Nichols romped on the raider's deck, and Midshipmen Mason and Browne fished with barbless, bread-baited hooks for albatrosses. They caught a pair of the great birds and cut off the feet, the skin of which were sometimes used to make tobacco pouches.

By eleven that night the last of the *Delphine's* instruments and cabin stores were aboard. The destruction crew, under

Bulloch, pulled off in the whaleboat. A few moments later, flame shot up from the companionway and began to spread over the deck. Fire ran along the lines until they burned through and snapped in the air like flaming whips. The yards came thundering down, and the ship began to move before the wind; then the flames leaped into the shrouds. The cotton exploded into a mass of fire, flared fiercely for a few minutes, and died away, leaving the *Delphine* a fiery skeleton, surging and tossing on an angry ocean. The flames reflected in the massed clouds and outlined the ghostly form of a wide-winged albatross, kiting against the wind.

In the excitement of watching the fire, no one had thought about the destruction crew. Now it was realized they had not returned. Anxious eyes searched for the whaleboat in the tossing waves, but none found it. Lanterns were fastened aloft. Apprehension grew. Then suddenly a cry rang out, "Ah, there. Throw us a line."

The whaleboat was made out fifty yards to windward, on the crest of a huge wave. A moment later a coil of rope sailed away from the deck of the *Shenandoah* through the air rendered half opaque by the spray of breaking waves. It was caught by a man in the boat, and they were dragged alongside. The destruction crew came hand over hand up the lines, the whaleboat was hoisted up on its davits, and the *Shenandoah* moved away from the glowing debris of its latest victim.

Captain Nichols stood at the stern, watching his ship. He looked about to cry; everyone pitied him. Fred Chew, who hated to see anyone unhappy, even a Yankee, approached the skipper and tried to comfort him.

"Just think, Captain," Chew began, "upon what small actions important results depend. Why, if at daylight this morning you had changed your course one-fourth of a point, you would have passed out of our reach or sight."

Nichols raised himself from his sorrow. Angrily he turned on his would-be comforter. "That shows how damned little you know about it," he exploded. "This morning at daylight I just did change my course a quarter of a point, and that's what fetched me here."

5

New Year's Day at sea was a time for stock-taking. With the memory of the flaming *Delphine* still sharp in their minds, with two women and a small boy among the prisoners aboard, the officers of the raider entered 1865 with feelings of pride — and an uneasiness akin to guilt, an urge to justify their mission of destruction. On New Year's Eve, Waddell entered in his notes:

> Thirty-first of December closed the year, the third since the war began. And how many of my boon companions are gone to that bourne from which no traveler returns? They were full of hope, but not without fears, when we last parted. They have fallen in battle in defense of their homes invaded by a barbarous enemy. War, when waged by unprincipled and brutal civilized men, is always more savage and inhuman than when waged by the untutored savage of the woods. The Yankees in their invasion of the South came with all the vices and passions of civilized men added to the natural ferocity of the savage. They had no magnanimity or chivalry; they fought on a calculation of profit. This fact never left my mind, and reconciled me to the destruction of property which was captured. I felt I was fighting them more effectually than if I were killing the miserable crowds of European recruits which they filled their armies with. For two years they waged war against the South without attempting to interfere with slavery; it was only when they found the negro could be used for killing the white people of the South and serve as breastworks for Northern white troops that they declared him free; it was a new element introduced into the contest, and a very powerful one. They cared nothing for the unhappy negro; they preferred his destruction to that of their white troops.

Cornelius Hunt, in his account of the cruise, had this to say:

> The new year, wearing all the languid beauty of a Southern clime, opened upon me just as I was about to be relieved from duty on deck. The weather was fine, with a light, variable wind blowing, and the stars threw their silvery shimmer over the quiet water. Everyone on board, save the officer of the deck, the quartermaster, the lookout, and the man at the wheel, were wrapped in slumber. Such were my surroundings when the ship's bell, striking the hour of twelve, announced the death of eighteen hundred and sixty-four and the birth of eighteen hundred and sixty-five. Many thousand miles from home and friends, with the broad Atlantic all around us, and our adventurous career just begun, we did not forget the day, and at eight o'clock in the morning we unfurled our banner to the breeze, and there at our peak it waved, the emblem of a young nation which for four years had struggled, God only knows with what self-denying patience and resolution, for liberty.

6

St. Paul Island, a dead volcano, thrusts its bald, basalt head a thousand feet out of the Indian Ocean. It lies halfway between Melbourne and Cape Town, and except for its volcanic sister, Amsterdam Island, the nearest land to the north is Ceylon, four thousand miles away. Even with the sea calmed to a soft swell, the sun bright, and the winds gentle, St. Paul looked desolate as the *Shenandoah* approached.

Waddell had a dual purpose in visiting St. Paul. He wanted to check his chronometer against a known landmark, and he hoped some whalers might have congregated in the harbor — a sheltered spot inside the rim of an old crater. But Lillias Nichols, coming on deck the morning of January 2, and seeing the dead cone of the volcano, remembered the captain's threat to maroon her there. The thought of months and years on that dark and desolate beach shook her. But she was not going to beg favors of any rebel. She stood at the rail, nursing her anxiety, as the bleak rock drew nearer.

Cornelius Hunt, walking the deck, saw her staring across the water and stopped to talk. Already he was on friendly terms with her husband; they had spent the previous evening in a bull-session during the earlier part of his watch. He noticed she was blinking back tears and he guessed the reason.

"Surely, Madam," Hunt began good-naturedly, "you do not think you are to be left in this out-of-the-way spot."

"That is my husband's expectation," she said, and added, with another look at the lonely island, "and I presume his fears are not without foundation."

"Let me assure you to the contrary then."

Hunt remained beside her as the *Shenandoah* cruised through the kelp beds surrounding the island. She did not speak to him. Eventually he asked, "Would you be good enough to inform me how your husband or yourself came to imagine that the commander of the *Shenandoah* was capable of leaving a whole ship's company in such a place?"

She hesitated a moment, then, staring at the water, said slowly, "When I said we must be put ashore, he said he would put me ashore here if I asked."

"He was joking. You should not have taken him seriously."

"They tell terrible stories at home about the outrages committed upon defenseless men and women by your rebel cruisers. The papers have been full of them, and I suppose they are at least founded on fact."

Hunt chuckled at the thought of himself as a pirate. "I'd like to see one of those papers," he remarked. But Mrs. Nichols, still uneasy about the island, did not keep up the conversation. She retired to her cabin.

Captain Waddell had given permission for a party to go ashore in a small boat and scout the island for any stores which might have been left by Yankee whalers. Except for the boatload of men who had rowed in at Madeira to pick up the *Laurel's* papers, none of the raiders had been on land since leaving London. There was no lack of candidates to man the oars of the whaleboat for the long row in. Only officers were chosen: Grimball, Scales, Lining, Browne, Mason, Smith, McNulty, and Codd. With much envy the disappointed majority watched the boat until it was out of sight around a point of land to the lee.

The entrance to the bay was tricky. The sea had worn away the outer edge of a small crater; it swept in to form a deep, landlocked harbor. Debris from the crumbled wall formed a reef across the mouth of the bay, and even in easy weather the water was white and dangerous. Several times the whaleboat scraped rock in twisting through the channel. If a small boat had difficulty entering the harbor, a whaler would be in real danger. Grimball, who was in charge of the landing party, did not expect to find any Yankee provisions.

But, drawing nearer the shore, Grimball was astonished to see houses roofed with coarse grass. Several small boats were tied to a rude wharf. The Confederates landed and advanced on the settlement, each man alert, each ready with his gun. No one opposed them, no one greeted them. The houses were deserted, but poultry pecked in the yards; the sheds were filled with barrels of salted fish and penguins.

Detailing two men to watch the boat, Grimball set out with the others to explore the island. On the beach they found footprints, fresh and clear. They came to the hulk of a wrecked ship that had been hurled far up on the beach; it seemed to have been there a long time. A hole had been knocked in the battered stern, and, looking in, Mason saw a makeshift cot, covered with fresh grass.

Uneasy but excited, the party continued the search. The men fingered the guns and cutlasses with which they were festooned. At the far side of the island, a low escarpment thrust out into the ocean. Clambering over it, Mason stopped suddenly and raised his hand in warning. The others cautiously pulled themselves up beside him. Below, seated on a rock, were two men, fishing. They were bearded, sunburned and, except for faded blue pants, naked. The guns of the landing party turned on them. "Ahoy," drawled Grimball, "who are you?"

"*Mon Dieu.*"

The men were French. They came annually from the French island of Bazaruto, off Mozambique, on the east coast of Africa, to spend the summer fishing. In June, when the weather began to get bad, a ship would call for them and carry their catch to market. Visitors were a rare treat for the fishermen, and they loaded the Confederates with presents – dried fish, salted fish, smoked fish, a few eggs, and a live penguin.

By six o'clock the landing party was back aboard the *Shenandoah.* The officers were equally proud of their sunburn, their blisters, and the penguin which padded about the deck looking at once absurd and dignified and emitting a call like the bray of an ass. A sailor tied a rag around the bird's neck, and as the penguin rocked away, fussing angrily, Lillias Nichols joined in the general laugh and said, "Like an old woman, for all the world." It was her first pleasantry. In his notes that night, Waddell confessed, "She has tamed down somewhat, and I rather admire the discipline she has her husband under."

Later in the evening, while Hunt was standing at the stern and watching the white froth of the wake streak the green of the ocean, Mrs. Nichols came from her cabin and stood beside him, her hands behind her back.

"I brought you this from my library," she said at last and, handing him a magazine, walked away. Her present was an illustrated weekly, printed in New York, and containing an account of the cruise of the *Alabama.* Hunt enjoyed the story hugely. The officers and crew of the *Alabama,* nearly twenty of whom were aboard the *Shenandoah,* were described as "a pack of rascals whom Morgan, the buccaneer, or the leader of the Indian Sepoys would have expelled from their several commands, lest they should have become contaminated by evil associations."

Hunt shared the magazine with his shipmates. For some time afterward the libeled *Alabama* veterans were joyfully shunned as rapists and robbers by their fellow raiders.

7

Whale ships bound from New Bedford to the Arctic could take two routes. Some went west around Cape Horn; this was shorter but the weather was worse. The others went east around the Cape of Good Hope. A few of this group usually paused at Cape Leeuwin, the southwestern tip of Australia, where right whales were to be found.

Aboard the *Shenandoah* most of the junior officers were convinced the raider should also cruise these waters, stalking the hunters. But Waddell was in a hurry. He was willing to spend a few days hunting Yankees off the arid coast of Western Australia, but he wanted to reach Melbourne before January 26, when a British mail steamer was scheduled to leave for London. It would be the last steamer for a month, and the skipper wanted to report to Bulloch on the successful progress of the voyage. The only official word he had sent the Confederate agent concerned the sad story of her shorthanded departure from Madeira. Waddell had been deeply discouraged when he wrote that first message, and he was anxious to repair any damage his pessimism might have done his prestige — and to have the report forwarded to America in time to be heard at the Confederate Congress.

The winds remained light. Hoping to have time to visit Cape Leeuwin before going to Melbourne, Waddell decided to risk raising steam. But after an hour under power, the ship vibrated to the familiar grating. The *Shenandoah* went back under canvas, O'Shea returned to work on the propeller shaft, and the prow swung south, away from the cape and toward the port. The junior officers grumbled. They felt that far from trying to reach Melbourne before the mail steamer left, Waddell should avoid it. No use advertising their position. "By no means ought we to get in before this steamer sails," Dr. Lining wrote in his journal, "as it will spread our arrival all over the world."

Dissension was reflected in minor incidents. One day the quartermaster appeared on deck with a hugely black eye. Grimball, who was on watch, called out, "What's the matter with your eye, Hall?"

"I fell down the ladder, sir."

"Fell down the ladder?" said Grimball.

"Yes, sir."

"Did I understand you to say you fell down the ladder?"

"Yes, sir."

Grimball shook his head. "Hall, that ladder gave you particular hell."

The quartermaster flushed. "No, he didn't, sir. In the first part of the fight he struck me in the eyes and got the better of it, but after I got under weigh, sir, I made a monument of his nose."

"Some ladder."

The party of the second part proved to be Sylvester, a cabin boy. His nose was, indeed, monumental, but the crew agreed he had beaten Hall badly.

Among the officers there were only verbal squabbles. Waddell, still distrustful of the abilities of Fred Chew, worked out an arrangement which would keep the Missourian off the bridge; he named Chew master of the captured chronometers, assigned him to wind them daily, and gave his watch to Joshua

Minor. Chew accepted the change without protest, but Midshipmen Mason and Browne, who outranked Minor, protested having to work under an inferior officer. Waddell paid no attention to them, except to pass a few sarcastic remarks about "what his officers would let him do before long."

Even the captive captain of the *Delphine* joined in the chorus of criticism of Waddell. Nichols remarked to Grimball one night that he thought the skipper was overanxious. "If I had a ship as large as this and five men in a watch, I'd like to see my mate call me before seven bells unless something very particular occurred." Grimball repeated the conversation to Waddell, who shouted, "The man is a liar, sir, a liar!"

Nichols came in for his own share of torment. He was intensely jealous and could not conceal his worries about the attentions the young officers were paying his wife. Lillias had begun to coquet with her captors, and they were not unresponsive. Dr. Lining, whose first mention of her in his journal had been, "A finer-looking woman I have seldom seen, physically," expanded his praise and added, "She is a much better woman than I thought she was at first."

Even young Mason succumbed to her Yankee charm. "She is really quite a handsome woman, has a genteel look about her, almost a refined face, but occasionally she brings out some ungrammatical expression which dispels the illusion," he said at first. And later, "I have now come to the conclusion that she is not such a Tartar as I thought. She has a delightfully clean look and is always dressed neatly, even very well dressed, and what is still more important she dresses in good taste; in appearance she is quite queenlike when compared to Mrs. Gilman and Mrs. Gauge, our other two lady prisoners; and although Mrs. N does not have as much to say as they did, what she says is *beaucoup plus spirituel et plus à propos.*"

Nichols, unhappy over his wife's social success, always edged into any conversation she had with the Confederates. "The fool and ass," exploded Lining, "a man obliged to suspect his wife and to have to keep his eyes on her to prevent her doing wrong! I shall now go on talking to her to plague him, if nothing else."

Not even the animals got along. The pigs taken from the *Delphine* were put in the same pen as those belonging to the *Shenandoah.* "They did not seem to relish the idea of being obliged to mess with rebels," Mason remarked. "Or perhaps our good Confederate pigs were insulted at being obliged to take in the Yankees. At any rate they kept up a tremendous noise all night, and in the morning, in the mid-watch, I went forward and noticed them lying apart in the pen, the Confederates on one side and the Yankees on the other."

At daylight on January 17, while standing a hundred miles off the southwestern coast of Australia, the *Shenandoah* came in sight of a sail to port. She swung out in chase. The quarry was a pretty ship, a clipper, obviously American-built and very fast. It was mid-morning before the cruiser came within hailing distance. The clipper matched the *Shenandoah's* English ensign with one of her own.

Not satisfied, Waddell dispatched a boarding party. They returned with the captain and the ship's papers. New England-built, the clipper *Nimrod* had been sold the previous year to an English firm. Her captain, described by Hunt as "a grand-looking old fellow, with tremendous white whiskers, which gave him something of the look of a venerable polar bear," felt he owed the Confederates a debt of gratitude for helping him get so fine a ship; he paid the debt with a dozen bottles of ripe old brandy. The *Nimrod,* at first regarded as a candidate for kindling, sailed away as the *Shenandoah's* best friend.

A few days later the wind shifted to the west, the most unfavorable quarter for Waddell's purposes, and at the same time the ship met an easterly current which nudged it off course.

With only a few days left to catch the Melbourne-London steamer, Waddell again ordered steam to be raised. ("An extravagant expenditure of coal," said Lining, in his journal.)

For nearly twenty-four hours the *Shenandoah* pushed along in sight of another sail. Waddell, studying her through his glass, decided she was the *Nimrod.* His subordinates disagreed. She was bigger, and she had a different cut. They suggested a chase, but Waddell, still thinking of the mail, overruled them.

Lillias Nichols, who now frequently dropped into the wardroom to join the officers at checkers and backgammon – she did not play chess – listened to the grumbling of the younger men with studiously concealed delight. She, too, had seen the sail. She recognized it at once: the *David Brown,* a Yankee, owned by her father.

"We caught the January mail," Mason remarked ruefully long afterward, "but we did not catch the *David Brown.*"

8

The *Shenandoah* sighted the heads of Port Phillip at noon on the 25th. An hour later, a pilot boat was bobbing in the swell alongside. The pilot, Edward Johnson, showed his surprise on learning the raider's identity.

"We thought you was the *Royal Standard,*" he told Waddell. "We telegraphed Melbourne that's who you was. She's due from London. Why do you want to get into the harbor?"

"Why do you ask, sir?" Waddell snapped.

"No offense, Captain, but my orders is rigid about belligerent cruisers. They has got to have a reason to come into the harbor."

Waddell explained that the propeller needed repairs. The pilot was satisfied. He took the helm to bring the ship in.

At the heads the health officer came out to inspect the cruiser. She passed. "You have a great many friends here," the health officer remarked to Dr. Lining, "and some enemies." Returning to shore, the health officer telegraphed the news ahead to Melbourne that a Confederate raider was coming into port.

As the *Shenandoah* glided through the heads and across Hobson's Bay toward Australia's southernmost metropolis, a fleet of yachts and pleasure craft came out to meet her. Some dipped their flags as the warship passed. On others the passengers stood and waved. A few watched her glumly.

The raider dropped anchor at six o'clock on a beautiful midsummer afternoon. Lieutenant Grimball went ashore with a message from Captain Waddell to His Excellency, Sir Charles H. Darling, K.C.B., Captain General and Governor-in-Chief of Victoria State.

> SIR: I have the honor to announce to your excellency the arrival of the C.S.S. *Shenandoah*, under my command, in Port Phillip this afternoon, and also to communicate that the steamer's machinery requires repairs and that I am in want of coal.
>
> I desire that your excellency grant permission that I may make the necessary repairs and supply of coal to enable me to get to sea as quickly as possible.
>
> I desire also your excellency's permission to land my prisoners.
>
> I shall observe the neutrality.
>
> I have the honor to be, sir, your most obedient servant,
>
> J. I. WADDELL

While waiting for Grimball to return with the Governor's answer, Breedlove Smith, the paymaster, checked the parole papers of the prisoners. Mrs. Nichols had signed none. Smith made out a parole — a promise not to bear arms or do anything to the detriment of the Confederate cause — and brought it to her to sign.

"I am not a prisoner of war," she protested. "Captain Waddell has said so. He says the Confederates do not take women prisoners."

"It is only a formality, madam," Smith explained. "We can release no one who does not sign a parole."

"I shall not consider it binding."

Smith shrugged. She signed the paper and, handing it to him, met his eyes squarely, "The first thing I shall do ashore is go straight to the American Consul."

"I am sure you will, madam."

"Is there anything you want little Phinny to sign?"

"No, madam. We are much more afraid of you than we are of him."

Lillias strode off to her cabin to pack her belongings.

The *Shenandoah* was already surrounded by a crowd of small boats. The occupants, including representatives of all the Melbourne newspapers, clamored for permission to come aboard and inspect the raider. Waddell refused. No visitors would be allowed until the ship had been formally admitted to the port. The reporters protested — the Governor was out of town; it would be hours before Grimball reached him, and after that a council meeting would be necessary. But Waddell was adamant: No entry permit, no visitors.

An old gaffer on a tiny sailboat begged to be allowed aboard. The guards refused. He climbed the spar of his little vessel and, when the swell was right, leaped across into the *Shenandoah's* mizzen chains and scrambled aboard. The officer of the deck later confessed that there was something so audacious in being boarded by a single individual that he did not know whether to surrender the ship to the white-haired invader or to toss him overboard.

"I'm the only genuine Confederate in all of bloody Austrylia," the old fellow explained, "and I guess that gives me the right to come on board any vessel that flies my country's flag."

He was permitted to stay aboard until midnight.

Seated at his desk in his cabin early the next morning, putting the final paragraphs on his report to Bulloch, Captain Waddell overheard a conversation in the adjoining stateroom.

"If those chronometers and sextants were mine, I guess I'd make him give them to me," Mrs. Nichols was telling her unhappy husband. "I made him give me back all our books, didn't I?"

"All but one, dear," Nichols said gently.

Waddell smiled to himself. In looking over the *Delphine's* library before turning it back to Mrs. Nichols, Lieutenant Whittle had found a copy of *Uncle Tom's Cabin.* He hurled it overboard.

A few hours later the officer of the deck reported that without permission Mrs. Nichols had hailed a passing launch and asked to be taken ashore.

"Let them go," Waddell said wearily, "as long as it is not the ship's boat they use."

Lillias Nichols' farewell words as the launch bore her away to freedom were, "I wish that steamer may be burned."

THUNDER DOWN UNDER

MELBOURNE, aged thirty, was a thriving community with fifty thousand inhabitants, gas lights, metaled streets, paved footwalks, a bluestone town hall, and a split personality.

Australia's southeastern metropolis had been founded in 1835 by two rival groups, one made up of business and professional people, the other of tradesmen and workers. From this schizoid start it rapidly developed several distinct personalities, none of them compatible.

There was a Melbourne of English officials, who wished that the Yarra were the Thames and who tried hard to make a little London out of the free-and-easy frontier town. For the merchants, Melbourne was the side door to a rich continent. The Melbourne of the seamen was a waterfront town of brothels, bars, and brawls. There was another Melbourne for the diggers – Australia's forty-niners – the adventurers of the world, many of whom had come Down Under to the rich diggings at Ballarat when the pickings grew slim in California. And to the liberated convicts, men who had served their time, Melbourne was a place to start a new life on a new continent. Most of the convicts were courageous men, though they wryly spoke of "leaving our country for our country's good." Their offenses had been primarily political – they asked more democracy than England was willing to give. Now, having paid the penalty, many had added to their rebellious yearning for natural rights a convict's anarchic loathing for authority.

All these were Melbourne in 1865, an excitable city, passionately political, seething with conflict, always eager for diversion.

For Melbourne a Confederate raider was something new.

2

Fifty-six-year-old Sir Charles Henry Darling, governor of Victoria, was a military man but not altogether unintelligent. After successive attempts at imposing army authority on English civilians in colonies around the world had brought him nothing but trouble, he recognized a truth which often escapes the military mind: men resent arbitrary orders. From then on, in disgust or wisdom, Sir Charles followed a laissez-faire policy which some called lazy and others called enlightened. He was the most widely popular governor in the history of Australia.

When Lieutenant Grimball delivered Waddell's note asking permission to land, the Governor referred it to the Executive Council, which met the next day. The colony of Victoria was bound by British foreign policy. Its attitude toward belligerent men-of-war stemmed from a note written by Earl Russell in 1862, in which international law was interpreted as follows:

> Vessels belonging to a belligerent power are not allowed to enter a neutral port unless they require supplies, coal, etc., or need repairs, and they must comply with the following conditions:
>
> They must take in their necessary supplies as soon as they can, as much coal only as will enable them to get to the nearest port in their own country, or to the next port of destination, and then leave the neutral port of refuge as soon as possible.

The Council decided the *Shenandoah* should be allowed to pick up provisions and stay in port until the propeller band was repaired. At three o'clock word of this decision reached

Waddell. No mean propagandist, his first action was to open the ship to visitors.

Word that the "Rebel Pirate" was in port had been carried in the morning papers, along with the rumor that Captain Semmes of the *Alabama*, the most notorious sailor alive, was aboard. All day long, sightseers had crowded the short railroad running from Melbourne proper to the waterfront towns of Sandridge and Williamstown. When news spread that the ship could be visited, every craft in the harbor began to haul visitors out to her.

"The multitude of absurd questions with which we were plied by the gaping crowd would have made a stoic laugh," Hunt complained good-naturedly. "A large percentage of our visitors seemed to entertain the notion that human beings were removed from the vessels we captured, or not, as convenience dictated, prior to their destruction, and solemnly queried of us as to the manner in which the Yankees bore themselves while waiting the approach of the devouring element upon a burning ship, or waiting to be engulfed with a scuttled one. But notwithstanding this hard character they were ready to ascribe to us, they vied with each other in showing us every courtesy in their power, and the ladies in particular were well pleased when they could secure the attendance of a gray uniform to escort them on their tour of inspection."

Though disappointed not to discover Captain Semmes aboard, the Australians found the courtly Waddell a suitable substitute. Melbourne newspapermen were quick to spot a pair of famous surnames on the list of officers – Lee and Mason.

Midshipman John Thomson Mason was the adopted son of James Mason, a Confederate diplomatic agent, looked upon as a hero by many Englishmen. Early in the war, the elder Mason had been the center of a storm that threatened to blow England into the struggle on the side of the South. Appointed as an agent to Great Britain, Mason and a companion, Slidell, slipped through the blockade to Cuba and caught the British steamer *Trent.* The next day, the *San Jacinto,* a Union gunboat under Captain Wilkes, stopped the *Trent* on the high seas and removed the runaway diplomats.

The Northern press went wild with joy; it had been a long time since the papers were able to announce any kind of a victory. The public, smarting under the defeats of '61, uneasy at the impotence of Northern arms, treated the capture as an omen of triumph. The Secretary of the Navy congratulated Wilkes on his "great public service;" the Secretary of War issued a commendation; the House of Representatives voted thanks for his "brave, adroit, and patriotic conduct." Only a few fusty historians ventured to suggest that seizure on the high seas was what we had fought the War of 1812 to outlaw.

In England a decidedly dim view was taken of Wilkes' exploit. The British press called for release of the captives and a full apology – or war. The Government ordered the Navy, arsenals, and dockyards put on war footing. Troops were shipped to Nova Scotia, and the bands played "Dixie" as they sailed.

In due course, the United States decided Wilkes had been wrong. With appropriate apologies, the captive commissioners were put aboard a British ship off Boston. "It is gall and wormwood," Secretary of the Treasury Chase confided to his diary, "but I am consoled by the reflection that the surrender . . . is but simply doing right, simply proving faithful to our own ideas and traditions under strong temptation to violate them."

The Trent Affair had made a British hero out of the Confederate agent, and the presence of a member of his family aboard the *Shenandoah* was welcomed by Melbourne society.

On Sunday, seven thousand persons made the short railroad trip from Melbourne to Sandridge to see the raider. Other thousands came in rigs, on horseback, or on foot. A steady procession of small boats crossed to the raider. Her decks were so crowded that many of the visiting craft had to stand off, unable to unload their passengers until some visitors left and made room for newcomers. Dr. Lining had great difficulty returning to the ship from a visit ashore and remarked sourly, "Several very pleasant gentlemen came aboard, but a great deal also of Riff-Raff."

In return for their hospitality, the *Shenandoah's* officers were invited to all the social affairs of the colony. Most elaborate was a great ball at Ballarat, the mining center forty miles north of Melbourne. The officers, dressed in their best uniforms, polished and primped as for an Annapolis inspection, took the two-hour train trip across a mining area – which Lining described as "so thoroughly perforated and undermined by shafts sunk in pursuit of the precious ore that if the whole town tumbled through, some fine day, it would be no matter of especial surprise to any one" – and reported, ready for dancing duty, at Craig's Hotel.

The affair was, according to Hunt, "decidedly recherché. The wealth and beauty and fashion of Ballarat were out in full force. Every attention that kindness and courtesy could suggest was shown us, and more than one heart beat quicker at such convincing evidence of the existence of sympathy in this country of the Antipodes. Many a gray uniform coat lost its gilt buttons that night, but we saw them again ere we bade a final adieu to Australia, suspended from watchguards depending from the necks of bright-eyed women, and we appreciated the compliment thus paid, not to us but to our country. God bless the gentle women of Melbourne and Ballarat."

3

Not everyone in Melbourne shared the pleasure of the gentle ladies at the arrival of a boatload of handsome young

Confederate officers to add gold braid and glamour to the season's affairs. William Blanchard, for example, was most unhappy.

Blanchard, a businessman, had become American Consul when Virginia-born James Francis Maguire "followed his state" in 1861. Energetic and outspoken, Blanchard spent an unhappy tour of diplomatic duty. Not only were the Colonial officials hopeful that America would be split into two hostile nations, but most Australian working men, unlike their English counterparts, sided with the South – they hated authority, they thought the struggle of the Secessionists was the fight of all colonial peoples, and, having cruelly mistreated the native aborigines, they had little sympathy for colored men.

Though the Melbourne majority were Southern sympathizers, a hard core of Federalists had formed around Blanchard. Some were aboard the three American merchantmen lying in the harbor, some were native Australians, some were Northerners who had crossed the Pacific during the Australian gold rush. Upon the *Shenandoah's* arrival, this cotorie launched a diplomatic offensive aimed at having the ship seized as a pirate or, at least, forbidding her to enter the port.

When Blanchard came to the Consulate on Thursday morning, January 26, he knew from the morning papers that the Confederate raider was in the harbor. But he was surprised to find eight refugees from the *Delphine* already ashore and waiting in his office. All eight protested that they were under parole not to communicate anything detrimental to the Confederate cause or that might lead to the capture of the *Shenandoah*. By judicious questioning the consul gathered enough material to write a good description of the raider, which he included in a report to Mr. Adams in London and the American consul at Hong Kong. These letters left on the British mail steamer that also carried Waddell's report to Bulloch.

Blanchard was still questioning Captain Nichols when, at three-thirty in the afternoon, a note arrived from the Commissioner of Trade and Customs. It announced that the *Shenandoah* was in port and that Waddell wanted to land prisoners. Would the Consul look after such prisoners if they were landed?

In reply, Blanchard, whom the Australians sometimes described as "bilious," by-passed the Commissioner and wrote sourly to Governor Darling protesting the landing of the ship on the ground that she was the *Sea King,* that she had not entered any port since leaving England and was, consequently, not a cruiser but a pirate.

The Australian answer that the ship was obviously a belligerent did not improve the terrible-tempered Mr. Blanchard's disposition. But it did set his course. Although he continued, none too hopefully, to pound away at the Australian interpretation, he devoted most of his efforts to stripping the *Shenandoah* of her crew.

The refugees had reported the *Shenandoah* shorthanded. Several had said that the impressed crewmen, if sheltered from arrest, would probably jump ship. "I informed the crewmen that I would protect all persons that had shipped (under duress) from captured American vessels," Blanchard reported to Secretary of State Seward. "I did this with the view of liberating the men, of reducing her crew, which was mostly made up of such impressed men, and of obtaining information that the men I then had would not give on account of their parole."

The policy paid dividends. Eight of the impressed seamen jumped the *Shenandoah.* Some came ashore on liberty and did not return, some slipped away on the boats that brought visitors to the raider, and one man swam.

As each deserter reported to the Consulate, Blanchard took his testimony that the *Shenandoah* was really the British *Sea*

King. Finally he forced the Australian authorities into the position of admitting that the two vessels were probably identical. But then, though they conceded that the ship might be captured were she to return to England, the officials contended that as Colonial administrators they had ground for such a seizure only if an offense were committed in Australian waters.

Blanchard, though objecting to such an interpretation, could only play by the local ground rules. So he busied himself trying to prove that Waddell was violating the Foreign Enlistment Act.

Waddell was worried. The continuing desertions seriously threatened the *Shenandoah*. He asked the waterfront police to help him round up the runaways, but they refused. Ordinarily cooperative, the police protested that desertion from the raider was a political rather than a maritime matter.

Rumors began to circulate on the *Shenandoah* that the American Consul was paying a hundred pounds bounty to any man who jumped ship. A hundred pounds was a great deal of money. Waddell began to cut down on liberties; he was afraid to let men go ashore where they might be met by American agents. Morale sagged. An Australian officer in a confidential report to the Government described the crewmen as "ill-mannered, slovenly, and undisciplined."

The obvious solution was to recruit new members along the Melbourne waterfront. There were plenty of unemployed and adventurous seamen in the port. But two difficulties were apparent: the Foreign Enlistment Act and the possibility of enrolling Union saboteurs.

"I had employed a carpenter to make and put up a bureau in my cabin," Waddell reported in his notes on the voyage, "and while he was engaged about it, fitting it to the side of the vessel, he told me he had heard in a restaurant some

Americans discussing the feasibility of smuggling themselves on board, and after the steamer was at sea to capture her. I was in bed during the reception of that *morceau delicieux* of intelligence and replied, 'If it is attempted they will fail, and I will hang every mother's son of them.' "

Another Southern sympathizer warned Waddell that Northern agents planned to tie a torpedo to the cruiser and blow her up. A double watch was kept at night. Any boats seen approaching were promptly challenged. Waddell's orders were to fire after the third challenge, but though scarcely a night passed during which a suspicious craft was not sighted, all swerved away into the darkness before the third threat.

4

The Colonial authorities grew impatient with their guests. The Confederates soon outstayed their welcome. The Governor kept prodding Waddell to make sure that repairs progressed as rapidly as possible.

A party of Australian engineers had inspected the *Shenandoah* soon after her arrival and certified that repairs were necessary before she could proceed to sea as a steamer. ("The lignum vitae staves, forming the bearing for the forward end of the outer length of the screw shaft are entirely displaced.... The inner sternpost bracket, in which the staves of lignum vitae are fitted, forming also the support for the foremost end of the screw frame, is fractured on the starboard side to the extent of about four inches.")

It was necessary to dry-dock the cruiser. She was towed to the patent slip at Williamstown, two miles across the bay from Sandridge, and lighters came alongside to remove her cargo. Before the job was completed, a sudden storm whipped across the bay. It gained in intensity through the night.

"At 11 P.M. she parted the stern lines and was driven sideways against the breakwater," Lining reported in his journal.

"Our bow lines still holding on kept us free forward. Fortunately we had a lighter on either side, and in this instant it acted as a fender. All hands were on deck working to fend her off with coils of rope, bales of hay, etc., the stevedores helping manfully. A little before midnight the bow hawser also parted and we were entirely driven on the breakwater. By that time however we had got her pretty well fended off, and she was soon made quite comfortable as there was no sea on and the lighter fended us off well. I don't think I ever saw the wind blow harder than it did about midnight. It nearly took me from the forecastle. A steamer and pilot were sent for to get us off, but the winds blew so that we could not be moved safely and we lay there until morning."

It took two days to work the ship onto the patent slip. Even when she was in place, work progressed slowly. Day after day the government objected that the job was taking too long; day after day Waddell complained that Australian workmen seemed in no hurry. Impasse.

The Government's uneasiness about the *Shenandoah* was soon to increase considerably. On Friday, February 10, the American Consul forwarded a new set of affidavits from former crewmen of the raider. They not only buttressed Blanchard's contention that the *Shenandoah* was the former *Sea King*, but they declared flatly that several men were aboard, and wearing Confederate gray, who had not arrived with the ship. One of these men was identified as "Charley," a cook.

Confronted with statements, sworn to and in proper form, that the Foreign Enlistment Act was being violated, the authorities had to act. The information in the affidavits was forwarded to the Williamstown police, a warrant was made out for the arrest of Charley, and on Monday evening, Police Superintendent Thomas Lyttleton went to the patent slip where the *Shenandoah* still lay.

Captain Waddell was not on board. The policeman was escorted to Lieutenant Whittle. When Lyttleton said he had come to arrest a cook named Charley, Whittle showed him the ship's articles and asked him to point out the name of the man in question. There was no cook named Charley on the list.

"I shall have to search the ship," said Lyttleton. He handed Whittle the warrant.

The Virginian studied it, handed it back. "That is all right," he said, "but you shall not go over the ship."

After a brief argument, Whittle suggested that the policeman return the next day, when Captain Waddell would be present. It was agreed.

On Tuesday morning Lyttleton tried again. Waddell received him courteously and listened to his statement that he had a warrant for the arrest of one Charley, who, in violation of the Foreign Enlistment Act, had joined the *Shenandoah* in Melbourne.

"I pledge you my word of honor as an officer and a gentleman that I have not anyone on board," Waddell said solemnly, "nor have I engaged any one, nor will I while I am here."

"I am sorry, sir, but I have sworn information that the persons I want are wearing the uniform of the Confederate States and are working on board."

Waddell flatly denied this. He offered to let Lyttleton look at the ship's articles. The policeman explained that he already had seen them; he said he would have to search the ship.

"I am sorry, sir, but I cannot permit that."

Lyttleton showed him the warrant.

Waddell shook his head, "I cannot permit a search."

"Sir, I must try to execute my warrant even if I have to use force."

"And I, sir, will use force to resist such a search. And if I am overcome, I will throw up my ship to your government and go home and report this matter to my government." Waddell reined in his temper and resumed, more evenly, "I dare not allow you to search the ship, sir. The deck of a man-of-war is national property. This is Confederate territory. It would be more than my commission is worth to permit a search. Such a thing would not be attempted by your government to a ship of any other country."

As Waddell talked, his anger swelled up again. "It is only by courtesy that you were allowed to come on board at all, sir. I think that a great slight has been put upon me and upon my country by your government in sending you aboard the ship with a warrant, a police warrant. I believe, sir, that the word of the master of a ship, of an officer and gentleman, should be taken in preference to that of men who had probably deserted from the ship and have been hired by the American Consul to annoy us. If I allowed you to take one man from my ship, you might come afterward and take fifteen or twenty. If such warrants are to be honored, the American consul would perhaps lay an information against me as being a buccaneer or pirate. I think, sir, that I have been very badly treated in this port. I get no cooperation from you in regard to my deserters, and yet you come and offer such an insult as this."

"Then, Captain, you refuse to allow me to look for the man for whom I hold a warrant in my hand."

"Yes, sir. I refuse. I will fight my ship rather than allow it."

Superintendent Lyttleton left. He reported Waddell's action to the Governor, who at once summoned the Executive Council into extraordinary session.

The problem before the Council was ticklish. The ordinary course of law had been frustrated by Waddell's refusal to allow the execution of the warrant. Yet, to execute it might lead to violence and a quarrel with the Confederacy.

The Council came up with a compromise. The Commissioner of Trade and Customs was instructed to write Waddell asking him to reconsider his determination to resist by force the execution of the warrant and to inform him that, pending his reply, permission to repair his ship and take in supplies was suspended. The Governor told the Chief Commissioner of Police to send a force to the slip to see that no Australians worked on the repairs; this force was not to molest the *Shenandoah,* its officers or men. The Chief Commissioner telegraphed the Williamstown station, four miles away:

> I have to direct that you communicate with Mr. Chambers, the lessee of the patent slip, that the governor in council has given directions that he and all other British subjects in this colony cease and desist from rendering any aid or assistance or perform any work in respect to the said Confederate ship *Shenandoah,* or in launching the same. You will proceed at once with the whole of the police at your disposal to the patent slip and prevent at all risks the launch of the said ship. Superintendent Lyttleton and fifteen men, also fifty of the military, proceed at once to Williamstown, telegraphing anything that may occur direct to me.

A Confederate sympathizer copied the telegram and gave it to Waddell before the police arrived. The captain immediately made arrangements with the slip managers to keep the workmen aboard until the repairs were complete. He was sure the police would not try to board her, and the workmen could eat and sleep with the crew until the *Shenandoah* was ready to be launched.

At four o'clock the police took over the slip. They cleared the yard and refused permission for any Australians to go aboard the cruiser. A little later, a force of artillery was seen approaching on the road around the bay from Sandwich to Williamstown, but it turned back — recalled by the Governor. At 6 P.M. a Goverment messenger delivered the Trade

Commissioner's letter to Waddell; he told the skipper he had been instructed to wait for an answer.

Waddell let him wait a long time, until ten o'clock. Then he gave the messenger two letters. The first informed the Trade Commissioner that the *Shenandoah* would get to sea by the 19th unless some unforeseen accident occurred. The second was in reply to the Commissioner's letter asking Waddell to let the warrant be served:

> SIR: I am in receipt of your letter of this date, in which you inform me that you have been directed by his excellency the governor to allow the execution on board the *Shenandoah* of a warrant issued upon sworn information according to law, alleging that a British subject is on board this vessel who has entered the service of the Confederate States in violation of the British statute known as the Foreign Enlistment Act; that it is not consistent with British law to accept any contrary declaration of facts, whatever respect be due to the person from whom it proceeds, as sufficient to justify the non-execution of such warrant; I am then "appealed to to reconsider my determination" and your letter concludes by informing me that "pending a further intimation from me" the permission granted to repair and take supplies is suspended.
>
> I have to inform his excellency the governor that the execution of the warrant was not refused, as no such person as the one therein specified was on board; but permission to search this ship was refused. According to all laws of nations, the deck of a vessel of war is considered to represent the majesty of the country whose flag she flies, and she is free from all executions except for crimes actually committed on shore, when a demand must be made for the delivery of such persons and the execution of the warrant performed by the police of the ship. Our shipping articles have been shown to the superintendent of police, all strangers have been sent out of the ship, and two commissioned officers were ordered to search if any such have been left on board. They have reported to me that after making a thorough search they can find no person on board except those who entered this port as part of the complement of men.

I therefore, as commander of this ship, representing my Government in British waters, have to inform his excellency that there are no persons on board this ship except those whose names are on our shipping articles, and that no one has been enlisted in the service of the Confederate States since my arrival in this port, nor have I in any way violated the neutrality of the port.

And I, in the name of the Government of the Confederate States of America, hereby enter my solemn protest against any obstruction which may cause the detention of this ship in this port.

I am, etc.,

JAMES I. WADDELL

Less than an hour before the two notes left the ship, Constable Alexander Minto of the Williamstown water police saw something else leave her. Minto was making his usual rounds in the police boat, he later testified, when he noticed a boat hauled up to the gangway of the *Shenandoah.*

"One of the officers of the *Shenandoah* was standing at the gangway; he had his uniform on. I saw one of the boatmen, George Nicholls, go on board, and in a short time, a second or two, four men, James Davidson, among them, came down to the boat. Another waterman (waterfront boatman) remained in the boat. When I saw the four men go into the boat, I hauled alongside and spoke to them. I asked them who they were and what they had been doing on board. I think the officer at the gangway could have heard me. They said they had been working at daywork on board. One of them had a bundle in his breast. I heard a call of 'George' from the ship, which I took to be from the officer at the gangway, and immediately I saw Nicholls come and slide down into the boat. The boat then at once pulled ahead. I followed them but lost sight of them on the water.

"I returned at once to the patent slip and ran up to the

railway station and saw two of them on the platform. I searched and found the two others in the water closet. I went to them and asked them why they hurried away from the ship so quickly. They seemed to hesitate and then said, 'Oh, the *Shenandoah* you mean.' They asked what I wanted, and spoke of the train having just started, and I told them there was another. I asked them to accompany me, and they did so. I took them to Mr. Lyttleton."

Mr. Lyttleton was glad to see them. He looked at the four men, and addressing the young Scotchman who gave his name as James Davidson, said, "I believe you are the very Charley I want."

Davidson laughed and said it was a great joke on board the *Shenandoah* about Charley being wanted; but, unfortunely, he wasn't Charley. He said he had been cooking for the wardroom mess.

"So was Charley," said Lyttleton dryly, and sent him to the lockup, accompanied by two constables. Davidson, whose reticence was not exemplary, told his escorts that he had been aboard the *Shenandoah* for several days; he was sorry he couldn't ship on her because he had sold all his belongings in the belief he was going abroad. "Charley's" three companions – Arthur Walmsley, William Mackenzie, and Franklin Glover – were also jailed on charges of violating the Foreign Enlistment Act.

These developments led to another special meeting of the Executive Council on Wednesday morning. According to the minutes, the officials mulled over the meaning of the arrests and Waddell's letters "noting the disagreement in the statements . . . with the indisputable fact that four men were seen to leave the vessel." The councilmen "passed from this subject, upon which His Excellency and the Council have no desire to dwell." While thus delicately avoiding the question of whether an officer and gentleman could also be a liar, they received another letter from the captain in question.

Waddell declared that he had been informed officially by the manager of the patent slip that the slip had been seized by the government to prevent the launching of the *Shenandoah*. This, he argued, amounted to seizure of his vessel. Therefore, he wanted to know whether this seizure had the approval of the Governor.

Enclosed in Waddell's letter was a note from the slip owner which said that the *Shenandoah* would be in great danger if she remained on the slip in stormy weather.

His Excellency was squarely on the spot, but he was helped off by the Crown Law officers. They reported that in their studied opinion Waddell was right: the Government had no right to execute a warrant aboard a foreign man-of-war. The decision opened the way for another easy compromise by 'Do-Nothing' Darling. Since the man for whom the warrant had been issued was now in custody, there was no longer any question of Waddell's interfering with justice. Consequently the ban against Australian workers on the *Shenandoah* could be lifted and the cruiser could be launched.

Darling sent Waddell a blunt letter. It announced the raising of the blockade. Then, after referring to the captain's oath that no one was aboard, it pointedly said that "in the opinion of the Government it was plain that the Foreign Enlistment Act was in the course of being evaded." It concluded that as soon as the *Shenandoah* was launched and loaded, it was hoped Waddell would put to sea.

The showdown over the *Shenandoah* had raised excitement in Melbourne to its highest pitch. During the night of the 14th, after the seizure of the slip, Confederate sympathizers plastered the town with placards announcing a public meeting at 3:30 Wednesday in the Criterion Hotel, a mass protest against the "action of the Government in seizing the *Shenandoah*."

Shortly before the meeting was convened, a notice was posted outside the hotel:

SHENANDOAH

THIS VESSEL HAS BEEN RELEASED BY THE GOVERNMENT

Question – Have the Government of this Colony any right to search the *Shenandoah* for the alleged offender Charley?

Answer – I am of the opinion that the Government have not the powers which they claim. A ship of war, commissioned by a foreign government, is exempt from the jurisdiction of the Courts of other countries. T. H. FELLOWS.

There will therefore be no meeting.

The crowd had gathered to howl its protests against the authorities. Release or no release, they wanted a chance to demonstrate. No one would admit having organized the meeting or take responsibility for carrying on. But several hundred demonstrators crowded into the hotel.

Out of the crowd rose Robert Kent to harangue his fellows. Standing on a table, he spread his arms for quiet. "Citizens. Fellow Australians. The issue we are met to discuss is large, very large indeed. It is not the issue of a single man, of a single cook, of a single captain. The issue is nothing less than whether peace or war is to exist between England, her colonies, and the South American Confederacy."

When Kent had concluded, George Robertson, a more homespun orator, arose and proclaimed himself the voice of common sense. He suggested that since no one had made any resolution and there was no business before the group, that it wait a few moments, then adjourn.

A voice from the crowd: "And I propose that meantime we all adjourn for nobblers."

"We can do that any time," snapped Robertson, "and not at your expense."

Phillip Cohen, a merchant, shouted for attention. He declared the seizure of the Southern ship was an insult to the Confederacy. "I would ask the meeting: if the *Shenandoah* had been a Federal ship, would the Government have dared lay a hand on her?"

"No," shouted the crowd. "No, no, no."

"No," agreed Cohen, "they would have shaken in their shoes. Had the *Shenandoah* been a war steamer belonging to the smallest, most trivial power of Europe, would the Government have dared touch her?"

Over the chorus of "no's" came the dissent of a lone Union supporter. "Certainly not. But they seize a pirate."

"My friend, this ship is no pirate. She is a crusader for liberty, a symbol of eight million men who are struggling for their liberty. It was an act of cowardice to seize such a ship."

John Quinlay, a lawyer, scrambled onto the table beside Cohen and identified himself as a friend of all downtrodden nationalities. "I propose a resolution. Be it resolved that we protest the seizure of the *Shenandoah* as likely to endanger happy relations with a state likely to be very powerful."

A doctor seconded the motion. "I regard the question as a colonist," he said. "The South is now engaged in a struggle in which this colony, or all the Australian colonies, may some day be involved — the struggle against imperial power."

Cheers and hoots and cries of "No, no" and "Hear, hear" echoed through the hotel.

"Yes," repeated Dr. Rowe, "the South is at war simply in support of a demand for the rights of self-government. As to the rumors about stowaways on the *Shenandoah*, gentlemen, I have it from Waddell himself that up to the time the ship was placed on the slip there was no one aboard. While she was on the slip, of course, it would be easy for the Federals to hide someone aboard her."

Rowe sat down. David McKay, an American, proposed that

the resolution be amended to read that the seizure was approved until it was made clear that the ship was not violating Australian law.

Cohen leaped to his feet, shouting that it was improper for either Northern or Southern partisans to interfere at a meeting of British citizens. There was general confusion. Several fights broke out but were quickly quieted. A Mr. Herberson fought his way to the table and stood looking down at the crowd. "The men who have preceded me," he began, "evidently made a mistake in addressing this audience as 'gentlemen.'" That ended Mr. Herberson's speech. He was hissed down.

Someone shouted for a vote on the resolution. McKay protested that his amendment was still before the meeting. In a moment of parliamentary condescension, the crowd voted on the amendment, walloping it soundly. The wording of the resolution was then toned down from "relations with a state likely to be powerful" to "with neighboring neutral states." The resolution was passed. The crowd surged, cheering and satisfied, into the street.

A scene almost as wild was staged in the Victoria Assembly the next day when James McCullough, the Prime Minister, outlined the Government's course of action:

> I think the course the Government have taken will justify us, not only in the estimation of the House (cheers), but I am sure it will be admitted that the Government have taken the proper course to carry out and support the intention of the British Parliament in respect to the Foreign Enlistment Act (cheers), and the intention of the Proclamation of Her Majesty with respect to the observance of neutrality. (Cheers.)
>
> There is no doubt that this man Charley, for whom the warrant was obtained, and of whom we were assured that he was not on board, was in the uniform of the ship – on various occasions at all events. (Hear, hear.) Now it appears to me and to the Government that if anything can be a violation of strict neutrality, that is it. (Cheers.)

My honorable colleague, the Minister of Justice reminds me that we have not yet proved that this man Charley wore the uniform of the ship, but we have the statement of various parties that such was the case; and as they are to be brought before the police court tomorrow morning, I have no doubt but further information will be received on the point. (Cheers.)

In the meantime, the Government have obtained what they really desired to obtain in the first instance — that all the parties who joined the ship illegally should be removed from the vessel. (Cheers.) That having been done, we have removed the suspension of leave to Her Majesty's subjects to carry out repairs and to assist the vessel off the slip. (Hear, hear.) Captain Waddell will, of course, be ordered to remove from this port at the very earliest possible date. (Cheers.)

A member arose to ask how the Government could be sure there were no more neutrals aboard. Was Waddell's word to be believed on this point? McCullough replied that a warrant was issued for only one individual and that the individual was now under arrest.

There were more cheers. The Assembly proceeded to other topics.

The following day a group of the *Shenandoah*'s officers, including Cornelius Hunt and Fred McNulty, were guests at a party at Scott's, one of Melbourne's leading hotels. As the group was about to be seated for dinner, a stranger entered the dining room, joined them, and almost at once launched into an anti-Confederate tirade. His invective was superb, but his guard was down. McNulty knocked him out with a single punch.

The riot was general. Knives and pistols were drawn, a few wild shots were fired into the ceiling, glasses and decanters sailed through the air, and after a short, fierce fight the field at Scott's was clear of Union sympathizers. The Confederates formed into a squad and marched off, singing, to the theater.

The next day the Union sympathizers won a victory. All four prisoners were remanded for trial on charges of attempting to enlist in the Confederate service.

5

A tug hauled the *Shenandoah* off her slip. Stores of lime juice, fresh vegetables, wine, rum, and bread were brought on board. The *John Frazer*, a British merchantman from Liverpool, opportunely arrived in port with a cargo of almost smokeless coal; the *Shenandoah* took on 250 tons. On Friday, the 17th, clearance papers were picked up and the raider raised steam. It was a signal many men had been awaiting.

Aboard the British steamer *Saxonia*, Captain John Blacker said good-bye to his first mate and ordered his Negro servant to bring his bags. Charley McLaren, who had been both barman and boxer at Ballarat, shook hands with his brother Robert. Harry Sutherland, a ship's carpenter, paid his bill at a Williamstown hotel. Cornelius Regan, a member of the Australian Naval Brigade, told his sister that he had to go "upcountry" on a visit. Shortly after nine o'clock, these men and thirty-odd others gathered in a patch of scrub near the Sandridge Pier. They waited until the police boat passed on its regular round.

From the pier, Constable Minto saw three watermen's boats draw up to the shore. The night was dark and cloudy, visibility poor. The constable could not see clearly, but he thought he made out a man, wearing an officer's uniform, giving directions. The little boats were quickly loaded and pulled away toward the *Shenandoah*. Minto made no effort to stop them. The police boat was away and he could not follow. He had no way of telling whether these men were recruits, or regulars returning from a final tour of the town's brothels and bars.

⸙ 6 ⸙

The evening of Friday, the 17th, was a time of frustration for the terrible-tempered Mr. Blanchard.

He was working on another letter to the Governor, calling attention to some new affidavits about the *Shenandoah's* recruiting program, when Andrew Forbes, a Union sympathizer, burst into the Consulate with the information that several persons were waiting on the Sandridge wharf to board a vessel that would meet the *Shenandoah* beyond the jurisdiction of the port. Forbes had heard this rumor from a man who claimed he was shipping.

Blanchard felt this was his big opportunity. If he could move fast enough he might catch Waddell in the act of violating the antirecruiting regulations. Asking a friend, S. P. Lord, to accompany them, he went with Forbes to the Crown Law Office.

The office had closed for the day but the Crown Law officer had returned to pick up some papers. Blanchard caught him. The officer refused to help: it was not his business to issue warrants, that was a matter for the magistrates. Or, he suggested, the Consul might take it up with the Attorney General or Minister of Justice, both of whom were at the Parliament. As for himself, he was late for dinner and did not intend to delay longer.

Blanchard, Forbes, and Lord hurried on. They went to the detective police. The police said they could do nothing; it was out of their jurisdiction. But, they suggested, if Mr. Forbes would sign an affidavit, a county magistrate might execute a warrant.

Off rushed the trio, this time going to Parliament. Blanchard sent word to George Higinbotham, the Attorney General, that they wanted to see him. Higinbotham, a Dublin-born lawyer-journalist with a fiery temper and a rasped tongue, was urbane but unhelpful. It was out of his jurisdiction. Why didn't the Consul go to Mr. Sturt, who would issue an affidavit on Forbes' testimony.

Off they raced to the office of Mr. Sturt, a mile away. Mr. Sturt listened to Forbes' story and declined to take the testimony. It was out of his jurisdiction. This was an affair for the waterfront police at Williamstown, across the bay.

Blanchard stormed back to his office and angrily wrote down Forbes' testimony himself. This document he dispatched in Lord's care to the Attorney General. Then he started with Forbes toward Williamstown. But when they neared the edge of the bay, the informer began to be nervous. He did not want to appear in Williamstown, where he was known, in the company of the American. It wouldn't be safe. He refused to go farther. Blanchard went back to his office.

At eleven o'clock, George Washington Robbins, a master stevedore, rushed in to say that boatloads of men and baggage were leaving Sandridge and crossing to the raider. The discouraged Consul asked Robbins to take his information to the waterfront police. The stevedore started at once. He ran back to the waterfront and began to row to Williamstown.

When well out in the Bay, Robbins saw a boat pull off from the *Shenandoah*. As it drew near, he recognized the oarsmen, a waterfront pair named Jack Riley and Robert Muir, who had been hauling recruits to the cruiser. They hailed Robbins but he did not answer. He wanted only to beat them to shore. Two backs proved better than one when thrown into oars, and the watermen overhauled Robbins' boat. Muir grabbed the gunnel while Riley raised an oar threateningly. "If you talk . . .," Riley began. Robbins batted him alongside the head with an oar, kicked Muir's fingers away from the gunnel, and rowed off toward the pier. He reached it ahead of his pursuers and disappeared into the nearby scrub. It was after four o'clock before he reached the Williamstown police station.

And at 4 A.M. the *Shenandoah* hove up her anchor. With Edward Johnson, the pilot who had brought her in, standing at the helm, she steamed across Hobson's Bay, between the heads, and out into open water. Waddell was pleased to use Johnson as pilot again. That worthy had run a steamer aground since bringing the cruiser to port. Shunned by merchant captains, he was so pleased to get another assignment that Waddell was certain he would not talk about the new additions to the crew.

The decks were cleared, the guns were loaded and rolled into position, and everything was ready for action in case a Union cruiser was lurking outside the harbor entrance. There was none. At 1 P.M. the pilot was dropped. He took ashore with him letters from some of the Melbourne recruits. For the veterans aboard, the parting was disappointing.

"The pilot left us with his good wishes," Waddell wrote, "but the parting was not accompanied with those home feelings which cluster around the heart when shaking the hand of the man who would so soon return to our native soil. A feeling of impatience hurried him over the side, and no regret was entertained for the separation."

Several vessels were in sight. Since they would report the course the *Shenandoah* took, Waddell had her stand south until dark. Under cover of the summer night, the raider turned toward Bass's Strait, the passage between Australia and Tasmania, opening into the Tasman Sea and the Pacific.

"A surprise awaited us upon getting fairly outside," Hunt wrote blandly. "Our ship's company had received a mysterious addition of forty-five men, who now made their appearance from every conceivable place where a human being could conceal himself from vigilant eyes. Fourteen of the number crept out of the bowsprit, which was of iron and hollow, where they had come very near ending their existence by suffocation; twenty more turned out of some water tanks which were dry;

another detachment was unearthed from the lower hold, and at last the whole number of stowaways were mustered forward, and word was passed to the Captain to learn his pleasure concerning them.

"Captain Waddell soon made his appearance, not in the best humor, and without any circumlocution demanded of our new recruits to what country they belonged and for what purpose they were there. The old sea-dogs chuckled, rolled over their tobacco, hitched up their trousers, and with one accord, protested that they were natives of the Southern Confederacy, and had come on board thus surreptitiously for the purpose of joining us.

"There was something absolutely refreshing in the effrontery with which that motley crew had first stolen on board, at the moment of our leaving port, and then claimed the privilege of remaining on the ground they were our countrymen. I verily believe half the nations of the earth had contributed to the proposed accession to our numbers but sailors change their nationalities as readily as they do their names; besides, we really needed their assistance, and as they had come through no connivance of ours, we determined to consider it providential, and they were all enlisted. A few who were not seamen, we made available as marines. Good men and true they proved, and very useful before our cruise was ended."

7

The *Shenandoah* dropped out of Melbourne's sight, but she was far from being out of Melbourne's mind. The circumstances of her departure stirred up a new controversy. The Victoria papers printed rumors that Waddell had shipped from forty to eighty men before leaving port. Riley and Muir drew jail sentences for assaulting Robbins. The affair came to its climax in mid-March with the trial of James "Charley" Davidson and his fellow recruits.

The Case of the Captured Cook became a symbol. It was not merely Charley who was on trial, but the *Shenandoah*. Southern sympathizers wanted an acquittal to clear the questioned honor of the ship's officers – to them the issue was whether the Colonial Court would, by implication, call Waddell a liar. The authorities wanted a conviction to show that they had done their best to enforce the Foreign Enlistment Act; to them the issue was Australia's neutrality.

The courtroom was packed when the case came before his Honor, Mr. Justice Molesworth on March 17. The men were to be tried separately, Davidson first.

Defense Attorney Aspinall staggered the prosecution with a sneak punch: he called on them to prove that there was a war in progress. If there was no proof of war, there could be no proof of violation of the Foreign Enlistment Act. A panicky officer for the prosecution sent a subpoena to the American Consul, ordering him to appear to testify that the Confederate States were a government. Mr. Blanchard blew up with a bang. He wrote to the Governor that the invitation was a deliberate insult, that the Colonial authorities had allowed the ship into port because she was a belligerent and now asked him to prove that she was. The Governor replied that it was all a mistake.

In the meantime the judge ruled that there was prima facie evidence of a war. Then Aspinall demanded that the prosecution prove that the *Shenandoah* was really a cruiser and not a pirate: it would be no violation of neutrality to join a pirate. The judge ruled that the *Shenandoah* must be considered a cruiser.

These rulings left matters directly up to the jury. Only if their sympathy for the South outweighed the evidence of a violation of the law could Charley be freed. In his closing plea, Aspinall put matters on just that basis.

"Gentlemen," he told the jury, "this is the most ridiculous State prosecution ever brought before twelve men. The State has looked ridiculous in everything it has done concerning the *Shenandoah*. Superintendent Lyttleton marched up with fifty men, supported by Mr. Vernon with all the artillery, for the purpose of capturing a cook. But, like the King of France, they all marched down again. With their array of military might, gentlemen, they captured the *Shenandoah* on the patent slip, and then they dropped it like a hot potato.

"The Crown would have the jury believe the country is about to be plunged into a war, all because this man Charley has cooked a few chops for the officers of the ship while on the patent slip. What a case to make a State trial of! Do you gentlemen believe that Her Majesty is trembling upon her throne because Charley cooked a few sausages? Or that because the Attorney General is prosecuting this case, the Confederate States care a fig whether Charley was cooking chops or hominy there?

"But, gentlemen, I ask you this. What sort of justice is it which brings Charley before us? He is no loafer. He is a working man, a man who believes in giving labor for money received. He was seeking to earn a living by honorable employment. Why then has he been seized upon to be made a scapegoat? Mr. Landlangs, who manages the slip, went to great length in putting the ship in repair and making her ready for war. He is allowed to pass scot-free. But the man who fried potatoes on the patent slip stands before you a State prisoner, awaiting his fate. Is this British justice? Charley, the cook, subverting the British constitution — that is the proposition submitted to the jury.

"In order to convict this man, the jury must believe that he was engaged aboard the *Shenandoah*. But the Attorney General proved that he was not engaged, that he was refused, that he was told to leave the ship by the ship's officers. Of course, the Attorney General in his wisdom considered this evidence that he had been engaged. But intent and attempt are very different things. A man might go on a ship merely in the hope of getting employment.

"The Attorney General, it seems, insists on a conviction, though he tells you he does not intend to press for a heavy penalty. There is significance in this, gentlemen. It is plain that the intention of the prosecution is to prove that Captain Waddell and the officers of the *Shenandoah* are liars. Though the defendant only be given an hour's imprisonment, if the jury convicts it will go forth through the American press that a jury of a British colony has pronounced the officers of a Southern ship guilty of violating a treaty and of neglecting their own honor and position. This would do more to create a war than any act of the defendant. The fact, of course, is that the officers of this vessel so faithfully maintained their position that they would not even have Charley as cook.

"If any war comes out of this affair, it will be from the method adopted by the Colony in dealing with the vessels of foreign powers. It is a method which has outraged the feelings of representatives of belligerents.

"I have not the least anxiety for my client. I do not believe the Executive would dare to carry out any sentence upon him. But I wish to protect the Southern flag from unmerited insult. I should like it to be said that whatever the Government of this colony thought proper to do, a jury of twelve men could not be found to sanction it; and, for the credit of the Colony, I do not want it to be said that political feeling has been allowed to determine the matter, and that a stigma has been unjustly put upon the character of the officers of the *Shenandoah*."

The jurymen were in chamber only briefly. When they

returned, the courtroom crowd fell silent. The foremen arose: "Guilty of attempting to enter the service of the Confederate States of America. Not guilty of entering the service of said Confederate States."

The Judge nodded. He made a short speech. A breach of the laws of the country had been proved; but it was not to be said that the defendant had been guilty of an infringement of moral duty, as persons of his rank of life might not, and probably did not, know the important results which might follow from such unlawful acts. As the defendant had already been imprisoned for more than a month, a small further punishment would suffice to show that the neutrality laws must be strictly maintained. "I sentence the defendant to be imprisoned for ten days."

Suppressed applause ran through the audience.

Two of Charley's companions were released – one because he was an American, the other because he was seventeen. The third pleaded guilty to attempting to enlist and also received a ten-day sentence.

Australia considered the case closed. Though the *Shenandoah* officers stood "convicted" as liars, no declaration of war, not even a protest, came from the Confederacy. Before news of the trial reached Richmond, no government remained to be insulted.

BIG SPACE

THE Pacific lay open before the *Shenandoah*. Never before had a raider known such an opportunity. From Pole to Pole, from Hawaii to Hong Kong, there was not a Union cruiser to oppose her. The only American warship in the Western Pacific, the sailing sloop *Jamestown*, was laid up at Shanghai for repairs.

More than a year earlier, the *Alabama* had ventured into the Java Sea. She won a long race from the *Wyoming*, a fast Union steam sloop commanded by Captain David McDougal. The *Wyoming* had had the most exciting career of any Northern ship in Pacific waters during the war. Besides hunting the *Alabama*, it had fought Japan – single-handed.

In July 1863, the sloop had gone to Yokohama. Japan at the time was in turmoil. The foreigners who had followed Admiral Perry to the forbidden islands were unpopular, the Japanese talked about tossing them into the sea. The *Wyoming* was supposed to convince local warlords that it was expedient to be kind to merchant Christians.

Arriving at Yokohama, McDougal learned that an American merchantman had been shelled while passing through Shimonoseki Strait, which connects the Inland Sea with the Sea of Japan. Off went the *Wyoming* to investigate. She found the strait well fortified and guarded by three warships – a steamer and two sailing vessels – belonging to the Prince of Nagato.

Outnumbered, outgunned, in unfamiliar waters half-the-world away from home, McDougal by all rules should have retreated. Instead he steamed into the strait. The batteries on shore and on the Japanese warships opened up, and the *Wyoming* engaged them. The battle was brief and violent. A shot from the American exploded the steamer's boilers. One of the sailing ships was hulled below the waterline and left sinking; the other was damaged. A shore battery was knocked out. That was as much as the *Wyoming* could accomplish alone; she could not defeat six forts. McDougal withdrew to count casualties: four dead, seven injured. The ship, hulled eleven times, was badly battered, a circumstance which hampered its hunt for the *Alabama* a few months later.

But now, in 1865, there was not even the *Wyoming* to challenge the *Shenandoah.* Of the Union ships assigned to the chase, the *Iroquois* was still en route to Singapore, limping across the Indian Ocean under short canvas. The *Wachusett,* at Boston, had just been detailed to the pursuit. Her captain, Robert Townsend, accepted the assignment with a flourish:

> I am very grateful for the confidence the Department is pleased to repose in me, and I will faithfully endeavor to prove that it is not misplaced. Duty, as well as inclination, will induce me to follow up, within the scope of my orders, the *Shenandoah,* and strive to win the last sprig of laurel left for the Navy to add to its glorious chaplet gathered in this war. . . .

A fast ship in an era of slow communications, the *Shenandoah* had every advantage of surprise. Though the telegraph had been invented, the absence of ocean cables slowed dispatches down to steamer speed. The raider reached Melbourne on January 25; it was March 11 before the news reached London, another ten days before it crossed the Atlantic to Washington. The Navy Department promptly ordered the sloop *Wyoming* back to the Pacific. In a letter to the *Wyoming's* new commander, the Secretary of Navy declared:

> Recent intelligence advises us of the arrival of the rebel steamer *Shenandoah* at Melbourne, Australia, and it is believed that she will make the straits and passes to China the field of her piratical operations. It is therefore highly important that you should take your departure at the earliest practicable day and reach your station without unnecessary delay or detention en route.
>
> Your chief and first object will be the pursuit and (should you be so fortunate as to overtake her) the capture or destruction of the *Shenandoah.* Hence you are expected and directed to follow her wherever she may go, unless it be to the Pacific Coast of America or this side of the Cape of Good Hope. Should you encounter her anywhere this side of the Cape you will pursue her without regard to the orders to proceed direct to the East Indies. If on reaching Batavia you gain no tidings of the corsair it will be well to remain there, or in the vicinity, until you learn something definite of her movements. . . . You may consider the limits of your station as extending as far north as Macao, China, and you are at liberty to go beyond that point should an emergency require it.

Information about the *Shenandoah* trickled in slowly and by strange, roundabout routes. On April 21, the Commander of the U.S.S. *Cyana,* at Panama, forwarded to the Secretary of the Navy a note from the American Legation at Lima, Peru, written April 11, containing a translation of an item from the Lima *Comercio* of April 7 of an extract from the Sydney *Morning Herald* of January 27, announcing the arrival of the *Shenandoah* in Melbourne. A few days later the Commander sent along a similar note from the Legation at Santiago de Chile, in which the Ambassador moaned:

> If this report be true we shall doubtless soon learn of her presence in the waters of Chile, and the American whaling and merchant vessels trading at the South Pacific ports will be in imminent danger.

I have frequently invited the attention of our government to the unprotected state of our commerce in this vicinity, and beg to request, if it can be done without prejudice to the public interests, that a vessel . . . be detached for service upon the coast of Chile at the earliest possible moment.

Rumors put the raider everywhere. In February, the skipper of the U.S.S. *Connecticut* reported from Bermuda that the *Shenandoah* was expected to meet the Confederate ironclad *Stonewall* soon at that port. In April, the U.S.S. *Wachusett* reported from Martinique that "It should not be surprising if the *Shenandoah* turned up hereabouts at any time." The same month, the Commander of the U.S.S. *Suwanee* heard at Bahia, Brazil, that "the *Shenandoah* has been seen to the southward of this port." And two weeks later the same worthy reported, "It is believed that she crossed over some time since to the Cape of Good Hope." In May, the skipper of the U.S.S. *St. Mary's* wrote the Secretary of the Navy from Callao Bay, Peru:

It is rumored that certain parties in Callao (Englishmen, of course) have received information that the rebel steamer *Shenandoah* is on her way to this coast. I am looking out for her, and should she come will try to do all that can be done with a sailing vessel to prevent her doing any injury to our commerce. It is natural to suppose that the pirate contemplates visiting the Chincha Islands, where there is a large number of American vessels loading with guano. Therefore I have decided to go there myself, and will sail tomorrow, or as soon as the wind will permit me.

Some of the rumors were founded on fact. Some grew naturally out of the absence of authentic information. And many were launched deliberately by Confederate sympathizers or British shippers who wished to frighten American merchantmen into staying in port, or to make neutral merchants think twice about entrusting goods to American bottoms. This war of nerves was effective. When the *Iroquois* reached Singapore late in March, a dozen U.S. ships were tied up at the British base, unable to get cargo or afraid to put to sea.

2

Meanwhile the *Shenandoah,* object of all the speculation, and fountainhead of all the fears, was cruising north, bound for the Okhotsk Sea.

After the strains and tribulations of the month at Melbourne, Waddell found it pleasant to be back at sea. The first night out was a thing of midsummer beauty. The moon shone bright, the atmosphere was clear and cool, the brilliance of the sky moved the captain to enter in his notes a lone snatch of poesy:

> While the stars that oversprinkle
> All the heavens seem to twinkle
> With a crystalline delight.

The brilliance of the moonlight was more fortunate for the steamer than for poetry. The *Shenandoah* was slightly off her course. Shortly after midnight, Grimball, the watch officer, sighted land dead ahead. Had the night been stormy, or even overcast, the cruise would have been over. As it was, the helmsman was able to haul her round, avoid hitting Tasmania, and point her into the Bass Strait.

Waddell had intended to raid the Lord Howe and Norfolk Islands which lay between the east coast of Australia and the northern tip of New Zealand. Ordinarily their harbors were the bases for thirty or forty ships making up the South Pacific whaling fleet. But the wind hung at east of north, forcing the

Shenandoah to beat back and forth – south of east, then north of east.

The great distances of the Pacific which protected the *Shenandoah* from pursuit also aided her quarry. Not knowing when he might be able to coal up again, Waddell turned down suggestions that they raise steam. If the cruiser couldn't make Lord Howe Island under canvas, he said, they would have to miss visiting there. Besides, he reasoned, the long layover of the *Shenandoah* in Australia had probably scared the whalers out of these waters.

Dissension, stilled at Melbourne, arose again as day after day passed without sighting a Yankee. "Have not seen a sail since losing sight of Cape Howe," Lining wrote, a week out of port. "I thought we were going to cruise on the Northern Coasts of New Zealand and between that and Sydney but now we seem pressing right on, not going near land, consequently we never see a sail. How I do wish some people could stick to one thing at a time and not be as vacillating as the wind. We ought to have caught several prizes before now."

North of New Zealand, the weather went sour. The ship was caught in a revolving gale. "Never in my twenty-three years service had I seen such a succession of violent squalls," Waddell declared. "She was enveloped in a salt mist and tossed about by an angry sea like a plaything."

For the first time the *Shenandoah* was forced to lie to, her topsails close-reefed, and a tarpaulin in the mizzen rigging. For four days she tossed about in the storm. The lookouts strained their eyes peering into the mist to watch for land ahead. The firemen kept the furnaces ready in case steam were needed to keep the ship off shore. At the end of four days the gale was over. A flat calm descended on the tropic sea, broken only by midday torrents of rain. "Nothing in sight, not even a bird," remarked Lining. "This region seems to be the abomination of desolation, as the very birds have deserted us and for several days we have not seen one, nor has even a fish been in sight. Of course we can't expect to catch a prize in such a place as this."

There comes a time in any adventure when the flavor of excitement is lost, when the tasks that once were diverting become tedious to the point of torture, when the recreations which once filled the time begin to rattle emptily in each age-long day. For many men aboard the *Shenandoah* that point was reached during the fourth week out from Melbourne, when the ship lay becalmed under the equatorial sun. Not since the *Delphine* appeared in the Indian Ocean had they seen a Yankee sail. Three months without a prize. The grumbling was not confined to the officers; the men, too, were bored and unhappy. One enterprising sailor boosted his fellows' morale by clambering through the propeller shaft, working into the hold, and siphoning off fifty gallons of the officers' rum.

On Friday, March 24, the *Shenandoah* found a breeze. After a few hours under sail, she raised Drummond Island, a little jewel of the tropics, full of exotic fruits and malarial mosquitoes.

As the ship approached the island, a canoe put out from shore. Crew and officers crowded to the rail as the dugout approached. It was manned by three natives – short, copper-skinned, and, except for a remarkable array of tattoo-marks, stark naked. They had brought a boatload of fish and fruit to trade for tobacco, the only article which interested them.

To the surprise of all hands, one of the *Shenandoah's* Malay seamen began to talk to the natives. At first his shipmates thought the Malay was merely making up gibberish, but it was soon apparent from the delight of the natives that the man knew their dialect. Whittle saw an opportunity to gain information. Through a series of seamen interpreters, who turned his questions from English into Portuguese into Malay, he had the seaman ask how many whalers had been seen around the island recently. The natives replied there had been none for months.

Bitterly disappointed, Waddell ordered steam raised. Dr. Lining asked permission to go ashore to make a brief study of the natives' way of life. He was refused.

As the propellers began to turn, the natives in the dugout shrieked with surprise and horror. The *Shenandoah* was probably the first steamer they had seen. They paddled cautiously in her wake, staring at the troubled water astern, trying to learn what magic made the ship move. At a hint from John Grimball, the engineer "played a stirring solo upon his steam whistle, and, with every appearance of consternation, the natives took to their paddles and only paused when they had placed a safe distance between themselves and the screaming monster."

Having had their little joke, the raiders let steam go down and with all sail set moved off before the Southeast Trades.

That night they again crossed the Equator. There was no celebration.

Shortly before sundown the following Wednesday, the pleasant cry of "Sail Ho" sounded unexpectedly from the lookout. The speck on the horizon swelled into a sail bearing south. Before the tropic sunset faded from the sky, the ships were close enough for the *Shenandoah's* twelve-pounder to sound the signal for the stranger to heave to. She ran up Hawaiian colors. Waddell, not satisfied that she wasn't American, and hoping, in any event, to learn the whereabouts of some whalers, dispatched a boarding party under Bulloch.

The sailing master was met at the rail by Captain Hammond of the *Pelin.* Hammond was an American citizen, but his ship was properly registered as an Hawaiian. Though Bulloch told him that the *Shenandoah* was a Union cruiser, the *Miami,* the captain remained suspicious and uncommunicative. From a junior officer one of the boarding party learned that five Yankee whalers had been lying in a harbor on the southeast side of Ascencion Island when the *Pelin* called there a few days before.

Under steam and sail the raider raced off for Ascencion, hoping to head off the Yankees before they could start north.

TROUBLE IN PARADISE

ASCENCION, the Flower of the Pacific, is a lovely little island that drifts in and out of history like flotsam before the trade winds. One of the Caroline group, it is now known by its native name, Ponape.

The first western ship to raise Ponape's jungled shore was a Spanish caravel sailing from Manila to Mexico in 1565 with an announcement of the conquest of the Philippines. The discovery was important. Ponape, unlike most of its mid-Pacific neighbors, is no mere coral spangle; it is the top of a drowned volcano. Streams of fresh cold water pour down its basalt and granite sides – and fresh water can mean life or death to sailors.

The natives proved something of a problem to their Spanish discoverers. Ponape's brown-skinned, tattooed warriors were tougher than most of their Micronesian contemporaries. The island was large enough to support five different tribes, and the males kept in fighting trim with raids on each other's palm-thatched villages. Contemptuous of pain – the men scarred themselves with sea shells in their youth and at maturity underwent mutilation of the right testicle to prove they could suffer in silence – they fought with bone knives and spears tipped with the spines of sea wasps. But spears and stoicism were no match for muskets. The Spaniards took what they wanted from the island.

As the Iberian Empire withered, the stream of traffic between Mexico and the Philippines dried up. Ponape was forgotten. When in 1823 James O'Connell, a Dublin-born adventurer, was cast upon its shore from a foundered Australian whaler, he waited six years for another ship to come in sight. During those years, O'Connell and five other seamen, the first white men known to have lived on the island, were adopted by the local tribes. O'Connell married a brown princess, who bore him a son and daughter. He acquired – though under protest – a royal array of tattoos, and discovered on the northeast section of the island the mysterious ruins now known as Nan-Matal, but called by the Irishman "O'Connell's Cluster."

Nan-Matal, the Venice of the Pacific, is a monumental relic to a vanished race. Its huge buildings, forty and fifty feet high, are scattered over eleven square miles. The unhewn slabs of basalt which went into them are as heavy as the stone blocks of the pyramids. Archaeologists now believe the rocks were brought from a natural quarry on the far side of the island. They were probably dragged over a hill on a wooden slide greased with coconut oil, maneuvered onto rafts and poled fifteen miles to Nan-Matal. By what methods a primitive people hoisted the three-ton stones into place, no one knows. Such an engineering feat appears far beyond the abilities of the inhabitants of Ponape. The natives told O'Connell that the ruins were built by the Gods. Scientists, after studying skulls found in the burial vaults, disagree. Indications are that the city was the creation of a vanished negroid race; Ponape legend tells of a struggle between black and brown warriors for its possession, the blacks losing; O'Connell noted a negroid appearance among the slaves of the brown rulers.

Though without formal education, O'Connell was sharp-eyed and intelligent. On reaching America, he joined a circus as tattooed man and, while on display, wrote a fine, fantastic book, *Eleven Years in Australia and the Carolines,* in which he recorded his life as a Micronesian tribesman. It is a document of considerable sociological importance. Though the islanders had some strange habits (dogs were the only livestock, and women nursed orphaned pups until they were big enough to be baked), the life he pictured was on the whole so idyllic that a reader can but wonder at his anxiety to catch the first boat.

Coinciding with the publication of the tattooed sociologist's report on Ponape was the rediscovery of the island, this time by American whalemen who stopped to slake their thirst, and who brought the pox to Paradise. Fresh water, fine harbors, tropic fruits, abundant fish, and finely formed women made the Carolines an attractive base for ships cruising in the Central Pacific en route to the Arctic. During the forties as many as sixty ships visited Ponape each season.

Soon after the Yankee whalers came Yankee missionaries to preach against lust, liquor, and laboring on Sunday. A fine feud developed between the hunters for whales and the fishers for souls. It was climaxed when Bully Hayes, a consummately unpleasant character, invited an unsuspecting divine aboard his whaler to hold Sunday service, then sailed off to maroon the soul-saver on a surf-washed rock north of the Marshall Islands. The misplaced missionary was never again heard from.

In time the feud flickered out. The whalemen realized the men of the cloth would never talk the natives out of their love of strong liquor. Thereafter, shipmasters and missionaries sought each other's company in the inevitable manner of Americans away from home. So it was that on the morning of April First, 1865, the skippers of three American ships and an Hawaiian bark anchored in Lod Harbor on Southern Ponape, left their vessels, and started around the island in a whaleboat to visit the Reverend and Mrs. Edward Doane.

A few hours later, the mates in charge of the anchored whalers saw a black steamer standing across the mouth of Lod

Harbor. It seemed to be seeking the channel through the coral reefs into the narrow lagoon. One of the mates asked an escaped Australian convict, who went under the name of Thomas Hardrocke, to paddle out and pilot the stranger in. Hardrocke obliged.

⸙ 2 ⸙

Before dawn on April First, the *Shenandoah* nosed slowly through a fog thick enough to be carved. After daybreak the equatorial sun thinned the mist. By 6 A.M. the jungled peak of Totolom, Ponape's 2500-foot mountain, was in sight. Shortly after eight a masthead lookout shouted, "Sail ho. Four sail in a harbor."

A small boat having been spotted coming out from shore, Waddell gave orders to stand by. The boatsman wore nothing but tattered cotton pants. His skin was mahogany brown, his body fearfully tattooed. The men on the *Shenandoah* were amazed when he hailed them in English and, coming over the side, introduced himself as an Australian, Tom Hardrocke.

The *Shenandoah* flew no flag. Looking around, Hardrocke asked Whittle the ship's nationality.

"American."

"You have countrymen in the harbor who'll be glad to see you."

"No more so than we to see them," Whittle replied serenely.

For thirty dollars worth of whiskey and tobacco, Hardrocke agreed to paddle ahead of the ship in a canoe to show the way in. Waddell, fearful of a trap, warned the pilot it would be worth his life to run the *Shenandoah* on a reef. To emphasize the point, he strapped on a pistol and climbed down into the canoe with him.

As the *Shenandoah* slid into the harbor, the whalers raised their flags in her honor. Three ran up the Union colors, the fourth raised the flag of Oahu.

The lagoon was narrow. The raider dropped anchor in fifteen fathoms near the harbor entrance, blocking any possible escape. A razor-edged reef rose in the center of the lagoon; to keep the tide from swinging the *Shenandoah* onto it, a pair of hawsers were run from the ship's stern and looped around palm trees on shore.

These preparations complete, the starboard gun crews took their positions. Four prize crews of six men each climbed into the ship's cutters and whaleboats. The signal gun was sounded – scattering the natives who had lined the shore to study the steamer – and the Confederate flag was raised.

As the prize boats pulled off toward their trapped prey, Thomas Hardrocke stood on the raider's deck, looking with bewilderment and some anger at the strange flag and the ready cannoneers.

"What is this, matey?" he asked Dr. McNulty.

"All answered in a word, my hearty," replied the assistant surgeon. "Those four ships are prizes to the Confederate government."

"And what the bloody hell is the Confederate government?"

"The best and biggest half of what was the United States of America," boomed McNulty in his best brogue. Ten years' residence in Connecticut had not dimmed his Irish love of oratory. "The Yankees didn't sail the ship of state to suit us, so we cut adrift and started on our own hook."

"The devil you did. So then you're Jeff Davis's men. I never thought I'd live to see that flag." Hardrocke spat on the deck. "What are you going to do with your prizes?"

"Set them on fire by and by, after we have taken what we want out of them."

"Well, you and the Yankees must settle that business to suit yourselves. If I had known what you were up to, maybe I shouldn't have piloted you in. I don't like to see a bonfire made of a good ship."

Within an hour the four prize teams were back with the mates and papers from the whalers. Waddell was particularly pleased with the capture of the whaling charts; they were not only more recent but far more detailed than the naval charts supplied the *Shenandoah*, or the charts taken from the *Edward*. "With these in our possession," he told the officers exultantly, "we not only hold a key to the navigation of all the Pacific Islands, the Okhotsk and Bering Seas and the Arctic Ocean, but the most probable localities for finding the great Arctic whaling fleet of New England without a tiresome search."

John Grimball and his team had bagged the *Edward Carey* of San Francisco; Smith Lee, the *Hector* of New Bedford; Fred Chew, the *Pearl* of New London; and Dabney Scales, the *Harvest* of Oahu. The latter proved to be a problem ship. She had an American register, an American master, the same American mates who had made her previous voyages, and American flags in her hold, but she also had a bill of sale showing her transfer to Hawaiian owners. Most of the *Shenandoah's* officers felt the change legitimate, but Waddell, noticing some technical irregularities in the transfer, declared the *Harvest* forfeit. All four ships were condemned. Their total value was estimated at $116,000.

The mates of the whalers were confined in single irons in the *Shenandoah's* forecastle. The crews were put to work transferring stores of bread, salt meat, liquor, and winter clothing from the whalers to the raider.

Late in the afternoon, a small boat was seen coming through the channel. Glasses trained on it revealed the oarsmen to be the missing shipmasters, returning from their visit with the missionaries. The captains observed the activity in the harbor, guessed what was wrong, and began to row a rapid retreat.

An armed crew from the *Shenandoah* started after them in a cutter. At the end of an hour's chase, the fugitive skippers were captured.

The record of their remarks about their fate is lost to history, but they do not appear to have been polite prisoners. For the first time Waddell was discourteous to brother captains. He confined three of them to single irons, and the fourth, who had taken part in sinking the Great Stone Fleet off Charleston and was "disposed to be impertinent" drew double irons and a gag.

3

Waddell wanted to talk over the disposal of the captured ships with the native king. On Sunday, April 2, he dispatched the pilot, Hardrocke, who spoke the language, and Master's Mate Hunt, to invite His Majesty aboard.

"As we neared the beach," Hunt wrote later, "a crowd of natives rushed down to meet us, armed with stones which they hurl almost with the precision of a rifle ball, with swords manufactured from sharks' teeth, the edge of which are dipped in a subtle poison that leaves certain death in any wounds they inflict. The appearance of this heathenish multitude was anything but conciliatory, but a few words from the interpreter explained the real object of our visit, and when they learned it was to do honor to their king that we had come, their unfriendly demonstrations subsided, though there were still two or three ferocious-looking villains who eyed us askance, and I have no doubt considered what sort of roasts or barbecues we would probably make.

"His majesty was not in his customary abiding place, a little bamboo hut near the beach, barely large enough to contain four persons, but at a sort of Government house farther inland, where some sort of festivity was in progress. Two or three of his chiefs volunteered to escort me thither, and leaving my men in the boat and accompanied by the interpreter, I set forth for the first time in my life to pay a visit to royalty. It was more of a walk than I had anticipated, and the way led over some steep, rugged ascents, hard enough to climb under that broiling sun, but there was much to amuse me in observing the manners and habits of this strange people, and in gaining a better insight than I had before been able to do into their domestic economy.

"Once in passing a native hut I observed a dog with his brains beaten out, but still retaining his skin and entrails, lying by the side of a rude oven, already prepared for his reception; when I returned a few hours later, a woman sat before the still smouldering embers gnawing the hind leg of the animal, to which the hair still adhered.

"In the process of time I arrived at the place where the king was holding his temporary court. It was a rude, extensive building, built of bamboo, with a high peaked roof and eaves which extended nearly to the ground, and in it were assembled some three hundred of the most hideous-looking beings it was ever my fortune to behold. The most of them were armed like those we had met on the beach with stones, and bone swords, though a few of them had spears, and I am free to confess to feeling anything but comfortable as I stood in the presence of that fiendish looking multitude, with no attendant save the demoralized Englishman who had perhaps degenerated into a worse savage than any of them. But it was too late to turn back, even had I been disposed to do so, and assuming as nonchalant an air as possible, and feeling to see that my revolver was convenient to my hand I entered the building.

"His majesty was seated on a platform raised a few inches above the floor, and on my entrance arose to meet me. He was a miserable little savage, scarcely more than five feet high, naked with the exception of a tappa made of grass worn about his waist, and smeared from head to foot with coconut oil. Like most of his followers he wore thrust through a hole made in the lobe of his ear for the purpose a huge misshapen tobacco pipe, an arrangement which however convenient did not add in the least to his personal appearance.

"A number of his subjects were employed in making *gorwa,* a kind of intoxicating beverage, manufactured from roots crushed between stones and afterwards left to ferment; an industrial pursuit upon which he seemed to look with peculiar favor.

"The old pilot presented me in due form, and I at once made known my errand. The King listened, looked round distrustfully a few moments, and showed himself a true diplomat by asking by way of answer to see my sword and revolver. Having examined these to his heart's content and taken another deliberate survey of his followers, probably querying with himself meanwhile whether they would be able to protect him against one desperate Confederate should he feel disposed to make a prize of him, he advanced another step in our negotiations and invited me to take a drink. As this was a branch of diplomacy in which I had had some practice, I complied and touched my lips to the coconut cup containing the vilest smelling, most nauseous compound upon which a man ever attempted to get 'salubrious.'

"These formal points of court etiquette disposed of, we returned to the real business in hand, and after a little persuasion, my royal host condescended to favor me with his company, but to effectually guard himself against any machinations that might be meditated against his peace and dignity, he gave his ugly person a fresh coating of coconut oil, and announced himself in readiness for the proposed excursion.

"Back to the beach we wended our way, the King and a few of his chiefs and my insignificant self taking the lead, and the whole vagabond colony following at our heels.

"On reaching the shore, the King was accommodated with the seat of honor in the boat, while I placed myself out of olfactory range of the peculiar perfume belonging to him and his retinue, and ordered the men to give way. As we glided seaward at least a hundred boats put off and followed in our wake, each containing from three to five natives, and all keeping at a respectful distance behind, out of deference to the great man who preceded them."

As Hunt and the royal party paddled out from shore, the officers of the *Shenandoah* gathered on deck. Waddell had ordered them all into dress uniform, and they oozed sweat. The war canoes, decorated with faded bunting and colored cotton, swung in a semicircle around the cruiser. The king's boat drew alongside. The Confederates came to attention.

"His majesty came up the side very cautiously," Waddell wrote in his notes, "and, arranging his apron, seated himself between the headboards of the gangway, smelling furiously of coconut oil, a protection against mosquitoes and almost anything else, and blocking the passage to the hereditary prince who was hanging on outside the vessel to a manrope.

"The pilot was still in the gig. It was impossible for me to speak to his majesty. He was therefore very unceremoniously introduced to the deck by motions of head and hand. He stood perfectly erect, as if expecting a submissive bow from all present; and after his retinue reached the deck and arranged themselves in their respective orders and with respect to their sovereign I was presented to his majesty by the pilot, who simply said, with a backward motion of his head, 'That's the king, sir.'

"I invited his majesty and suite to my cabin, and the officers were asked to witness the proceedings, for such things are interesting: the absurdity makes it so.

"The topic for discussion was postponed till after the introduction of the pipe and schnapps, not a bad introduction, as it was a sort of prelude to something else which interested me more, and my august visitor became quite at ease, although greatly impressed by the objects of capture which were in the cabin, and its general appearance.

"He said to the interpreter, 'I wish to spit, but don't like to spit on the carpet.'

"A spittoon was supplied such as are generally used on shipboard, made of wood and filled with sand. I observed then for the first time that the lobes of the ears were split and seeing a pipe handle pushed through and suspended in the opening of the lobe, I understood the use made of them.

"A few glasses of Schiedam drew forth friendly sentiments from his majesty. The pipe and schnapps having performed their office, and when the king and his court felt themselves comfortably seated, the conversation was introduced, through the interpreter, by explaining the position of the ship and the character of the war, which, I said, was so familiar to his majesty it did not need repetition; to which his majesty grunted. I think he questioned his intelligence on that subject. He drank more often than anyone else, and never sipped his liquor – drank bumpers.

"I said the vessels in port belonged to our enemy, who have been hostile to us for four years and will be always so until the end of time. 'Then,' said he, 'you don't like one another.'

" 'No,' said I, 'it is incompatible with virtue that the South should ever be reconciled to the North again. Blood has been spilt; life has been taken; our countrywomen have been outraged, and the unprotected have been driven into the forest for shelter while their homes are destroyed by fire. I am ordered to capture and destroy their vessels whenever it shall be in my power to do so, and if your majesty's laws of neutrality' (here he looked confused) 'would not be violated, I will confiscate the vessels in port. And as there is very little in them which the steamer requires, I propose to present their contents to your majesty, which you can make use of as you may wish, and when your tribe have finished with them I will take them to sea and burn them.'

"His majesty, after a short conference with his chiefs, said, 'We find nothing conflicting with our laws in what you say; there are shoals in the harbor on which the vessels can be run and there destroyed.' But he desired that I would not shoot at them for the shot would go on shore and hurt some of the tribe. I agreed to all his views.

"Among the stores which had been brought to the steamer were seventy down-east muskets, which had been for trade with the islanders, and two dozen infantry pants and coats. The pants would answer for the marine guard which I hoped to be able to recruit for the steamer. I said to his majesty, 'My fasts on shore are very insecure. A wicked person could cut them at the very moment when, for the safety of the vessel, they should hold on. If such an accident should happen to the vessel a flaw of wind might drive her on that rock.' (I pointed to it.) 'Several of the men from the Yankee prizes are on shore, having deserted their vessels as soon as our flag was hoisted. Now, I desire your majesty will station one or more of your warriors to guard the fasts, with orders to shoot anyone who should go within prescribed limits.'

"He replied, 'Have the warriors, but have no muskets and ammunition.'

"His majesty was now on such familiar terms with me that I could, without evoking royal displeasure, make suggestions and crack a joke at his expense, and I do not think he considered me undignified, for he frequently addressed me as his dear brother.

"I struck a bargain with his majesty by offering him the seventy very dangerous muskets and some ammunition if he would guard the fasts. He accepted the gift and sent his order for guarding them, which was promptly obeyed. No one knew the character of the musket in the hands of the guards, but I would have preferred the muzzle to the chamber as far as danger was concerned.

"His majesty expressed a desire to examine the steamer, and when he was informed of the pleasure it would afford me to accompany him, I handed him a sword which I begged his acceptance of, as it might prove of value to him at some future time. That sword was once United States property, and was found on board the schooner *Lizzie M. Stacey* in the North Atlantic.

"His majesty did not exactly understand its use or manufacture. He was induced to belt it to his naked waist and some one of his chiefs hung it to his right side, which caused me to ask if his majesty was left-handed. His majesty eyed the weapon suspiciously, and his expression of countenance conveyed such doubt as to the propriety of having it so near his royal person that I was quite overcome with laughter, and I endeavoured to conceal from his majesty my merriment, when I observed him unbuckling the belt, evidently not well satisfied.

"I told him it was absolutely necessary he should have the sword during his visit through the ship, and he reluctantly removed his hand from the belt. We had reached the engine room hatch and were in the act of descending to the engine room when I saw his majesty's legs entangled with the sword and the hereditary prince assisting to disengage it. He could not descend the ladder with the sword to his side, so he removed it, and the prince took charge of it.

"The machinery excited his surprise and amused him, and his expression of wonder was communicated by a cluck of the tongue, which his retinue echoed. He forgot his dignity and rested against a part of the machinery; he became smeared with a white coating that is used to prevent rust."

After the royal party had inspected the ship, the king returned to shore to give orders for the plunder of the captive ships. Aboard the raider the crew was busy holystoning coconut oil from the deck.

✓ 4 ✓

The *Shenandoah* lay deep under the weight of her booty.

Prize crews combed the four Yankee ships for gold, nautical instruments, guns and delicacies. Boatload after boatload of special supplies were hauled over to the raider. The *Harvest,* most richly provided of the captives, was hauled alongside and her entire food supply transferred as well as five tons of prize sperm oil. The other three ships were rammed onto shoals in mid-harbor. The natives were told to pick the bones.

Never was there such a potlatch. Hundreds of canoes darted about the lagoon, and the ships swarmed with scavengers. Everything was taken – bread, tobacco, bits of irons, hand lances, clothing, fluke chains, strips of wood, broken glass, hooks, blubber spades, sailcloth, doors, barrel hoops, old copies of San Francisco and New Bedford newspapers, bulkheads, cordage, Bibles from the Boston Missionary Alliance, salt pork, a mermaid figurehead, try pots, stoves, paint, patent medicines "for illnesses contracted in a sailor's youth," spars, hammocks. No stevedores ever unloaded ships with more loving thoroughness, though their technique was a bit elementary.

"Not having sense enough to rig a tackle and hoist out the casks of flour, meat, sugar, molasses, etc.," young Mason reported, "they broke them all open in the ship's hold, loosing half and making a most horrible mess. They then stripped all the sails off the ships, cutting them out in pieces. I was much amused at one poor fellow who got up as far as the royal yard and trying to get the sail down, in his passion for cutting, cut away the royal lift, which of course cockbilled the yard and left him swinging about between wind and water much to his astonishment and discomfiture."

When the ships were almost empty and the sterns floated high, a flotilla of dugouts clustered at their sides. Working in teams, the warriors stripped the copper sheaths from the hulls. With the long strips laid across four canoes, they paddled, chanting, to the shore. As each ship was picked clean, the king sent word that it was ready to be burned.

The *Pearl* was the first to be put to the torch, and a day later the *Hector* and *Edward Carey* were destroyed. The *Harvest*, because of her stores of oil and the question of her nationality, was spared for several days.

The burning of the ships stirred the *Shenandoah* crew deeply. It was an impressive spectacle.

The prize crews pulled away from the *Hector* and *Edward Carey* shortly after noon on a humid, breathlessly hot day. The only sounds were the chirping jungle noises from shore, the creak of the oarlocks, the hissing and crackling as the tide rose against the smouldering embers of the *Pearl*. The smoke rose in a straight, narrow column before mushrooming over the lagoon. It was flat calm, so still that even with the incitement of turpentine and tar the fire made slow headway through the new victims. But eventually the flames could be seen running along the deck of the *Hector*, licking up the masts, darting out of the portholes. Suddenly the scattered sentinels of flame on the *Hector* drew together into a mass; the ship puffed in a ball of fire.

Aboard the *Shenandoah*, the whaler's captain, Amos A. Chase of Saccarappa, Maine, watched her burn. He had sailed on her for seventeen years. She was his life. "She was the fastest whale ship in light winds I ever saw," he said afterward. "She was a good, strong, substantial ship. Why, to show how strong she was, when I was coming out of the Arctic in the season of 1864, we struck a cake of ice, the ship going free on the starboard tack, which turned the ship right round on the opposite tack. We sounded the pumps immediately, expecting she was stove in at the bows, but found she did not leak any and never after did we find that the ship suffered any injury from that collision with the ice."

The *Edward Carey* had taken no whales during the season and, not being oil-soaked, was slow to burn. But by mid-afternoon she, too, was ablaze from bowsprit to masthead.

As the ships flared up and the roaring and hissing of fire and water filled the shallow cup of the harbor, the tattooed warriors on the beach, who in silence had watched the white men's preparations for the sacrifice, broke into a war dance. Rude music played on nostril-flutes, the rhythmic thud of hands on fish-skin drums, the shrieks and breast-beatings of the ritual dance underscored the terrible sounds of the burning ships.

The whalers burned through the night. The glow from the fires outlined the figures of the dancers on the shore and threw weird shadows against the screen of banyan trees.

By noon of the second day, three charred keels lay like tombstones on the tide-washed shoals.

5

With his drooping moustaches neatly brushed, his gray and gold uniform pressed, his sword buckled on, and his second lieutenant and interpreter in attendance, Captain Waddell set out to repay the visit of royalty.

As they were rowed ashore in the gig, Hardrocke, the interpreter, briefed the captain on the latest gossip from His Majesty's bedchamber. King Ish-y-paw, it was said, had a few months earlier been smitten by the charms of a local lass who found his attentions not unwelcome. The affair was idyllic except for the unfortunate fact that the king already had a consort who, though unlovely, was quite durable. Polygamy was practiced by the tribe, but local court etiquette allowed a king only one queen at a time. Suddenly the queen died. Her passing was marked by symptoms of *kiti*, a potent Ponape poison, but no questions were asked. The following day the king married his *enamorata*. As court gossip went, this seemed to Waddell to be up to European royal standards.

The hereditary prince met the Captain and his suite at the landing and escorted them to the royal residence. For the duration of the *Shenandoah's* visit, the king had moved from the big Government House in the interior to his cabin by the shore. The hut was small, only about six by eight feet. It was set on piles to keep out flood tides and the overflow of the nearby stream during the rainy season. The walls were of interlaced vine, the roof of coconut leaves. A pair of rickety steps led to the open door.

The prince ushered Waddell in. The palace was unostentatious. His Majesty's throne was a grass mat in a corner to the right of the entrance. There were two wooden chairs, a wooden box, and a battered old trunk to complete the furnishings.

The royal couple were seated on their mats, their hands and chins resting on their knees. Neither arose on Waddell's entrance. The queen politely ignored him, as was court custom; the king gestured for him to take the seat of honor atop the trunk. Hardrocke was left to choose a chair.

As his eyes grew accustomed to the darkness, Waddell decided that "the queen was downright ugly, the first really ugly woman I have ever seen." He wondered what her predecessor must have been like.

After the opening politenesses, the king asked when the *Shenandoah* would leave. Waddell replied that he expected to sail the next day.

"And when will you kill your prisoners?"

"They will not be killed, your majesty. We will parole them and leave them here."

The king seemed uneasy at the idea of the former proprietors of so much of the tribe's new treasure being left on the island. His visitor reassured him by reminding him of the muskets; Waddell had noticed members of the palace guard seated in the yard outside the hut, anointing the weapons with fish and coconut oil.

"But why do you burn the ships and not kill the men?" the king asked. "You said they were your enemies."

"In civilized warfare we destroy only men who are in armed resistance to us," Waddell replied. "When men lay down their weapons they are set free if they promise not to fight us again."

The King thought it over before relaying his objection through the interpreter. "War can never be considered civilized, and people who make war on an unoffending people, as you said these men did, are bad people and do not deserve protection."

Waddell, who was inclined to agree, parried the statement with a remark that freeing prisoners was a custom which could not be changed. The king, who knew about taboos, understood.

As he rose to leave, Waddell said that he would report to his President the kindness which had been shewn the *Shenandoah* and the respect paid by Ish-y-paw to the Confederate flag.

"Tell Jeff Davis he is my brother and a great warrior," the king replied through Hardrocke, "and that I am very poor, and that our tribes are friends, and if he will send your vessel for me I will go to see him in his country. I send these two chickens to Jeff Davis, and some coconuts which he will find very good." He handed Waddell two dead hens wrapped in coconut leaves, and a woven basket filled with coconuts.

The captain gave the king a silk scarf.

The king thereupon gave the captain the royal princess. All

of Hardrocke's interpretive skill was needed to explain Waddell's ungallant rejection of the gift. The maiden was finally withdrawn. In her place Waddell received a belt woven of coconut fiber and wool.

In spite of these gifts, Waddell thought the king "a selfish old beggar until the schnapps and pipe warmed him. He did not consider it undignified or selfish to ask for whatever he fancied and show displeasure if refused. He is, however, not unlike his brother sovereigns of the world in that particular."

6

Members of the *Shenandoah* crew were allowed ashore daily to disport themselves. Each man was issued a few ounces of tobacco to use in his negotiations with the natives. The Confederates proved as popular with Ponape's debutantes as with the social set of the Colony of Victoria. The king's sister was found to be a particularly obliging hostess, and Dr. Lining wrote wonderingly of the number of visitors she attracted daily.

Young Mason felt it necessary to go into school-boy French to describe Ponape morality. "*Pour la vertu, il n'y en a pas. C'est une grande honneur que d'etre la maitresse d'un homme blanc. Les jeunes filles depuis l'age de huit ans sont tout aussi polissonnes que les autres. Il faut dire que c'est ainsi dans toute l'isle. C'est leur religion. En arrivant sur le balleinier, j'ai trouvé une treulaine de femmes qui s'ammuisaient sur les officiers de cas navies prennent toujours les filles du Roi ou des chiefs.*"

The other major tourist attraction was Nan-Matal. On Sunday, April 9, Hunt and Lining found a native whose love of tobacco outweighed his fear of the tribal taboo surrounding the ruins. Persuaded by a pound of rough-cut, he guided a party in the captain's gig to the Metalissian Venice which lay a few miles northeast.

Sail was raised, the gig ran from the lagoon, idled over the languorous swell, slid past the crumbled breakwater onto the smooth, green surface of another lagoon. Along the far shore rose a rampart of black stone, the outlying building of the hundred which lay along the clogged canals of the forgotten citadel. The stronghold was made of prisms of basalt, six-sided, about twelve feet long, four feet thick, and laid alternately lengthwise and crossways to make walls reaching forty feet above the lagoon. The rocks were rude, unhewn; no effort had been made to fit them. The crudeness of the construction added to the impression of barbaric power, of a savage competence startling and menacing to the visitors.

The sailors fell silent as their craft slid under the shadow of the black walls. They stared uneasily at the rampart, as though half expecting a host of warriors to leap shrieking into sight. Yet the only sounds were the hiss of water against the moving boat, the slap of small waves against the rocks, the wind moving across the jungle. Their guide grew uneasy; the visitors by ridiculing his fears were able to suppress their own.

They rowed down narrow canals between huge buildings. They began to talk, their voices at first loud with nervousness. As time passed and they became accustomed to the dead city, their remarks began to reflect curiosity rather than caution. They clambered over the sides of the ruins, stared down into the courts, walked back into the jungle where more buildings, still larger, stood festooned with enormous vines and supporting banyan trees on top of the twenty-foot thickness of their walls.

They sighted a great building, far larger than any of the others, its gateway flanked by parallel lines of thirty-foot stone pillars. Inside were a maze of walls with low doors alternately at the extreme left and extreme right. Here, in this twisting passageway, a dozen men could stand off an army. Creeping through the low portals, the Confederates were assailed by an awe bordering on terror. The splutter of their torches was loud in the heavy dead air; the scent of decaying vegetation and the peculiar damp, cold feel of old rock oppressed them. They came to a narrow room floored with great flat slabs of basalt. A stairway led into a pit. Bats brushed their faces and rushed off into the darkness as they awkwardly descended the uneven steps. The bottom of the pit was covered with a litter of sticks, coconut shells, rocks. Kicking through the debris, one of the sailors turned up a skull. Its empty sockets seemed full of menace in the flickering light of the torches. The trespassers stayed only long enough to assure themselves of their courage.

As they rowed back south of Lod Harbor, the tourists debated the mystery of the empty city. Hunt and Lining, who had had the usual classical education of young Southern gentlemen, recalled the ruins of Rome and Egypt, which did not aid greatly in understanding this jungled Venice.

All agreed with Hunt that "it is certainly a relic of considerable antiquity, and whoever erected it had no contemptible knowledge of the application of mechanical powers." They did not believe it could have been erected by the natives who now lived in thatched huts, and one can only speculate at their reaction had they been told the current theory — that it was built by Negroes.

"The generally received opinion among seamen," wrote Hunt, "is that it was built by some of the ancient Spanish buccaneers as a repository for their ill-gotten gains, and a place to retreat in time of danger."

While the raiders debated the disappearance of a civilization on that Sunday evening of April 9, half a world away, in the courthouse at Appomattox, Robert E. Lee surrendered the Army of Virginia to Ulysses S. Grant.

7

The *Harvest* was burned. The Yankee captains were unchained and given their choice of staying on Ponape or being put ashore on Guam. They preferred Ponape. Hardtack was landed for the crews of the four whalers; additional coconuts and fresh water were taken aboard; the ultimate visits were paid to the king's sister and her associates; some schnapps was sent ashore for His Majesty. These details taken care of, the *Shenandoah* was again ready to put to sea. Steam was raised.

Thomas Hardrocke came aboard to guide the ship back through the channel. The hawsers were untied from the palm trees. Her stern swung free. The crew heaved at the windlass, and the anchors were tripped, not to be lowered again for eight months.

Shortly before noon on Thursday, April 13, the *Shenandoah* started out of the harbor. The Ponapeans lined the shore, many of them carrying the doubly dangerous down-east muskets Waddell had bestowed upon the tribe. A few bearded faces were seen ashore, and the sight of the stranded seamen aroused differing reactions aboard the raider. Waddell wrote:

"We left to the care of the king and his tribe, 130 disappointed whalers, who had been accustomed to ill treat the natives and cheat them, besides introducing loathsome diseases never till then known to the tribes."

Hunt took a more lighthearted view. "I should mention that this island is provided with a missionary, unexceptionable in faith and practice I should infer, as he hailed from the goodly Commonwealth of Massachusetts, so it was fair to presume that the morals of our discomfitted foes would be well cared for during their stay in his diocese. The reverend gentleman did not pay his respects to us, but he doubtless considered us unregenerate heathen, not worth saving, if indeed divine mercy was for such as we."

Late in the afternoon, Hardrocke shook hands with the captain and mates, collected his fee as pilot, wished the ship well, and went over the side.

The *Shenandoah* turned her prow north, a ship without a country, bound on a mission which was to take her almost out of the world, and destined to wreak more destruction in a shorter period than any timbered warship in history.

***

TYPHOON

THOUGH steam had come to stay, the canvas-clouded Yankee Clippers still reigned as queens of the Pacific. As fast as they were beautiful, capable of cruising 350 miles in a day, the clippers raced across the widest open spaces of the world, carrying gold from San Francisco and Acapulco, timber and furs from Astoria and Victoria, tea and rice and spice from Hong Kong and Akyab and Singapore.

Waddell placed the *Shenandoah* across the track of the westward bound vessels that took advantage of the trade winds between 17 and 20 degrees north latitude. The raider beat back and forth in the area between Wake and Saipan. Lookouts mounted their perches and swung glasses along the cloudless horizon. But not a sail was sighted.

The weather was wonderful. "In all the course of my sea life I never enjoyed more charming weather," Waddell wrote. "The sun shone with splendid brilliancy, the moon shed her peculiar luster from a dark-blue vaulted sky, while the vast mirror below reflected each heavenly body and flashed with sprightliness as the great ocean plow tore the waters asunder, and for ten consecutive days I would stand for hours on her deck gazing at that wonderful creation, that deep liquid world."

Even wonderful weather can be a bore. Whittle kept the newly formed marine guard busy drilling in the uniforms captured at Ponape; prize crews drilled in boarding tactics;

the boatswain busied others at minor repair work. But the failure to find victims left everyone feeling dull and let down.

"I only wish this trip were over," the ship's surgeon noted in his journal after a particularly peaceful day's cruise.

And a master's mate spoke of "weeks of idleness, with nothing to break the tedious monotony. The watches turn out and in, yawning, the lookouts mount aloft, and sleepily throw a glance over the broad expanse of water – at seven bells the master comes up with his sextant, to 'take the sun,' and work out the position of the ship with his logarithms – in the forecastle tough yarns are spun by solemn-visaged old sea-dogs, and at night perhaps a violin or banjo furnishes entertainment for a little knot; but with every expedient that can be resorted to, and the working of the ship, a light labor with so many hands to assist in it, the time drags wearily, and if one has not the resource of some mental occupation, it falls in the course of time just short of unendurable."

After two weeks of idling through these latitudes, steam was raised. The *Shenandoah* pushed north between the Marcus and Los Jardines island groups to reach the area of westerly winds where California-bound clippers might be expected.

Clouds began to veil the sun. The winds were from the west but unsteady in force. The days were cold and foggy. Waddell studied the barometer with particular interest.

The twelfth of May dawned cloudless and calm, but in mid-afternoon the mercury in the barometer plunged. The surface of the ocean was gray and roiled. Waddell later said that if it had not been for the falling barometer, he would have thought the sea stirred by a tide rip; warned by his instruments he ordered sails to be reefed. There arose a little cloud out of the sea, like a man's hand. It grew in size and blackness as it swung down from the northeast. It smashed against the ship like a mailed fist. Under the blow the *Shenandoah* heeled over until the ends of her lower yards were wet with spray whipped from the tops of waves. She righted herself and, in her captain's words, "started like the affrighted stag from his lair, bounding off before the awful pressure. Squall after squall struck her, flash after flash surrounded her, and thunder rolled in her wake."

The storm swelled through the night. At daybreak the ship was scudding along before the typhoon at nearly twelve knots, though under close-reefed foretopsail and reefed foresail. The hatches were battened, preventer braces were fastened in the yards, the fires in the galley were doused. The ship was buttoned up against the roughest blow it had yet encountered.

Crack! The report sounded like a cannon shot, but it came from above. Looking up, the men on deck saw the great sheet of canvas which had been the main topsail kiting away in the gale. The leech ropes had broken, the sail had run down, and under the fury of the hundred-mile wind the canvas was torn from the yards. The few streamers of cloth still fast to the spar jerked and snapped in the pulsing wind.

The ship needed her sails if she was to be controlled in the storm. The officer of the deck gave the desperate order: the maintop team must go aloft to make repairs.

Muttering curses around the knives they held between their teeth, the seamen started aloft. The ship was plunging through terrific seas, perched at one moment on the crest of a wave, then sliding down into a gray-green trough, continually pitched from side to side, the hull timbers groaning under the strain, the rigging shrieking like a devil's violin. The shreds of canvas from the main topsail lashed about menacingly. A blow from one of these wild whips might knock a man into the sea or onto the deck.

The few sailors below who were not too busy at tasks of their own watched anxiously as their friends worked up the shrouds. Sometimes gusts of particular ferocity pushed them against the ropes so firmly they could not move; sometimes it billowed them out over the sea so that only the clamp of their elbows hooked around the lines held them from death. But they kept climbing.

They reached the spar and inched out along it. The ship rolled wildly; the yard ends alternately brushed the white-toothed waves, then pointed straight up into the mist of flying spray. The seamen carefully cut away the remnants of the mainsail. One after another the strands flew off through the driven mist. Then, carefully, with the casual precision of men who live their jobs, the team of Portuguese and English and Malays and Hawaiians and Germans and Swedes and Frenchmen worked the new sail into place, secured it, sheeted it home. With the aid of the ship's revolving yard they close-reefed the canvas against the blast. Then, their work magnificently accomplished, they climbed down.

They reached the deck just as the storm landed a crushing blow that staggered the *Shenandoah.* A great wave broke in over the side of the ship as it wallowed in a trough. The comber carried a seaman overboard, but the backwash hurled him back over the rail, frightened, shaken, unhurt.

The deck was waist-deep in water. The ship trembled under the burden. She settled lower and lower, as though pushed down into the turbulent sea by an invisible hand. For the second time on the voyage, the order was given to smash out the ports. The crew waded to the bulwarks and knocked the casings loose. The danger drained away.

Freed of the water, the *Shenandoah* rolled more heavily than ever. The royal yards were sent down on deck and secured in the fore, main, and mizzen rigging. A tarp was rigged to break wind.

"On, on, we rush," wrote Hunt, "now rising to the summit of a mountain wave, then darting with almost the velocity of light down the dark, shining declivity, while behind us the sea reared its crested head, threatened to engulf us at once and forever. Thousands of right whale birds were hovering over the ship as though speculating upon the position of affairs and wondering whether we would be able to weather the tempest."

Toward evening the storm let up. The *Shenandoah* had been blown a hundred miles out of its course. Waddell gave up any hope of finding prizes in these wild waters and ordered the course be shaped directly for Amphrite Strait which led through the Kurile Islands into the Okhotsk Sea, where part of the North Pacific whaling fleet spent the spring.

But the 45th parallel north latitude seemed more like a barrier than a navigating convenience. The typhoon was followed by a cloudburst, the cloudburst by another typhoon. For a week the *Shenandoah* tried to push north. Each time it was shoved back by northeast winds. At last the storms subsided into fog interspersed with flurries of snow.

On Sunday, May 21, land was sighted.

****

BEYOND THE KURILES

TWENTY DAYS after leaving the tropics, the *Shenandoah* was in sight of the snow-covered Kuriles, a volcanic festoon strung between northern Japan and the Kamchatka peninsula. The Kuriles were beautiful – but not attractive. Glimpsed through a moving veil of fog, the peaks glittered with the winter's snow; purplish tundra covered the highlands, black cliffs dropped sheer into the dull-green sea.

The air was as chill as the islands. The crewmen delved into their duffelbags and sea chests. They brought out pea jackets and overcoats. Woolens were issued. Lining, as surgeon, ordered the men to stay off the deck as much as possible. His hard-drinking assistant, McNulty, joyfully superintended the issue of extra grog. The officers set up a small stove in the wardroom.

On Tuesday, May 21, the raider raised steam and worked carefully through Amphrite Strait into the Okhotsk Sea. Waddell was nervous. When Fred Chew was slow clewing up the topsails, the skipper bawled at him, "Make haste, Mr. Chew, I don't want to go on shore here." They were still under steam at the time, and the shore was three or four miles off. The junior officers looked at each other and shook their heads.

The weather grew steadily colder. Patches of floating ice appeared. The lookouts were doubled. At night and in the fog men listened uneasily to the thump of the floes against the copper-coated hull; in clear weather they stared in amazement at the mirages.

"The most beautiful optical illusions I ever witnessed were about Kamchatka," Lieutenant Whittle recalled years later. "When not foggy the atmosphere was a perfect reflector. We saw prominent points seventy miles distant. We would see a snow-clad peak direct and above it, inverted, the reflection, peak to peak, with perfect delineation; or we would see a ship direct, and above it the reflection of the same ship, inverted, masthead to masthead, just as if you put your finger to a mirror and would see the finger and reflection point to point."

The mirages and double portions of alcohol were not enough to make the Okhotsk popular.

"I do not suppose there were half a dozen men on board, who, of their own accord, would have selected that cruising ground, notwithstanding the inducements it offered," Hunt said. "But our orders were to proceed thither and nothing short of the probable destruction of the ship would have been regarded as an adequate excuse for not carrying them into effect."

Waddell, growing ever more cautious as the gap between himself and his young subordinates widened, took no unnecessary chances in the ice-clogged sea. He kept the ship under short sail and set a course so far from the volcanic shores that Lining complained, "We are again committing the fault of keeping too far from the coast. We ought to know by this time that whalers fish close along the coast. Will we ever learn by experience?"

From the charts captured on the whalers at Ponape, Waddell had learned that a concentration of Yankee ships might be expected at Shantaski Island, northwest of Sakhalin. The *Shenandoah* worked through increasingly thick drift toward that rendezvous.

2

At noon on Saturday, May 27, while the *Shenandoah* was working in light fog along the southern edge of a field of floe ice, a lookout announced a sail on the other side of the ice. She was standing on a course roughly parallel to the raider. All through the early afternoon the two ships cruised side by side, separated by about five miles of ice. Around three o'clock the lookout sighted a channel through the floes. Under extra canvas and flying the Russian ensign to avert suspicion, the cruiser entered its first pursuit since leaving Ponape.

Shortly after four o'clock the stranger was overtaken. When within a quarter mile of the Yankee, the gunners fired a blank shot. The Confederate flag was raised. The whaler did not change her course; still under full sail she ran past the stern of the *Shenandoah*. As she slid by, Whittle shouted at her, "Heave to on the starboard tack, damn quick." The ship hove to.

Dabney Scales headed the boarding party. He was accompanied by Joshua Minor, who, before the war, had sailed these waters on Yankee whalers, and John Blacker, the British captain who had jumped ship to join the *Shenandoah* in Melbourne.

They were met at the rail by Captain Ebenezer Nye of Cape Cod Bay.

"Captain," said Scales, "you are a prize to the Confederate steamer *Shenandoah*. I order you take your ship's papers and go with your officers on board the *Shenandoah*."

Nye looked at him blankly for a moment, scratched his head, laid in a fresh chew of tobacco, and remarked, "Well, I s'pose I'm taken. But who on earth would have thought of seeing one of your Southern privateers up here in the Okhotsk Sea. I know some of the pranks you fellows have been playing, but I supposed I was out of your reach here."

"Why, the truth of the business is, Captain, we have entered into a treaty offensive and defensive with the whales," Joshua Minor said with a smile. "We are up here by special agreement to disperse their mortal enemies."

The old captain looked at the young officer a moment before replying. "All right, my friend," he said at last. "I never grumble at anything I can't help, but the whales needn't owe me much of a grudge, for the Lord knows I haven't disturbed them this voyage, though I've done my part at blubber-hunting in years gone by. But it's cold talking here; come below and take something to warm your stomach while I get my papers."

There was plenty of stuff for stomach-warming aboard the bark *Abigail.* Nye had shipped a huge quantity of liquor, some of good quality for his personal pleasure, some cheap but powerful to be used in trading with northern natives, whose palates were not particular. Included in the stores were fifteen fifty-gallon barrels of Monongahela Whiskey, eleven barrels of gin, eight barrels of rum, one barrel of pure alcohol, 736 gallons of brandy, one barrel of Indian Antidote ("A fine beverage that I had been some years manufacturing"), thirty-six dozen bottles of cider, thirty dozen cordial, twelve dozen bitters, ten dozen Schiedam schnapps, one and one-half barrels port wine, forty cases port wine, one barrel cherry rum, ten dozen bottles of malt wine, ten dozen ginger wine, twenty-four cases of claret, and eight dozen bottles of champagne cider.

While Nye and his mates were being rowed back to the *Shenandoah* with Master's Mate Minor, the rest of the boarding party discovered the alcoholic contents of the hold. An impromptu celebration was started.

Aboard the raider, the sedate proceedings of a drumhead prize court were under way. The prize proved to be one of the oldest whalers afloat. The *Abigail* had been built in Amesbury,

Massachusetts, in 1810. She was twelve years older than her master, who had commanded her since 1852. The bark was condemned to be burned. Orders were issued to bring her crew aboard. Captain Nye took the bad news calmly, but one of his mates, a Baltimorean named Manning, attacked him angrily:

"You are more fortunate in picking up Confederate cruisers than whales. I'll never go with you again, for if there is a cruiser out you will find her. You've caught a whaler again this time." Turning to the astonished officers of the *Shenandoah,* Manning explained that Nye had previously lost a ship to the *Alabama* in the Atlantic. It was the first of many lies he told them.

A party in a cutter was sent to bring the *Abigail's* crew aboard. They found the Yankee still in the hands of her own men. The boarding officers and crew were staggering about below, knocking the tops out of whiskey casks and tossing down corn liquor by the cupful. The Confederates in the cutter told the *Abigail* men to get in their own boats and row over to the *Shenandoah;* then they went below to sample Captain Nye's stock-in-trade themselves.

The captured crewmen obeyed orders. They gathered their belongings and rowed over to the raider. One of them, noticing the *Shenandoah's* telescoped funnel for the first time as he came over the side, loudly remarked that he "had not expected to take steam home, and to tell the truth would just as lief trust to sail."

Waddell was surprised at the arrival of his prisoners unaccompanied by any guards. He ordered the Yankees put in irons in the forecastle. Another boat, under the command of Whittle, was dispatched to the *Abigail* to learn what had happened to the two boarding parties.

Whittle found them floundering about below, half-drowned in whiskey. He ordered them topside. They refused to come.

He sent his men down to haul the drunks from the hold. The sober citizens caught a few of their sodden fellows and carried them up on deck, but on returning for more, they paused to celebrate their success. Soon pursuers and pursued were equally determined not to abandon the *Abigail.*

Whittle signaled the *Shenandoah* for reinforcements. A party of marines were dispatched — with foreseeable results. The marines rapidly overhauled the headstart of the earlier crews and soon achieved a superb state of stupefaction.

Waddell sent over a party of officers. They appropriated Captain Nye's private stock for themselves and set about getting drunk in a gentlemanly fashion. Eventually a little group of willful, abstinent men herded their fellows onto the deck, maneuvered them into the boats, and got them back aboard the raider. The seamen were dropped on deck and told to sleep it off. The drunken officers were locked in the wardroom. Lynch, the ship's carpenter, and McNulty, the assistant surgeon, had to be handcuffed and tied into bed.

"It was," Hunt estimated, "the most general and stupendous spree ever witnessed. There was not a dozen sober men on board the ship except the prisoners, and had not these been ironed, it might have proved a dearly bought frolic."

Young Mason was shocked. "Had it been merely the men who became intoxicated it would not have been so bad," he lamented, "but I regret to say that some few of the officers committed themselves. One, an Irishman of mean birth, who is our youngest engineer, but a low blackguard, the carpenter and boatswain, both of them Englishmen — all of these fellows we were obliged to appoint at the commencement of the cruise for want of others. The carpenter, Mr. Lynch, behaved so badly that the captain confined him in irons and actually had him triced up and gagged, an everlasting disgrace for an officer, but such men as these have neither pride, principle, nor honor; they have joined us when we were forced to take them, simply for mercenary motives and only serve to disgrace us and discredit our cause. Wonderful to say, the gunner, who is the worst of the party, did not get drunk on this occasion. I have no patience with such 'cannaille' for they are a disgrace, most emphatically a disgrace to the uniform they wear."

When the officers and men had sobered sufficiently, they were ordered to start transferring supplies. The *Abigail* was an old hulk and had little to offer in the way of cabin equipment, except a stove, which Waddell took for his stateroom. Most of the plunder gurgled as it was brought aboard. Twenty-five barrels of corn whiskey were taken "for medicinal purposes." Every member of the prize party – all men with a broad social outlook – thoughtfully concealed on his person a few bottles of Captain Nye's personal stock – for use in case of epidemic.

A lookout reported a sail. A whaling bark was seen moving through the floes in the distance. But before the hung-over crew could get the raider under weigh, a fog squall blotted out the prey. When the weather cleared, the sea was clear. Waddell was furious. He wrote an official order to the executive officer:

> Sir: Private appropriation of prize property is prohibited. All articles sent from prizes to the ship must be sent to you, to be transferred to the paymaster's department. You will be pleased to call the attention of the officers to this order, and require rigid adherence to it. Any violation of it, coming under your observation, must be brought to my knowledge.

The order was ignored. The men kept their private caches of liquor. On Sunday, half the crew was drunk again.

Twenty-four hours after the *Abigail* was sighted, she was put to the torch. After standing by for two hours to make sure the fire did not die out, the *Shenandoah* steamed slowly away, leaving the ancient ship a mass of flames amid the sub-Arctic ice floes.

The alcoholic content of the *Shenandoah* remained high. The day after the *Abigail's* destruction, Lining wrote, "Things getting worse and worse. Lynch drunk, Marlow our steward drunk, Hopkins the officer's cook in the same state, and some of the men. In the evening the Captain sent for Scales and put him under suspension for having brought off a beaker of whiskey which he had put into Blacker's room until he could draw it off. Pitched into Blacker. Found a box of liquor in Codd's room, which ought to have been in the hold, but which had been stopped on the way down. Chew put on watch."

And the next day: "Worse and worse do things go and many are the changes that take place. Smoking in the engine room prohibited. Blacker sent out of the cabin into the steerage. Boatswain's mate broken and disrated. Chew put on watch again and Bulloch only to do Master's duty. Blacker having repented, or rather said that he had left the Cabin because he did not not want to act as a spy of the Captain on the other officers. Whittle reported it to the captain who pronounced it a falsehood. Had Blacker up in the Cabin and sent for Bulloch and myself to act as witnesses to what he had said when going into the cabin this morning with a letter. Blacker said that he had used such an expression and had drawn the inference that he wanted him to act as spy, from which he had said last night. Captain then asked him if he, the Captain, had ever given him an order or requested him to inform him on any officer. Blacker said no. Then the Captain told us why he had sent Blacker out of the Cabin. How Blacker had told him that there was not another drop of liquor in his room when he had afterwards found out that there was part of a keg from which Scales had taken what he wanted and turned the rest over to Blacker. 'Such, gentlemen,' said he, 'are the circumstances.'

. . . . A charming day overhead. Sun bright, sea smooth, while on board all is stormy."

But by Wednesday, "Scales was restored to duty this morning and things have settled down to their old course."

3

On the evening of Saturday, June 3, while the *Shenandoah* was coasting south along the Siberian mainland near latitude 58, longitude 151, Captain Waddell, who usually dined alone in his cabin, paid one of his rare visits to the officers' mess in the wardroom. He came in full uniform and brought with him several bottles of champagne. It was a state occasion — the fifty-seventh anniversary of the birth of Jefferson Davis.

After a meal of fresh pork — there had been pigs aboard the *Abigail* — the Confederate officers offered toasts to the success of a government that no longer existed, and to the health of a frail man who, far from being a president, was then a prisoner at Fortress Monroe.

The celebration was interrupted when the watch officer sent word that the barometer was falling, the wind rising. Waddell went on deck to study the situation.

It was shortly before midnight. The arctic sun had just set; visibility was good in the twilight. The *Shenandoah* lay about twenty miles to the windward of a great field of floe ice. If the ship were hove to against the expected gale, the wind might drive her onto the floes. Pounded against the twenty-foot cliffs of ice, she would break up as surely as though smashed against some rock-bound coast. A passage had to be found through the ice field.

Fresh lookouts clambered aloft. The ship was put under steam. As the freshening wind began to sing through the rigging, the ship approached the ice. The wind gained force every instant. By the time the lookouts spotted a path through the field, it was blowing a gale. The ice was shifting. There was the possibility that the cruiser might be trapped in the channel, but it was a chance that had to be taken. Not even steam would hold the *Shenandoah* off the ice in a northern gale.

With necessary but infuriating slowness, the helmsman steered the cruiser along the lane of black water between the twenty-foot walls of the floes. At last she came out into clear water and soon was lying to under close sail. At that moment the storm broke with full force.

The floe was to windward. In Waddell's words "that ice which a little time before was our dreaded enemy was then our best friend. The fury of the seas was expanded on it and not against the sides of the *Shenandoah,* and it acted as a breakwater for her. She lay perfectly easy, while expended seas on the farther edge of the floe broke furiously, throwing sheets of water twenty feet high. It was a majestic sight, resembling an infuriated ocean wasting itself against an iron-bound coast."

The wind was strong and bitter cold. It carried a fine spray from the waves. The canvas-bare cruiser moved gently before it, drifting into the middle of another ice field. When the men came on deck Sunday morning, they found the ship surrounded by floes.

"On every side of us, as far as the eye could reach," Hunt said, "extended the ice field. As the ponderous floes came together, the crushed and mangled debris rose up into huge mounds of crystal blocks, seemingly as immovable and imperishable as the bluffs on shore. Indeed it was impossible, while gazing off over the scene of wildness and desolation, to conceive the possibility of an avenue of escape."

The ship was sheeted with ice. Waddell declares that "the braces, blocks, yards, sails, and all running rigging was thoroughly coated in ice from a half to two inches thick, so that it was impossible to use the braces. Icicles of great length and size hung from every portion of the vessel and her rigging. The fairy ship sparkled from deck to truck as if a diadem had been thrown about her, awakening exclamations of enthusiastic delight. The crew was ordered aloft with billets of wood to dislodge the ice and free the running gear. The large icicles falling from aloft rendered the deck dangerous to move upon, and it soon became covered with clear, beautiful ice. The water tanks, casks and every vessel capable of receiving it were filled. A supply of several hundred gallons of drinking water was not unacceptable, for it saved the consumption of fuel in condensing steam. As soon as the rigging was clear of ice, so that the braces would traverse the blocks without danger of chafe, warps and grapnels were run out on the floe and hooked to large blocks of ice. The ship was gradually worked out of it."

Waddell gave up any hope of reaching Shantaski or the Siberian mainland ports and turned toward Jonas Island, near the center of the Okhotsk Sea, another rendezvous for whalers. But that night the ship was again locked in the ice. The crew was openly frightened. The *Shenandoah* unlike the whalers, was not specially reinforced to withstand the pressure of the floes.

"As I lay in my berth," Hunt declared, "I could hear the huge blocks thundering and chafing against the side of the ship as though they would dash her in pieces. It was an anxious night to all on board. None of us were familiar with Arctic cruising, and consequently were to a great extent incompetent to judge of the imminence of the danger, but the hours of darkness wore away at last, without leaving us to mourn any serious accident. In a few places the copper had been chafed through, but this was about the greatest injury we had sustained, and soon after daylight the ice separated, through some unseen agency, leaving us free.

"But we had had enough of the route to Jonas Island, which

may be a most desirable locality for whalemen and other amphibious animals who enjoy a temperature below zero and have an affinity for ice fields and fogs; but for my part, I would not spend six months therabout for all the leviathans that ever poured their oily treasures into the coffers of New Bedford.

"The plain truth was, we were running too much risk in taking our cruiser through this sort of navigation for which she was never intended, and we reluctantly abandoned the idea of reaching the grand headquarters of the Okhotsk Sea whaling fleet."

The *Shenandoah* started back toward Amphrite Strait.

4

Off the coast of Kamchatka a ship was sighted, dim in the foggy distance. The officers were undecided whether she was a bark or a brig. If a bark, she was probably a whaler, if a brig, probably an American. Waddell decided she was a brig. No chase was made. The decision led to new dissension among the officers.

"There is a master's mate on board by the name of Minor," Young Mason confided to his diary. "He was a mate on board one of the ships captured by the *Alabama*. He shipped before the mast on that vessel and was afterwards made a master's mate by Captain Semmes. This person has been whaling a great deal and was in this sea several cruises; the captain has great confidence in his opinion and pays great deference to all that he says. Indeed, it is generally thought that our skipper pays rather too much deference to his opinions. It was he that pronounced the vessel to be a brig without doubt, when I am certain that she was never near enough to us for anyone to say positively what she was, however good an eye he might have. My candid opinion is that we lost a prize we might have had with ease."

Minor was a big man, nearly six feet four inches tall. Among his other duties he was caterer of the steerage officers' mess. His shipmates felt he took advantage of his size and position in allocating food. His playfulness was touched with sadism, and his teasing often crossed the line into torment. His favorite victim was his roommate, Lodge Colton, a small and gentle Baltimorean. One cold day in June, Colton had had enough. When Minor passed an insulting remark across the dinner table, Colton jumped up and shouted, "I've had enough of you. Get your sword."

Minor was startled. He had not expected this, and he did not want to fight. But there was no way out. His insults had been too barbed to be laughed off. He went with Colton to their room to get their swords. The other officers, as surprised as Minor, watched them, half-perplexed, half-amused. Knowing the two men, they were sure the combat would not be bloody. No one tried to stop it.

Noncombatants formed a rough circle about the duelists. They crossed swords and stepped back, on guard. Minor made a halfhearted pass at Colton, who stepped back. They glared at each other. Someone tittered. Each fighter waited hopefully for the other to stop the duel. No one moved. Colton closed in on his larger opponent but was careful not to press the attack too hard. Minor backed away before him.

"I don't think I ever saw a more absurd spectacle in my life," said one witness. "It was on the order of the stories in *Midshipman Easy*. Here were these two fellows with their naked weapons crossed. One was scared and the other afraid."

The duel died a natural death.

5

Captain Nye and the mates of the *Abigail* had been put on parole. When the *Shenandoah* was again in sight of the Kamchatka coast, the officers and crew of their last prize petitioned to be put ashore. They were certain they could survive until picked up by a Yankee or Russian whaler. After weighing the request against the temperature (15 degrees Fahrenheit), Waddell refused; he would not have it said that, even upon a written request, he had left thirty-five men stranded upon the Kamchatka coast in mid-June while the temperature still lingered below freezing.

The officers and men of the *Abigail,* with the exception of Second Mate Manning, a surly fellow, proved particularly popular aboard the raider. Of all the crews captured, the *Abigail's* took its captivity in the best grace, though the unheated forecastle was an unpleasant spot to spend an Arctic night. Every evening before being locked up, the men danced or had a sing-song on deck.

"The old Captain developed some new phase of Yankee eccentricity every day," Hunt reported. "It amused us, though it did not raise him in our estimation. Little by little it came out, partly from his own admission and partly from the casual remarks of his officers and crew, that he was a thoroughbred speculator in his own way. It was his custom on preparing for a voyage to lay in a quantity of cheap whiskey and secondhand clothing, which he retailed out, as opportunity offered, to his ship's company, or to the savages with whom he came in contact at such an advance on the first cost as would have frightened a Chatham Street secondhand merchant into serious apprehensions for the future well-being of his soul.

"He remarked rather gleefully to me, a day or two after the capture, that he guessed, after all, the loss of the old ship wouldn't swamp him. There was already another ship ready for him at San Francisco as soon as he got out of our hands, and another cruise would set him all right."

Nye spent long hours gamming with the Confederates. His favorite story was of the time he had been cast away in a boat near the Galápagos Islands with six other men. They sailed seventeen hundred miles in an open boat and for thirteen days lived on six biscuits and half a beaker of water. The young sailers listened quietly to Nye's stories, which they did not believe.

Most popular with the officers of the *Shenandoah* was the *Abigail's* first mate, "a staunch old sailor, true as steel to his own government, burly, bearded, and in his seventies." Young Hunt spent much time talking to him about Arctic sailing. Hunt was not without guile in this. After abandoning the search for the Okhotsk fleet, Waddell had decided to go north, not only into the Bering but beyond, into the Arctic Ocean. The skipper wanted any information his young subaltern could pry from the Yankee.

"The old fellow never dreamed that I had any other purpose than to satisfy a seamanlike curiosity. He took great pleasure in pointing out upon the charts the dangerous places, and in giving me a general idea of the difficulties to be encountered on a cruise in that direction."

Soon it became unnecessary to pump the old officer further. Second Mate Manning, the *Shenandoah's* Mr. Unpopular of 1865, volunteered to join the Confederates. He was an experienced pilot who for years had sailed with the New Bedford whalers. Though Waddell and his men despised Manning as a traitor, they reluctantly enrolled him as a brother officer.

"It is always unpleasant, though sometimes necessary, to accept the services of the most disreputable of men," said one of the mates. "As this was an opportunity which was not likely to occur again for securing a guide to the prize we sought, his overtures were received."

Thomas S. Manning was not an admirable man. A companion described him as "a Baltimorean by birth, anything by profession, and a reprobate by nature." His fellow officers on the *Abigail* swore that though he was an avowed Democrat, he sold his vote to the Republicans in 1864 for a drink of whiskey. Nevertheless he was not without influence and persuaded a dozen seamen – an Englishman, a Prussian, a Portuguese and nine Hawaiians, to volunteer.

Dr. Lining rejected two of the Kanakas as physically unfit and only reluctantly accepted the others. "I do hate to see our ship's company filled up with such men as these," he complained. "Won't we look beautifully while going into port with a crew made up with such people!"

On Wednesday, June 14, the *Shenandoah* again passed through Amphrite Strait having taken but one prize in three weeks. Safe behind the drifting ice which surrounded Jonas Island were ten whalers, all of them from New Bedford.

The *Shenandoah* turned again north.

WHEREIN THE WHALE SWIMS, MINNOW-SMALL

Between the outstretched arm of the Alaska Peninsula and the southern tip of Kamchatka lies a chain of islands now known as the Aleutians. The Bering Sea, shallow and cold, is held north of the Aleutian barrier; the Kuro Siwo, a warm flow, also called the Japanese Current, pulses through the deep Pacific just south of the islands. The collision of the warm, wet Pacific air and the chill winds from the Bering produces fog. In June fogs are almost constant over the archipelago.

The ultimate Aleutian Island is Attu, so far west that the international date line bends to keep it in the same day with the rest of the chain. Between Attu and Siberia are two more islands, known collectively as the Komandorskies, in honor of their discoverer, the Danish-Russian commander, Vitus Bering.

On leaving the Kuriles, Captain Waddell set a course which would take the *Shenandoah* between Attu and the Komandorskies. He wanted to hit halfway between them because "currents about detached portions of land are irregular in direction and force."

For a few hours after leaving Amphrite Strait, the ship boomed along before a cracking southwester. But then, according to Waddell's journal:

"The wind hauled more to the south and then east of south, producing a condensation of atmosphere which terminated in a thick, black fog, shutting the ship in an impenetrable mist to the eyes.

"I continued to run the ship northeast for the first twenty-four hours, and the wind having hauled still more to the eastward I deemed it prudent to steer ENE because I was without observations and the wind would give the current a set or direction to the northwest, which, if not considered and introduced into my reckoning, would force the ship too much away from a direct course and perhaps uncomfortably near the Komandorski Islands. I therefore allowed two points for drift in a northwest direction.

"At the end of the next twenty-four hours I was without observations again, and I knew from dead reckoning that the ship must be near the passage. The wind had drawn more from the land – then east – and the ship was headed more to the north. During the afternoon the wind fell light from northeast, which change in force of wind was pretty sure evidence of the proximity of land. Immediately with that change of wind the fog lifted a little and the cry of 'Land Ho!' was made.

"At intervals it could be seen ahead at a distance of not more than four miles. The ship's deck was in charge of Lieutenant Grimball, who, in obedience to my order, tacked the ship, having just enough wind to turn her around. It fell calm, leaving a fog denser than ever. That land was Copper Island.

"It is generally the case that a fog lifts so that objects are visible at a distance of five to six miles. That lifting frequently occurs on approaching land, which may be attributed to the rapid absorption of moisture by earth. The ship was thirty-seven miles in error of her reckoning, notwithstanding the allowance made for drift, etc. I ordered steam, furled sails, and entered the Bering Sea."

As the cruiser steamed past the snow-crusted, tundra-skirted island, the men heard a deep roaring, as though of heavy surf. The day was calm, the sea was light, and the white necklace of breakers which lay against the black sand was not spectacular enough to account for the sound.

Dabney Scales went up into the rigging with glasses. After studying the island, he shouted down an explanation for the noise: Seals.

The Komandorskies are one of the two great seal rookeries of the world. The bull seals had just returned from their mysterious migration to an unknown part of the Southern Pacific; they were fighting for the best positions on the breeding ledges. Their belligerent bellowings could be heard for miles. As the *Shenandoah* came nearer, the men could make out the sleek, gray-brown heads of the females that swam along shore trying to decide which bull to bestow their favors upon.

The price of seal skins was high, and some of the men looked longingly at the bleak breeding grounds. A few days of poaching on the Russian preserve would have made up for the prizes left untaken in the Okhotsk Sea. But the *Shenandoah* sailed on.

"The cruising in Bering Sea is not of a very delightful character," Waddell noted dryly. "Changes of weather are more sudden, and although the fogs do not last so many hours as they had done in the Sea of Okhotsk, they are more frequent."

For five uneventful days the *Shenandoah* tacked about through fog and mist, keeping north and east, in the general direction of Bering Strait. The weather was, at worst, squally and, at best, a foggy bore. On the 21st, the Siberian coast was sighted again. The following deadpan entry appears in the ship's log:

> At 1:30 p.m. made Cape Navarin bearing WNW, 15 miles distant.
> At 3:50 a sail reported to the westward; stood off in chase.
> From 4 to 6 p.m.: Chase proved to be a rock. Latitude 62° longitude 179° 57′ E.

After outsailing the rock, the *Shenandoah* entered waters flecked with offal — strips of lean meat from butchered whales.

Studying the currents, Waddell calculated that the whalers must be to the southwest. The cruiser stood toward the midnight sun which was wheeling along the horizon on the longest day of the year. Soon a smudge was seen against the sun – the thick, black smoke made by ships boiling blubber in their trying pots.

At 9 A.M. on Thursday, June 22, the lookout reported two sails off the port quarter. Under steam, the *Shenandoah* bore down on them.

2

In the spring of 1865 the whaling industry was in a bad way. This was due more to the distillation of kerosene than the devastation by Confederate cruisers.

Abraham Gisner, a Canadian geologist, discovered how to make kerosene out of petroleum in 1862. The following year the process was introduced in the United States. After that, oil for the lamps of America could be pumped from the petroleum fields of Pennsylvania. The sperm and the bowhead were no longer the best source of light.

The high point of the whaling industry had been reached in 1853. Two hundred thirty-eight ships went out after whales that year and brought back 103,000 barrels of sperm oil, 260,000 barrels of boiled-out whale oil, and 5,600,000 pounds of bone. No subsequent season could match this catch. As voyage profits fell under the impact of petroleum competition, more and more ships dropped out of the chase. By 1860 only 121 were left.

Then came the war. The Government purchased forty of the oldest whalers, filled them with rock, ran the Great Stone Fleet into position, and sank it off Charleston Harbor. Other whalers were caught in the South Atlantic by Confederate raiders. This led to the sale of others to foreign owners. Each year a few ships succumbed to storm and ice. In 1863 only forty-two deep sea whalers flew the American flag.

The scarcity of ships and the smallness of the catch raised the price of the products. Every voyage was almost certain to be either "greasy" or disastrous. Between 1854 and 1864 the price of sperm oil had risen from $124 to $178 a barrel, of whale oil, from $58 to $128, of bone, from $34.50 to $180 a ton. Even with war risks it seemed worth while to get back into the business. Old ships were refitted and put back to sea.

Eighty-five ships and barks made up the North Pacific Whaling Fleet in 1865. The *Shenandoah*, by June 22, had sunk six — the *Edward* off Tristan da Cunha, the *Hector*, *Pearl*, *Edward Carey*, and *Harvest* at Ponape, and the *Abigail* in Okhotsk. Of the remaining seventy-nine, ten were still around Jonas Island, eleven were moving north through the Pacific toward the whaling grounds.

Fifty-eight whalers were already in the Bering or beyond, in the Arctic, actively hunting. In the climactic week of its voyage, the *Shenandoah* captured twenty-three of them.

3

Never before had the *Shenandoah* been stalking two ships under sail simultaneously. To take one, without warning the other, called for both speed and precision. The two best prize crews — those led by Grimball and Lee, were alerted; the men strapped on their swords and sidearms. A gun crew moved into position by the forward cannon.

By 10 A.M. the *Shenandoah* was within olfactory range of the first ship, and by 11 A.M. within artillery range. Since the whaler was hove to with a whale alongside, no shot was fired. The cruiser steamed alongside, the Russian flag at her peak. A prize crew under Orris Browne boarded her.

Francis Smith of New Bedford, one of the oldest masters

afloat, met the boarding party at the rail. Browne told him to get his papers and proceed to the *Shenandoah.* He did not protest. While Smith was in his cabin gathering his documents, the mate of the *William Thompson* protested "My God, man, don't you know the war has ended."

"Did Grant surrender?"

"No. The Army of Virginia surrendered. The war is over."

"Sir, the war will not be over until the South is free."

Smith came back with his papers. He and his mates were sent to the cruiser. Browne and the prize party remained to guard the prize while the *Shenandoah* raced off after the second ship.

At 12:05 the *Euphrates,* another New Bedford ship, was overhauled. She responded to the *Shenandoah's* signal gun by running up the American flag. Lieutenant Lee and his boarding crew wasted no time in convincing her master, Thomas Hathaway, and his crew that any other ensign would have been better.

The *Euphrates* was condemned. Her crew, mostly Western Islanders with fine, picturesque names (Mana Joaquim José, Francisco de Brune Roncha, Thomas Francisco da Silva), went over to the raider in their own boats. The only booty removed by Lee was the sextant and three chronometers. The carpenter and his men rapidly battered down bulkheads, chopped open doors, and broke open the oil barrels. She was greasy with the product of two whales. She was burning brightly within three hours of her capture.

The raider returned to the *William Thompson.* Browne had loaded the whalers' own boats with provisions. These were being transferred to the Confederate when a masthead lookout cried, "Sail ho!"

"Where away?"

"Five points off the port bow and standing north."

A breeze had sprung up and, with the flaming *Euphrates*

an unmistakable danger signal, the stranger might well escape. Leaving the small boats still loaded with stuff from the prize, the *Shenandoah* broke out sail and under both canvas and steam entered her third chase of the day. About 7 P.M. she brought the fleeing whaler about with a blank shot across the bows. The ship ran up the English flag. Waddell did not believe it; she looked American. He sent Whittle aboard to investigate. She was the *Robert Townes,* of Sydney, Australia's only deep-sea whaler.

"And what ship is that?" the colonial captain asked as Whittle prepared to return to the raider.

Whittle looked him in the eye. "The Russian man-of-war *Petropawowka,*" he drawled.

For the second time, the *Shenandoah* hurried back to the *William Thompson,* passing en route the flame-wrapped *Euphrates.* This time the plunder was taken without interruption. At 3 A.M. of the 23rd, the biggest of New Bedford's ships, the $40,000 *William Thompson,* was put to the torch.

Once her victim was aflame, the *Shenandoah* sailed to the northeast, moving across the date line and back into Thursday, June 22.

She was half the world away from her starting point.

The second twenty-four hours of that Thursday proved even more profitable than the first. The *Shenandoah* steamed through fog and snow squalls into a field of mushy ice floes. Around noon the weather cleared. Five sail were sighted.

A solid mass of ice lay between the cruiser and the whalers. The *Shenandoah* worked cautiously around the floe. More sails came into sight. By 4 P.M. eight vessels could be seen from the raider's deck.

"The sun was shining with more than its accustomed radiance as we advanced toward them," Hunt reported. "As its rays were reflected from the glittering fields of ice, the effect was indescribably beautiful.

"Away on our starboard bow we could distinguish a boat and its crew gliding swiftly through the water, towed by a large right whale they had just fastened, and the vessel to which it belonged was standing slowly after, to keep it in view. Other ships we could see far off in the field ice, trying out the blubber of the ponderous animals which they pursue and capture with such consummate courage and skill; and upon the whole it was a scene of stirring activity well worth looking at.

"Seals in vast numbers were swimming in the water, or composedly floating on the drifting ice, and notwithstanding their cold bed, seemed to enjoy vastly the rays of the sun that for so small a portion of the year makes its heat felt in these high latitudes.

"On the starboard beam stretching away as far as the eye could reach was a seemingly unbroken sea of ice, while on the port beam rose up the cold, dreary shores of North Asia, as sterile and inhospitable a region as my eyes ever looked upon. The two vessels nearest us had foreign ensigns flying at their peaks, but the next three in order sported Uncle Sam's gridiron. . . ."

Displaying the Russian flag, the *Shenandoah* ran close to the stern of the nearest whaler. Black letters on her white hull announced her to be the *Milo* of New Bedford. She was " a staunch, but slow-sailing craft, evidently built expressly for this hazardous cruising, and well prepared to resist the drifting ice."

Whittle hailed her. "What ship is that?" Captain Richard Baker, her Connecticut-born skipper, shouted.

"Never mind," Whittle yelled back. "Come on board and bring your papers, and bear a hand about it."

Baker, who had thought the *Shenandoah* was in the employ of a company planning to lay a cable across the Bering Strait, realized his mistake. But not until he was on the deck of the raider and face to face with gray-uniformed, gold-braided William Whittle was he positive she was the *Shenandoah.*

"I had heard you were in Australia," Baker told Waddell, when taken before the Confederate captain, "but I didn't expect to see you up here. Haven't you heard the war is over?"

"Do you have documentary evidence?"

Bank had only the word of other captains who said they had seen the news in San Francisco papers.

"Then, sir, I must declare your ship a prize to the Government of the Confederate States of America." Waddell paused to let the Yankee realize his plight, then continued, "But as we have a great many prisoners already aboard and expect to take more shortly, I will bond your ship if you will agree to take our prisoners to the nearest port."

"How large a bond?"

Waddell studied the ship's papers. She was not a particularly expensive vessel, but she had aboard 200 barrels of oil. "Forty-six thousand dollars," he said firmly.

After a moment's hesitation, Baker replied, "I see how it is. I will give bond and receive the prisoners."

The fifty-year-old skipper, "a fine looking veteran, standing over six feet two and straight as an arrow," returned to the *Milo* and sent over his whaleboats to pick up the prisoners from the *Abigail, William Thompson,* and *Euphrates.* "Several of them," Hunt claimed, "shook hands with us at parting and expressed the hope that we might meet again under different circumstances. It was a sentiment in which we could heartily concur, and I must say that American whalers are officered by some of the grandest, noblest, most high-minded and generous men belonging to the great brotherhood of seamen. A kindness they seldom forget – to a friend their hand is ever open, and an enemy they can look upon as one who might have been a friend but for some political accident which it is out of their line of business to examine into very closely."

While the prisoners were being transferred, the breeze, which had been very light, suddenly freshened – a complication that Waddell had not anticipated. His plan had been to steam up to the becalmed sailing ships one after another. But two nearby whalers had already noticed the activity aboard the raider and the *Milo,* and they were already moving away before the rising wind. If one or both were not to escape, the raider had to work fast.

Waddell ordered Grimball and his prize crew to make sure the *Milo* behaved. Baker was commanded to send his sailors to the *Shenandoah;* without them the whaler could not escape. Once the Yankees were aboard and locked up, the cruiser set out after the fleeing whalers.

The two vessels were following different courses. One was threading between the ice floes, hoping to find a spot where the thin-hulled steamer could not follow. The other, under a complete array of canvas, was running before the wind toward Siberia, seeking the sanctuary of the three-mile limit.

Confident that his ship could outrun any whaler, Waddell ordered the lookouts to keep a constant watch on the course of the bark headed for the mainland. Then the *Shenandoah* took off after the ship fleeing through the floes.

The cruiser ranged alongside the ice field. A prize crew under Dabney Scales was put overboard in the gig. The cannoneers rammed a thirty-two-pound shot into the starboard Whitworth. The rifle spoke "in anger" for the first time. The shot arched in front of the runaway, barely missed the figurehead, and sent up a spray of chipped ice from the floe beyond. The Yankee did not cut sail.

Again the Whitworth spoke. The second shot ripped a hole in the whaler's main topsail. Moses Tucker, master of the *Sophia Thornton,* was convinced. The ship heeled around and began to work back in the direction of the prize boat that was pulling toward it.

Dabney Scales ordered Captain Tucker and his mates to go aboard the *Shenandoah*. They were confined in the forward coal hole, and the raider steamed away after the Siberia-bound bark.

The runaway was the *Jireh Swift*, of New Bedford, a beautifully outfitted bark that had been built at Dartmouth, Massachusetts, in 1853. She was one of the biggest whalers in the business, 122 feet long and weighing 428 tons. She was extremely fast. Her master, Thomas Williams, declared "I consider that on the *Jireh* I always had four hours a day more than any other ship of her class." If the breeze had been steadier, she almost certainly would have reached the theoretical safety of the waters within a marine league of neutral Russia. But the wind was variable.

After steaming for three hours, the raider came within artillery range of the Yankee. For the third time, the Whitworth rifle was called on as a convincer. The first shot, a near miss across the stern, ended the chase.

When Smith Lee and his boarding party reached the ship, the forty-six-year-old captain, his eighteen-year-old boatsteerer son, and the mates and men of the *Jireh Swift* had their bags and chests on deck, ready to be transferred.

Manning, the turncoat mate from the *Abigail*, told Waddell that the *Jireh Swift* was believed to have fifteen thousand dollars in cash aboard. But Captain Williams swore that he had less than a hundred dollars. A hurried search revealed nothing, and Manning's reputation for veracity being below par, the *Jireh Swift* was set on fire. She was aflame within thirty minutes of her capture.

Four more sail were in sight. The *Shenandoah* ran down the two nearest, but both proved to be foreigners. The other pair were so well protected by ice floes as to be unapproachable. Giving up on them, Waddell sailed back to the *Milo* and *Sophia Thornton*. En route he quizzed Captain Williams about the progress of the war.

According to Waddell's journal, "Williams stated he did not believe the war was over, but believed the South would yield eventually. He said the South had made a mistake in not sending a cruiser to the Arctic Ocean two years before, for the destruction of that whaling fleet, from which New England gathered her wealth, would have more seriously affected the Northern mind than a dozen battles in Virginia.

"That remark of Captain Williams," Waddell went on, "indicated a just idea of the Yankee character and its policy in the war. They made money by it, and for this reason they waged it. Politicians fed on fat contracts and immense Government expenditures, enriching the agents through whose hands the money passed. A high tariff taxed the people without their seeing it, while the manufacturers realized fortunes. The newspapers of the large cities, filled with details of battles, greatly increased their circulation, and their proprietors grew correspondingly wealthy. The Government stimulated business by issuing paper and creating a debt that it is intended the South eventually to pay. It was thus that the war was waged and continued, and it was only to be stopped on the mercenary principle of showing that it would no longer pay to keep it up. The Yankee captain spoke the genuine philosophy and morality of his countrymen."

Rejoining the two prizes about 9 P.M., the *Shenandoah* sent all prisoners aboard the *Milo*. The captain of that craft protested that he did not have enough supplies to feed three hundred men. With three more sails in sight, Waddell hated to waste time. He told the parolees to take whatever they wanted from the *Sophia Thornton*, but in return for this favor he insisted that, once they had transferred what they needed, they would set the ship on fire. Reluctantly the prisoners agreed.

To remove any temptation the Yankees might have to try to sail the *Sophia Thornton* into the protecting ice while the

Shenandoah was away, Waddell sent his carpenters aboard to saw down her spars.

"As we glided seaward," Hunt wrote, "still standing toward the frozen region of the Arctic Circle, we could see the disabled vessel, with her masts dragging alongside, and the paroled prisoners with their whaleboats, transferring from her to the *Milo* whatever suited their fancy. I have no doubt the craft was thoroughly ransacked, but ere the sun made its brief disappearance below the horizon, a bright tongue of flame shot heavenward, telling us that the prisoners had performed their distasteful task. A more unpleasant duty, I trust, will never be assigned to any of them. It is hard enough to see the oaken cradle in which one has rocked for so many weeks and months destroyed by the incendiary torch, but when necessity compels a sailor to light with his own hand the fire that is to consume the ship that he has learned to love, he has good ground for complaint against the fates."

One man who wasted no time telling off the fates was Ebenezer Nye, the skipper of the *Abigail,* whose Yankee eccentricities had so amused the raider's officers and whom they suspected of welcoming the destruction of his ship. No sooner had the *Shenandoah* steamed away, than Nye and First Mate George Smith put off in a whaleboat to sail north and spread the alarm. The risk was great. Nye was under parole, and if the *Shenandoah* turned back and caught him, he was liable to extreme penalties, even death. Nor was a small boat any craft to be taken between ice floes. Any sudden movement of the capricious Bering could crush the tiny craft like a mosquito between clapped hands.

The old skipper sailed 187 miles to Cape Bering, where he encountered the *Mercury,* which took him aboard. He warned five other whalers of the presence of the raider in northern waters. As best he could, Captain Nye had made up for the defection of his former second mate, Thomas Manning.

⸙ 4 ⸙

The brigantine *Susan Abigail* had been in San Francisco taking on goods when Lee surrendered. Her officers and crew heard the guns at the Presidio thunder in celebration. Some of them had drunk toasts to Grant and Old Abe in *tequila* and whiskey, listened to Mexican refugees talk about the "next war," in which the re-United States would drive Maximilian off the Mexican throne, sang the Battle Hymn of the Republic, carried torches in the parade along Market Street. By headline and hangover they knew the war was ended.

And, still inside the Golden Gate, they had lowered their flag when the black-bordered, black-columned papers were brought on board, announcing the assassination of Abraham Lincoln.

Only a scattering of rebel troops were still holding out west of the Mississippi when the *Susan Abigail* sailed out of San Francisco Harbor with a load of beads and bad whiskey to trade the Eskimos for furs.

So when a black-hulled, full-rigged ship steamed toward her in the Gulf of Anadyr at eight o'clock on Friday morning, June 23, the *Susan's* skipper suspected nothing. Called on board by a warship flying the American flag, he came up over the side wearing a superb fur parka and prepared to have a pleasant gam with a Union skipper. He was staggered to find himself a prisoner and his ship condemned.

"He didn't want to be burned," Lining reported, "because it was such a favorable season, and she was so well fitted out. A good reason for us!" And Hunt declared, "He begged very hard that his ship might not be burned as that was to be his last expedition to this part of the world, and he expected to clear about thirty thousand dollars, but his eloquence was all thrown away. Captain Waddell seldom took much notice of what prisoners said."

Five sailors shipped from the *Susan Abigail* – two Germans, an Englishman, a Scotchman, and an Irishman. They were less important for the strength they added to the raider's crew than for the reassurance they gave Waddell that the news of the Confederate collapse in the San Francisco papers aboard the prize was at least exaggerated.

"The papers," Waddell noted in his journal, "contained a number of dispatches, and among them was one that stated the Southern Government had removed to Danville and the greater part of the army of Virginia had joined General Johnston's army in North Carolina, where an indecisive battle had been fought against General Sherman's army; also that at Danville a proclamation was issued by President Davis, announcing that the war would be carried on with renewed vigor, and exhorting the people of the South to bear up heroically against their adversaries."

The Danville proclamation, issued only a few days before Davis's capture, said:

> We have now entered upon a new phase of the struggle. Relieved from the necessity of guarding particular points, our army will be free to move from point to point, to strike the enemy in detail far from his base. If, by the stress of numbers, we should be compelled to a temporary withdrawal from her (Virginia's) limits, or those of any other border state, we will return until the battled and exhausted enemy shall abandon in despair his endless and impossible task of making slaves of a people resolved to be free.

This call for continued resistance, for sudden blows against the enemy, fitted perfectly into the already formulated plans for the raid against the whaling fleet. The *Shenandoah's* officers agreed that they should continue their destruction.

"So far as we knew," said Hunt in writing of this decision, "our armies, though repulsed at many points and sadly depleted in numbers were still making a gallant stand against the Northern hordes, which eventually overran our unhappy country, bearing down all resistance before them; consequently our hearts were buoyed up with the thought that we were still aiding the great cause to which we had devoted our lives and fortunes."

As to the other news — the assassination of Lincoln, Hunt declared that "it occasioned a general feeling of astonishment and indignation throughout the *Shenandoah*. That one who sympathized with the Southern cause could have deliberately planned and executed an act that would strike with horror every honorable man, whatever his partisan sentiments might be, and thus redound to the discredit of the Government for whose success he professed to be laboring, seemed passing strange. It was even then shadowed forth in the papers we perused so far from the place of their publication that designing men would endeavor to fasten upon the Southern people at large, and especially upon their leaders, the odium of that hideous crime."

The failure of Captain Waddell to believe the San Francisco papers and the Yankee captains was a serious matter. It exposed him as never before to charges of piracy. Yet it was an understandable decision.

Waddell and most of his officers had left the South when Confederate power was at its height. Though the tide had turned before they sailed from England, the details of defeat were not known to them. The capture of the Army of Virginia was to them like the removal of a powerful piece from a chessboard. They did not think of it in terms of desperate little things — the blistered foot, the empty stomach, the horror of a march that seemed never to end, the cumulative despair of victories that brought no relief, of defeats that ate up miles and men and homes. Not knowing these details, the *Shenandoah's* officers were able, like some of Davis's advisers, to think of going on, to urge guerrilla warfare.

This inability to recognize defeat was widespread. Though cut in two and beaten in the border states, the Confederacy still covered a huge amount of territory. In March, when the situation was obviously critical, Captain Semmes of the *Alabama* had written to a friend in London:

> The State of Texas alone has within her limits all the materials, and is fast getting the appliances, for equipping and maintaining armies, and when you reflect that she has three times as much territory as France, and that countless herds of horses and beef cattle wander over her boundless prairies, you can well imagine with what contempt this warlike people regard the insane threat of subjugation. If our armies were driven across the Mississippi River, we could still fight the enemy for a century to come in Texas alone.

The *Index*, a Confederate journal published in London, after receiving news of later vintage than that in the hands of Waddell, wrote on April 27:

> The war is far from concluded. A strenuous resistance and not surrender is the unalterable determination of the Confederate authorities . . . and if the worst come to the worst there is the trans-Mississippi department, where the remnant of Johnston's army can find a shelter, and a new and safe starting point.

After learning of Johnston's unconditional surrender, the paper still argued that "the elements of a successful, or at least a protracted, resistance exist." And as late as May 25, in a piece entitled "Southern Resistance in Texas," the Southerners editing the *Index* said, "Such a war will be fierce, ferocious, and of long duration."

So, possessed of less information than their London kin, and doubting the authenticity of that which they did have, the officers of the *Shenandoah* decided to press on after the rest of the New England whalers. But their hearts were heavy.

"If it proves true it will be terrible," Lining confided in his journal. "First, that Charleston was captured; this I was expecting, as I did not think we could hold it against Sherman's army. Next that Richmond and Petersburg were taken. I was looking for their evacuation, so it did not surprise me much. But when I heard that General Lee had surrendered with the whole of the Army of Northern Virginia, I was knocked flat aback – can I believe it? And after the official letters which are published as being written by Grant and Lee can I help believing it? It is either true, or the Yankees are again publishing official lies. God grant it may not be true."

Young Mason, who, at nineteen, had been away from home two years, wrote that "it is difficult to believe this, but the accounts are so minute that there must be some truth in it. However, I put the best face on the matter possible, and try not to believe it. I am very uneasy about mother, Aunt E., and the girls as well as Tom, who has no doubt been in all these battles."

5

After setting fire to the *Susan Abigail,* the raider started under sail back toward the northeast. She passed the smouldering hulk of the *Sophia Thornton.* The men aboard the *Milo* had obeyed orders and burned her, but the preparations were not as thoughtfully thorough as those made by the Confederates, and the thick-hulled old ship still floated. The cannoneers suggested shelling her, but Waddell, unsolicitous of local shipping, left the wreck floating – another hazard for Yankee whalemen.

"There was a heavy ice floe in sight," according to Hunt, "which necessitated keeping a bright lookout on board for fear of running into it. Ships, sailing in the direction we were, always keep to the westward of the ice, on account of the current which sets so strongly toward that point of the compass. All day long the ice could be seen on our starboard beam, extending as far as the eye could reach. About six in the evening we discovered a sail, but the fog came on so thick we were obliged to abandon chase for fear of running into some unknown danger, from which we could not extricate ourselves.

"The most of the day the men had been busily engaged in killing hogs, of which we had an abundance, that had been captured with the prizes. Pork must be a favorite article of diet among whalemen, at least I do not recollect that we took a single vessel after entering the Okhotsk Sea that did not have at least half a dozen swine on board.

"We had now advanced so far north that night and day were mere arbitrary terms. For an hour or two there was a subdued twilight, or rather lack of sunshine, but at any time during the twenty-four hours there was no difficulty in reading ordinary printing without the aid of artificial light.

"No one can conceive until they have experienced it, the strange effect produced upon a native of the temperate zones by the endless day of the polar regions. There is something so supernatural and fantastic in the sight of the sun traveling perpetually round the horizon, just dipping beneath it at one point for a brief space, instead of seeing it at an angle of about sixty degrees as with us, that until you become in a measure accustomed to it, to sleep is almost impossible. But trying as is the long day, the night is infinitely worse, according to the testimony of all those who have experienced it.

"The morning of the 21st (24th) of June found us surrounded by a fog of unusual density, and we were under the necessity of lying to in consequence. Indeed, to see a ship's length in any direction was utterly impossible, and with huge fields of ice drifting near us, and anon crashing together with a report like thunder, our situation was anything but desirable.

"But this is only one of the many dangers incident to Arctic sailing. It is a region of terrors, which start up grim and formidable on every side, and absolutely without an attractive feature save the wealth borne on the backs of the great right whales, or worn in the shape of choice furs by the seals that inhabit its waters, and the foxes and sables that abound upon its icy shores; and for wealth, men will dare any peril, face any danger.

"Before noon the fog had cleared away, and a few hours later we sighted St. Lawrence Island, lying almost directly to the southward of Bering's Straits. It was impossible to approach very near it on account of the ice which increased in quantity as we advanced toward the Arctic Ocean. An immense field lay off our starboard bow, seeming as impenetrable a barrier as a similar extent of solid rock.

"The island is inhabited by a somewhat numerous tribe of Esquimaux, who carry on a considerable trade in furs with whalers and other vessels that visit these areas. They subsist almost exclusively upon the flesh of seals and walrus, which is generally eaten raw. How they can exist in a climate where for two months in the year the mercury freezes in the thermometer tube is a mystery.

"Twenty-five or thirty boats came off to us from St. Lawrence Island. They contained Esquimaux who brought with them a quantity of furs and ivory which they desired to barter for whiskey and tobacco. Their boats were ingeniously constructed affairs. The frame is something like that of a whaleboat, over which is stretched walrus hide, which renders them completely impervious to water. They are very light and much better calculated to traverse these icy seas than wood or even metallic boats. Few and simple as their implements are, these nomadic savages succeed in capturing a good many whales. They first blow a walrus hide, previously prepared for the purpose, full of air and to this they fasten one end of their harpoon line. Watching their opportunity they dart the harpoon into the whale, and they thus attach to him a great buoy, which materially interferes with his diving propensities. Another and another are attached in the same way, until the poor animal can no longer get below the surface and is in the end fairly worried to death."

The Confederates, especially Dabney Scales and Fred Chew, traded enthusiastically with the natives. Scales and Chew each left St. Lawrence with sealskin parkas, walrus *mukluks,* and specially carved ivory scoops for removing ear wax.

At 10 o'clock Sunday morning, June 25, while still within sight of St. Lawrence Island, the *Shenandoah* moved off under steam in chase of two vessels that appeared suddenly out of a clearing fog to the south. Neither fled. Within an hour the raider came up with the first ship. It raised the Oahu ensign. She looked foreign, and Waddell did not bother to send a boarding crew to inspect her but, instead, steamed away in chase of her companion, which proved to be the *Winslow,* of France. The raider swung back on her course. With Manning at the helm she steamed toward Bering Strait.

By three o'clock the *Shenandoah* was north of St. Lawrence again. A sail was sighted off the starboard bow. Since the newcomer was downwind, the cruiser went after her under fore and aft sail. At 5:10 they hailed the stranger. She raised the Union flag and, as the cruiser pulled up astern, she identified herself as the *General Williams* of New London. Waddell raised the Confederate flag and dispatched a boarding party under Smith Lee and Mason.

"Her captain was a miserable old whine of a Yankee," Mason commented. "He cried like a child when we told him his ship was to be burnt."

When the skipper tried to argue, Lee told him to go at once to the *Shenandoah.* "He took it very hard," said Hunt, "and was quite disposed to make a personal matter of it. As he came over the side with his papers he demanded in a blusterous, querulous manner what injury he had ever done us that we should hunt him like a wild animal and destroy his property.

"Of course we assured him that we had no feelings of personal animosity to gratify, that our blows were only aimed at his Government, though they might fall heavily upon private individuals; but this was far from satisfying him, and I believe to this day he is half inclined to the opinion that the *Shenandoah* went up to the Arctic expressly to look after his ship, through some spite conceived against himself by the Government of the Southern Confederacy."

The normally courteous Waddell had no use for the sniveling skipper of the *General Williams,* "a dirty old dog." He bluntly refused to listen to the pleas to spare the ship. After removing "thirty-four prisoners, three chronometers, one sextant, the other nautical instruments, and three hogs," Smith Lee set her on fire.

"The citizens of the wide-awake little city of New London must have been in a most flourishing financial condition, for the *General Williams* had more money on board than any vessel we captured," Hunt reported, but added, "I pray my readers do not permit their expectations to be raised too high. We did not make quite so good a haul as some of the old buccaneers used to when they fell in with a Spanish ship laden with specie; but we did secure out of that New Londoner the enormous sum of four hundred dollars. As I did not subsequently learn that any prominent New London house went down in consequence of that capture, I infer that they must have enjoyed a high degree of prosperity."

To the north were three more sails. The *Shenandoah* went after them. An almost solid mass of drift ice barred the way. There was not a breath of wind. Waddell, afraid that if he waited the three ships might take alarm from the flaming *General Williams,* ordered a course set straight through the floes.

Slowly the steamer moved down narrow channels toward the trio of becalmed whalers.

A sudden wind, an error in judgment by Manning, a mishap to the engine, and the raider's voyage would have been over, the nemesis of the New Englanders destroyed. But there was no gust, no mistake, no breakdown. In the 1 A.M. twilight the *Shenandoah* came into open water. Half an hour later she drew up behind the nearest of the whalers. On the high stern, Waddell could read her name: *William C. Nye*, San Francisco.

The *Nye* had left the Golden Gate in the early part of December, 1864. She cruised for four months in the vicinity of San Pedro, California, then sailed for the Arctic. She had taken 240 barrels of oil, and one of her whaleboats was in pursuit of a bowhead when the lookout sighted a steamer coming in from the south, under steam, with all sails furled.

"We did not suspect anything wrong, at first," Second Mate Fitch Way told reporters later, "and in one hour she came alongside of us. The steamer then hailed, telling us to bring to, which we did, and a boat came aboard of us. A prize master, who came in the boat, ordered Captain Cootey and his officers to go on board his vessel, saying we were a prize to the Confederate steamer *Shenandoah*.

"We went on board and signed a parole as prisoners of war, until exchanged. Our fourth mate refused at first to sign the parole, and the first lieutenant of the *Shenandoah* had him put in irons. He afterward signed it and was released.

"They broke open the trunk of Captain Cootey, but the steward of our ship had taken the money out of it and concealed it, with his watch, on his person. We were allowed nothing but a clothes bag apiece in the cabin, no trunks or chests being permitted. They did not allow the men even their bedding."

Waddell was in a hurry. The rising sun had revealed five more sails far to the north, and he wanted to get at them before the wind gave them an opportunity to scatter. The moment Captain Cootey and his mates were aboard, the *Shenandoah* moved over to the next bark, the *Catherine* of New Bedford.

Built at Rochester, Massachusetts, in 1831, the *Catherine* had recently undergone extensive refitting at Honolulu. She was, according to her skipper, William Phillips of Greenport, Long Island, "stout, stanch, and strong, had her cargo well and sufficiently stowed and secured, was well masted, manned, tackled, victualed, appareled, and appointed, and was in every respect fit for sea and the voyage." She had just captured a polar whale, and the crew was digging in the blubber when the raider came alongside. Half an hour later, the *Catherine* was flame-wrapped.

The *Shenandoah* steamed over to the third becalmed bark. James Clark, the master of the New Bedford bark *Nimrod,* guessed what was happening. Two years before, a ship under his command, the *Ocean Rover,* had been captured and burned by the *Alabama.* Helplessly, now, he watched the black cruiser approach, saw the small boat lowered and the prize crew pull off toward his vessel. Captain Clark went to the rail to meet his captor.

"My God, no!" he gasped as Smith Lee came up over the side.

Lee smiled. "We meet again, Captain." He had led the *Alabama* party that boarded Clark's other vessel.

The prisoners were hurried over to the *Shenandoah,* and the prize was fired almost immediately. She had aboard oil from seven whales, one of the great early-season catches in whaling history, which was one of the reasons Waddell refused to bond her, although he now had more prisoners than he could safely care for. (Also destroyed were a panama hat, a sable coat, and an ivory and teak fiddle belonging to First Mate Wellington Weaver.)

Like all whaleships, the three barks had been heavily manned. Their crews, plus those of the previous prizes already on the *Shenandoah,* totaled nearly two hundred – far more enemies than Waddell wanted around at one time, especially while finishing off the flotilla to the north. Lieutenant Grimball suggested the solution: "Put 'em in whaleboats and bring 'em along." Waddell agreed.

The mates and masters were confined in the coal hole. The shivering crewmen were loaded into twelve whaleboats which were taken in tow by the raider.

"It was a singular scene upon which we now looked out," Hunt declared. "Behind us were three blazing ships, wildly drifting amid gigantic fragments of ice; close astern were the twelve whaleboats with their living freight; and ahead of us were five other vessels now evidently aware of their danger but seeing no avenue of escape.

"It was a tortuous way we now had to pursue, winding about among the ice floes like the trail of a serpent. Six knots an hour was the highest speed we dared attempt, so intricate was the navigation, but we at length succeeded in penetrating the little fleet for which we were steering.

"We had learned from some of the prisoners that smallpox prevailed on one of the vessels, and we consequently gave her a wide berth, and turned our attention to the next in order, the *General Pike* of New Bedford, of which we soon made a prize."

Waddell, writing in his journal, said, "The *General Pike* had lost her captain, and the mate was in charge of her. He asked as a special favor of me to ransom the *Pike,* as I should have to ransom one of the vessels. I asked his reason, and he said, 'Captain, if you ransom the vessel her owners will think me well to do in getting her out of this scrape, and it will give me a claim on them for the command.' "

Waddell ransomed her, but he made no friend out of her acting master, Hebron Crowell, in doing it. In the *Pike's* log Crowell wrote the following white-hot entry:

> On the morning of the 26th of June, 1865, at 6½ o'clock, the *General Pike* being in lat. 64 d 30 m N, long 171 d 42 m W, saw a steamer on our starboard quarter, steering directly for us. At 7½ o'clock the steamer came up close under our stern and ordered me to come on board with my papers. She proved to be the English Pirate, thief or robber, *Sea King,* called *Shenandoah.*
>
> Waddel, the pirate chief, told me he should bond the *General Pike;* accordingly he had written what he called a ransom bond for $45,000, and I signed it by his order. The chief then said he should put about 160 men on board of me, but instead of that the brute, as he is, put 222 men on board, making with my own crew 252 men all told, crowded into this small ship.
>
> The pirate chief kept me on board his vessel about five hours. The only thing that he stole from me was the register of the *General Pike.* As I was leaving the pirate ship to return to my ship he said that if I did not have provisions enough on board to reach San Francisco I must cook Kanakas (Hawaiians) as I had plenty of them.
>
> All the masters agree in saying that they were promised their private property, but after getting them on board his vessel he robbed them of everything of any value, or allowed his officers and men to do it, showing plunder and robbery to be their object.

The *Pike's* officers were taken aboard the *Shenandoah* for temporary safekeeping, a prize crew was left in charge of the whaler, and the cruiser started toward her fifth victim of the day.

The bark *Isabella,* one of the best and biggest ships of the whaling fleet, was two years out of New Bedford. She had had a good voyage and was lying deep with $27,000 worth of oil in her casks. Her captain, Hudson Winslow, of Freetown, Massachusetts, had every reason to be content when he came on deck that Monday morning. But what he saw made him uneasy.

"I noticed a ship without sail," he said later, "and supposed her to be a whale ship at anchor, as there were a number of whalers in sight the night before. At 7 A.M. saw three large black smokes, which were the *Catherine* of New London, *William C. Nye* of San Francisco, and *Nimrod* of New Bedford, burning. I discovered a number of boats towed by the suspicious-looking vessel. The *Shenandoah* came by the bark *General Pike* of New Bedford and told the captain to come on board, then steamed up to the *Isabella,* not showing any flag, and sent a boat alongside with eight armed men, and told me that I was a prize of the *Shenandoah,* and ordered myself and my officers to take our things on board the *Shenandoah* and my men to go to the bark *General Pike;* then she steamed up to the bark *Gipsey,* which was about two miles distant at 9 A.M. and boarded her."

The *Gipsey* of New Bedford had been having a marvelously greasy voyage. She had left Massachusetts three years before and twice had trans-shipped oil at Honolulu. Already on her third venture into the Bering, she had taken three whales and had $10,000 worth of oil and bone aboard.

Dabney Scales led the boarding party sent to the *Gipsey.* Hunt, who was off duty, asked to go along. Permission was granted.

"The Captain who met us at the side," Hunt reported, "was terribly frightened. He was pale as a ghost, and could scarcely return an articulate answer to any question addressed to him. He evidently imagined he was to be burned with his ship, or at best run up to the yardarm, and could scarcely believe it when I assured him that no personal injury or indignity was intended.

"His cabin was a most luxuriously fitted-up affair for an Arctic whaler. There was a fine library, comprising some two hundred volumes, a beautiful writing desk, and indeed all his furniture in style and finish would have done credit to a well-appointed drawing room. He had also several cases of choice wines and liquors, which I destroyed to prevent the sailors getting at them, reserving a bottle or two with which to treat my crew when they returned, after discharging the duty assigned us.

"It had been the custom of the *Gipsey's* skipper to take his wife with him on his voyaging, but fortunately she had remained at home this cruise. In a little time the officers and crew of the *Gipsey* had been paroled and transferred to the *General Pike,* a few furs and trinkets were appropriated, and the torch was applied."

The *Shenandoah* steamed back to the *Isabella.* After unbending all the victim's sails and lowering protective mats, the raider lashed onto her and took on her water and provisions, a task that kept the tired crew busy until midnight. Just before the *Isabella* was burned, three of the Yankee captains made a last plea to Waddell to spare her. They argued that the war was over.

"Gentlemen," the Confederate commander replied, "I cannot believe what I read in the Northern papers. And as to our defeats in the field and withdrawal from Richmond, the war is not over yet. We only want to get you into the interior."

The *Isabella* was burned. The last of the prisoners were sent to the *General Pike,* which was then ordered to sail south.

Waddell was well pleased. "Within forty-eight hours, the *Shenandoah* has destroyed and ransomed property to the value of $253,500," he noted. "More than $200,000 of it was destroyed." But the possibility that the repeated Yankee protest that the war was over might have some foundation worried him. The chance that all this destruction was in vain burrowed into his subconscious. The following day he made a personal entry in the *Shenandoah's* log:

> The brig *Susan Abigail* sailed from San Francisco about the 19th of April, bringing papers dated to the 17th of April. I read from

one of the April papers dispatches for [of the] surrender by General Lee to General Grant and an announcement of a proclamation by President Davis at Danville to the people of the south, declaring the war would be carried on with renewed vigor.
J. I. WADDELL

The last shot of that war was soon to be fired. A few hours after making his entry in the log, Waddell was informed that a large number of sail were in sight to the north. He went on deck to study the situation. The craft were all downwind.

"I felt no doubt of their nationality," he said in his notes, "but to attempt the capture of any of them while the wind blew would mean the loss of the greater part of them.

"Lowered the smokestack and continued in the rear of the whalers, keeping a luff and retarding her progress as much as possible so as to arouse no suspicions among the Yankee crowd ahead."

Through the midnight twilight of Tuesday, on into the arctic dawn, the *Shenandoah* stalked the whalers.

"The morning opened with very little wind and a clear sky," Hunt recalled. "It was one of the pleasantest days we experienced from the time we entered the Okhotsk Sea until we finally got clear of these icy regions. There were eight sails in sight in different directions, and land was visible on our port beam, and about half past six we saw Diomede Island, about twelve miles distant.

"At eight o'clock we commenced what proved to be our last day's warfare against the commerce of the United States, by starting in chase of a sail we sighted a little way to the southward. At ten o'clock we captured the bark *Waverly*, of New Bedford, with 500 barrels of oil. Her officers and crew were at once sent on board the *Shenandoah*, after which she was set on fire, and we steered off to the northward, passing through an extensive field of ice, and at half past one neared a fleet of ten ships at the entrance of Bering's Straits.

"For the purpose of deceiving them we hoisted the U.S. flag, though there was not a breath of wind at the time and not a shadow of a chance for any of them to escape. It seemed as though the Fates had interposed to render our last achievement the most imposing and brilliant of the cruise, if not the war."

6

Early on the morning of June 28, the New Bedford whaleship *Brunswick* was moving north under light sail. Her captain, A. T. Potter, and her first mate, Caleb Babcock, were both in their bunks. Second Mate Andrew Jackson, a Canary Islander, was on watch.

Like most shipmasters, Potter slept lightly. At 3 A.M. he started awake. The officer of the deck had just yelled to the man at the helm. "Hard aport."

"Hard aport," the man answered.

"Steady," said Jackson, "steady." Then, a moment later, "Hard up, hard up, hard up." He was interrupted by a crash.

Captain Potter was thrown from his bunk as the ship crashed into the floe. Scrambling to his feet, he rang for the second mate and shouted, "Mr. Jackson, have you stove my ship?"

"No sir, I think not."

"Try the pumps."

"Aye, aye, sir."

While Potter was dressing, Jackson tried the pumps. He reported they were drawing no water. Potter ordered him to go into the forepeak and see if he could find any leak there.

The first mate rushed in, half-dressed and still sleep-drugged. "Try the pumps again, Mr. Babcock."

"Yes, sir."

As soon as he had climbed into his salt-stiffened clothes, Potter went on deck. Babcock reported that the pumps were now drawing water. A moment later, Jackson, his tanned face looking yellowish, came out of the lower hold and reported hearing water running in the bow.

Potter ran forward, looked over the bow, and saw she was dented in. He went down into the forepeak, saw two or three timbers cracked and broken. He ordered the flag hoisted, union down, as a signal of distress. The *Brunswick* limped toward the nearest ship, the *Congress.* Potter took the megaphone and called across the water. "Come aboard, Captain Wood. I have stove my ship."

Soon the skippers of several nearby whalers were aboard the stricken ship. Potter asked them to survey the *Brunswick* and determine whether she could be saved. This was a common practice, its purpose being to relieve the master of suspicion of having abandoned his ship for its insurance.

Potter went into his cabin and left the matter with them. They reported that the ship was not in condition to go to port for repairs. They condemned her.

Potter commenced dickering with his fellow skippers. He wanted them to haul the products of the two whales he had caught back to San Francisco. Ruel Cunningham, the master of the *James Maury,* agreed to carry the *Brunswick's* whalebone, but all the skippers, hopeful of filling their own casks, declined to carry any oil. While they were bargaining, two more ships, the *Hillman* and the *Martha* appeared in the distance, moving before a faint breeze. Potter knew that the *Hillman* had just left a large load of oil at San Francisco and would probably be empty. He decided to wait until she came up.

Before the new ships came alongside, a fog rolled in. When it lifted, Potter saw a black steamer cruising slowly among the whale ships. He thought it was the answer to a prayer. A steamer could, perhaps, haul him to safety; at least it could carry his precious oil quickly to San Francisco. He dispatched a mate to ask the stranger's help.

Pulling up under the steamer's black teak sides, the mate called to ask if the ship could come to the *Brunswick's* assistance. An officer leaned over the bulwark and shouted down, "We are very busy now, but in a little time we will attend to you."

The mate shouted his thanks, adding, "No hurry. The pumps will keep us afloat for a time."

"Which ship is the *James Maury?*" the officer asked.

A man in the *Brunswick* boat pointed to a nearby whaler.

"Thank you," said the officer. "We will come to you shortly."

The boat pulled away.

Lieutenant Whittle had inquired about the *James Maury* because Waddell had already determined she would be ransomed. While at Ponape, he had heard that the *Maury's* master, S. L. Gray, had died at sea of inflammation of the bowels. Mrs. Gray and her three small children were still aboard. Command had been transferred to the first mate, Cunningham. With her husband's body preserved in a cask of whiskey for a New England burial, Mrs. Gray had asked that the voyage be continued.

The *Shenandoah's* five prize crews were ready. Each was assigned two ships. The cruiser moved into a position where its guns commanded the entire fleet assembled around the stricken *Brunswick.* When all was ready, the boats started from the *Shenandoah,* the United States ensign was hauled down, the Confederate flag went up to the raider's peak, and a blank cartridge exploded in warning.

"All now was consternation," Hunt declared. "On every deck we could see excited groups gathering and gazing anxiously at the perfidious stranger, and then glancing wistfully aloft where their sails hung idly in the still air. But look where they would, there were no avenues of escape. The wind, so long their faithful coadjutor, had turned traitor and left them stranded whales to the mercy of the first enemy."

Fred Chew, who led the prize crew that boarded the *James Maury,* was met at the rail by Mrs. Gray. "The lady was very much frightened," one of Chew's companions said, "and besought him with tears in her eyes not to destroy the ship that had been her husband's home so long. As gently as possible he soothed her fears, telling her that no harm should befall her or the ship, through our instrumentality."

Cunningham, the acting captain, was sent to see Waddell. He signed a ransom note for $37,000. Waddell sent him back to the *Maury* with a message for Mrs. Gray. "I told her," he wrote complacently in his notes, "that no harm should come to her or the vessel; that I knew she was an owner of the vessel, and that the men of the South never made war on helpless women and children; although an example to the contrary had been set them by their Northern enemy, we preferred the nobler instincts of human nature."

In the meantime, Lieutenant Whittle was having trouble with the *Favorite.* Of all the ships in the group only she had not hauled down her American flag when the *Shenandoah* ran up the Confederate.

As Whittle and his boarding party approached, they saw the *Favorite's* master, a huge, gray-haired man, standing on the deck beside a harpoon gun. The captain held a cutlass in one hand, an old-fashioned navy revolver in the other. His men were crouched behind the ship's bulwark, sighting along their muskets.

"Boat ahoy!" bawled the captain when the *Shenandoah's* cutter was within hailing distance.

"Ahoy!" replied Whittle.

"Who are you and what do you want?"

"We come to inform you that your vessel is a prize to the Confederate steamer *Shenandoah.*"

"I'll be damned if she is, at least just yet. Now keep off, you, or I'll fire into you."

The captain began to sight the bomb gun used to hurl harpoons into the whales. Whittle decided the Yankee was crazy enough to do battle. He ordered his men to row back to the *Shenandoah* for instructions. When the news of resistance was shouted up to Waddell, he told the boat to come back. The *Shenandoah* then steamed alongside the whaler, matching her four cannon against the lone bomb gun.

The Yankee skipper stood his deck.

"Haul down your flag," Grimball shouted at him from the raider.

"Haul it down yourself, damn you," the old man shouted back, adding, "if you think it will be good for your constitution."

"If you don't haul it down, we'll blow you out of the water in five minutes."

"Blow away, my buck, but I may be eternally blasted if I haul down that flag for any cussed Confederate pirate that ever floated."

Waddell himself shouted orders for the prize crew to board the whaler. The cannoneers rammed shot into the Whitworth, ready to fire if the Yankees shot at the approaching boat. But though the skipper was not convinced, his officers and crew were. They had no desire to battle a cruiser with harpoon guns and pistols. They knew what one broadside would do. Throwing down their muskets and removing the cap from the bomb gun lest the skipper incite the raider by firing at it, the officers and men lowered the ship's boats and pulled away, leaving the master to defend his ship as best he might.

Still, Captain Young refused to yield. He substituted a bottle of whiskey for the cutlass and stood by the bomb gun. An old man, he had been under fire earlier in the war when sailing a supply ship on the Potomac. "Besides," he told reporters later, "I thought, I have only four or five years to live anyway, and I might as well die now as any time, especially as all I have is invested in my vessel, and I will have to go home penniless and die a pauper if I lose that."

Whittle's boat was now alongside the *Favorite*.

"Haul down the colors," Whittle shouted.

"I'll see you dead first," Young yelled back, waving his bottle.

"If you don't do it I'll have to shoot you." Whittle raised a rifle.

"Shoot and be damned."

Whittle lowered the gun and ordered his men to go aboard. They scrambled up the sides and found the captain sagging against his uncapped gun. He gave up without further struggle.

"It was evident," said Hunt, "that he had been seeking spirituous consolation; indeed to be plain about it, he was at least three sheets to the wind, but by general consent he was voted to be the bravest and most resolute man we captured during our cruise."

Waddell was less impressed. He ordered the captain put in irons in the forecastle and stationed a sentry by him with orders to gag him if he got saucy. "He was unable to take care of himself from drunkenness," said Waddell sourly. "His vessel was without a register, liable to seizure in profound peace by the police of the sea. All the captains and mates were more or less under the influence of liquor, and some of them swore their sympathy for the South, while others spoke incoherently of cruiser, fire, and insurance. A drunken and brutal class of men I found the whaling captains and mates of New England."

Aboard the punctured *Brunswick*, Captain Potter had realized he would not be rescued by the black steamer. With several of his mates he went to a safer ship. Second Mate Andrew Jackson was left in charge of the sinking whaler.

Jackson was bitter about the condemnation proceedings.

He was sure the ship could have been saved. He felt that Potter's fellow captains had been biased in their decision, that they were really interested only in putting the squeeze on the insurance company. Such co-operation was pleasant for Potter, but for Jackson, who had been on deck at the time of the wreck, it meant the probable end of his career. He decided to try to save the *Brunswick*. He cut anchor and, hoping the cruiser would be too busy with the unwounded vessels to notice, began to break out sail. In vain. A prize crew headed by Dabney Scales came alongside and carried Jackson off to the *Shenandoah.*

By five in the afternoon, the *Shenandoah* had rounded up ten prizes. In addition to the *Brunswick,* the *Favorite,* and the *James Maury,* there were: the *Hillman* and *Martha,* commanded by the Macomber brothers; the Baltimore-built *Covington,* with the oil of six whales already in her holds; the jinx-ship *Nile,* which had had eleven masters during the course of a two-year voyage; the forty-year-old *Nassau;* the oil-heavy *Isaac Howland* with a $35,000 catch already boiled out; and the *Congress,* commanded by hard-luck Daniel Wood of New Bedford, who four years earlier had lost the *Polar Star* in the Okhotsk Sea and only five months before had wrecked the *Fabius* on the coast of California.

They represented the cream of the New England fleet, the most daring ships and the most competent commanders. The ships were the best that could be built. Samuel Dammon, the man who had built the *Hillman,* talked in poetry when he spoke of her construction.

> "I worked on her every working day while she was building. Zachariah Hillman and I went into the loft and put the lines onto the floor and then we made the moulds. While we were making the moulds Jethro Hillman was at work in the yard on the timber. The material for her frame was to be of first quality white oak, this country growth. Her keel was rock maple. Her main

transom was live oak. Knight-heads were live oak. Apron was live oak. Side-counter timbers were live oak. Stanchions were locust. Her deck frames were of first quality Southern yellow pine timber. Her knees were first quality juniper. Her planks outside were the first quality white oak and Southern pine. The ceiling on the inside was the same. Her lower deck plank was of Southern yellow pine. Her upper deck was of first quality white pine. Her fastening were copper bolts and locust tree nails; these tree nails went through and through and were wedged on both ends, both outside and inside. The workmanship was done in first rate shape, as well as any ship ever built in New Bedford, or anywhere else. She was launched. Then she was sheathed and coppered. Her boat gear was put on, and all things were done to fit her for a whaler. The work was all done by the day. There was no contract work about her. Every part of her was salted on the stocks. All her deck frames and ceiling in between decks was varnished two or three coats. This was done to protect the wood and make it last longer. After the ship was launched she was hove out, and her bottom was graved and covered with tarred paper, which helped to preserve the oakum, and the bottom was then sheathed with pine boards put on with composition fastenings and then coppered as all other whalers are. When she returned from her first voyage, all that was done was recoppering and fitting what was necessary for another voyage. No repairs were necessary. I examined her thoroughly.

Their supplies were tremendous. The *Nassau,* for example, carried 321 barrels of salt provisions (118 barrels of beef, 203 of pork), 126 barrels of baked flour, 101 barrels of packed flour, 2475 pounds of butter, 502 pounds of dried apples, 1118 pounds of codfish, 800 pounds of sugar, 339 gallons of vinegar, 1037 pounds of coffee, 750 gallons of molasses. She also had 7150 fathoms of towline, 38 coils of Manila cordage, eight coils of tarred cordage, three new cutting falls and two old ones, 950 pounds of white lead, 75 gallons of linseed oil, and five tons of hoops.

The crews were the best sailors that could be recruited by world-roving captains. There were Anglo Saxons from New England, Portuguese from the Azores, Hawaiians from Oahu. Two of the ships had Negro officers; ability, not pigment, was what mattered in hunting whales. The crews numbered 336 men, too many to be transported south on the *James Maury*. Waddell, after looking over the ships' papers, decided to spare the *Nile*. He ordered the prisoners to proceed to the two vessels.

Nine men from the captured ships volunteered to join the raider. "They were all intelligent soldiers, men who had been educated to use the Enfield rifle and to respect military position," Waddell wrote later. "The enlistment of those men in the Confederate service was evidence at least that if they had heard any report of the military failure of the South they considered it so unreliable that it failed to embarrass their judgment in seeking service in the *Shenandoah*. It is not to be supposed that those men would have embarked in a cause which they believed to be lost. No, the failure of the South to establish herself was not known to any person who fell into my hands, or believed by such persons; for those waters are so far removed from the ordinary channels of commerce that it was simply impossible for authentic tidings of the progress of the American war to reach so remote a part of the world between the time of the actual overthrow of that Government and the capture of those vessels. Individuals may lie, but facts cannot."

By 7 P.M., all prisoners had been transferred to the *Nile* and the *James Maury*. Every man had signed parole, and cartels were furnished the ransomed ships explaining why they were without their registers. Then destruction crews began to move among the other eight vessels. By ten, all were burning.

"It was a scene never to be forgotten by any who beheld it," Hunt wrote. "The red glare from the eight burning vessels shone far and wide over the drifting ice of those savage seas; the crackling of the fire as it made its devouring way through each doomed ship, fell on the still air like unbraiding voices. The sea was filled with boats driving hither and thither with no hand to guide them, and with yards, sails, and cordage, remnants of the stupendous ruin there progressing. In the distance, but where the light fell strong and red upon them, bringing out into bold relief each spar and line, were the two ransomed vessels, the Noah's Arks that were to bear away the human life which in a few hours would be all that was left of the gallant whaling fleet.

"Imagination assisted us, no doubt, but we fancied we could see the varied expressions of anger, disappointment, fear, or wonder that marked the faces of the multitude on those decks as their eyes rested on this last great holocaust; and when, one by one, the burning hulks went hissing and gurgling down into the treacherous bosom of the ocean, the last act in the bloody drama of the American civil war had been played.

"Widely different were the arenas that witnessed the opening and concluding scenes. The overture was played by thunder and artillery beneath the walls of Sumter, with the breath of April fanning the cheeks of those who acted there their parts, while all the world looked on; the curtain finally fell amid the drifting ice of the Arctic seas; burning vessels formed a pyrotechnic display such as the children of men have seldom looked upon, while a grim and silent cruiser, that had, even then, no government nor country, and two weather-beaten whalers, filled with despondent prisoners, were the only audience."

Waddell, who kept his prose closer to the wind than did young Hunt, gave this description of the climactic scene of his cruise:

An occasional explosion on board of some one of the burning vessels informed me of the presence of gunpowder or other combustibles, and a liquid flame now and then pursued some inflammable substance which had escaped from their sides to the water. The heavens were illuminated with the red glare, presenting a picture of indescribable grandeur, while the water was covered with black smoke co-mingling with fiery sparks. Discharges on board often resembled distant artillery, and while that scene of destruction was going on, the steamer turned her head northward in search of additional prey."

6

Some of the men aboard the Yankee whalers had told Thomas Manning that a fleet of nearly sixty vessels had passed through Bering Strait, bound north, ten days before. Waddell, though taking a dim view of the turncoat's accuracy as a reporter, thought the tip worth investigating.

At 1 A.M., on Thursday, June 29, the *Shenandoah,* with Asia in sight on her left and America on her right, entered the Arctic Ocean.

A week earlier the northern waters had been clear. But now the currents had carried floes into the vicinity of the strait. "It was a desolate prospect that met our view," said Hunt. "We were at last launched upon the Arctic Ocean, within whose cold embrace was clasped the prize we so much coveted. But as far as the eye could reach extended one vast, unbroken sea of ice. To attempt to penetrate such barriers was sheer madness. The undertaking would have been attended with the gravest peril, even with the auxiliary of a vessel expressly fortified and strengthened for the rough encounter."

The weather was beautiful. It was the warmest day the Southerners had experienced since leaving the tropics. The ice-clogged sea was still as a mill pond, and numerous seals and walrus played about the *Shenandoah.* For several hours the ship cruised along the edge of the ice pack. No passage appeared.

At 10 A.M. the cruiser crossed the Arctic Circle. Waddell was faced with another difficult decision. Once before the ice had kept him away from a whaling fleet. If he turned back this time, there would be no second chance. With three ransomed ships en route to San Francisco, he could expect Yankee warships to be steaming north after him soon. A single enemy cruiser could cork the Bering Strait and block his escape.

Twice the ship hit ice floes. "I had no idea that ice even when it looks so rotten is so solid," Dr. Lining said. "It stopped us completely, although a small-looking cake."

After the second collision, Waddell was convinced that the danger was too great. "In consequence of her great length, the immensity of the icebergs and floes, and the danger of being shut in the Arctic Ocean for several months, I was induced to turn her head southward."

The sigh of relief that went up from the cruiser is echoed in Hunt's statement, "I do not think there was an officer or man on board who did not acquiesce in the wisdom of the decision."

The *Shenandoah* raced the drifting ice toward the strait. The ice got there first. The cruiser reached East Cape just as the first floes of a great field began to jam the narrow passage. There was nothing to do but enter the ice and hope. Very slowly, the *Shenandoah* moved south through the changing channels. The memory of what the ice had done to the thick-sided *Brunswick* cheered no one. But late in the afternoon, the raider entered comparatively clear water, swung past the smoking wrecks of three whalers that had not gone down, and caught a last view of the two prison ships which were idling south before a faint breeze.

Two unfamiliar sails appeared to the southeast. The *Shenandoah* ran down on them. One was French, the other Hawaiian.

A northwest wind sprang up while the *Shenandoah* was off St. Lawrence Island. Waddell ordered sail to be made. The fires were banked and the propeller triced up. When the sun dipped below the horizon and the golden fringe marked its progress westward, the ship was gliding along at six knots.

A Bering fog closed in with Arctic suddenness and, almost simultaneously, a lookout sighted pilot ice – sure sign of a large field of floes. Smith Lee, the officer of the deck, bawled orders for the sails to be shortened. Before the ship could be slowed down she crashed full tilt into a huge floe.

Officers were bounced from their bunks. Sailors tumbled from their hammocks. And to every mind came the same thought: she might be stove. Everyone rushed onto the fog-wrapped deck. The ship was slipping back off the floe. Her rudder grated against underwater ice, and one of the tiller ropes snapped.

Lee ordered all hands to work furling sail. The ship had to be kept from banging about among the floes. Several officers went below to see if the timbers below the waterline had given way under the impact. They reported everything fast, but the steamer was still in great peril.

The fog rolled back, revealing blocks of ice on all sides, twenty to thirty feet in thickness. A number of men went over the side onto the nearest floe. Warps and grapnels were run out and made fast by means of crowbars and kedges secured in the ice. Slowly the *Shenandoah's* head was swung around toward the only break seen in the field. While steam was being raised, cord mats were swung over to protect the cruiser's sides. Steam was gently applied. The *Shenandoah* nosed up against a large block of ice. Pushing it along before her, she pried apart the nearby floes.

The pale sun came over the horizon, dispelling the last of the fog. "Ahead of us and on both bows were great fields of floating ice extending to the utmost verge of vision, and for awhile it seemed as though we were to experience another jam, but ere long, another stretch of water opened, into which we steamed, more because it was the only space of open water than because it promised an avenue of escape, and continued our slow and painful progress southward, the ice parting before us as we advanced, as though on purpose to let our good ship through. After four or five hours of such anxious navigation, we sighted the open water again and finally, thank God! reached it, having passed almost scatheless the many perils by which we had been menaced."

The broken tiller rope was easily mended; after repairs it was better than ever. The impact had bent the gudgeons to the rudder, thus eliminating a thumping which the men had noticed whenever the steamer was running at more than ten knots. "The remedy," Waddell remarked rather dryly, "was severe."

The raider passed the Pribilof Islands, the greatest sealing grounds in the world, soon to come into American possession. Hundreds of bull seals were playing about the ship, "raising their huge bulks above the surface and uttering their strange roaring cry, and anon disappearing beneath the water." In the distance the Confederates saw the heads of thousands of smaller seals — females teaching the pups to swim.

Though still within the right-whaling grounds, no ships had been sighted by the *Shenandoah* since passing St. Lawrence Island.

"The time had arrived," said Waddell, "to take the steamer out of these constricted waters into more open seas, because if intelligence had reached any of the enemy's cruisers, which were parts of the squadrons of the Pacific or China stations, from the cartels which were sent from the Arctic or from other vessels which had received warning of danger from the drift of the wrecks or the illumination of the sky by the bonfires, or through the agency of foreign whalers, it would not have been difficult to blockade or force the Shenandoah into action, and to avoid such a result was my duty.

"It would not have been good policy or sensible to risk the steamer in a contest which, even if she had won, taking the most favorable view, would have materially injured and rendered her unfit for service until taken into a port where she could be repaired; and we knew too well what character of neutrality controlled the first naval powers of the earth to suppose that any Government bordering on the vast Pacific coasts would endanger its existence by receiving a Confederate cruiser for repairs, and thus incur the displeasure of the Washington Government, while England and France shrunk from such responsibility.

"Two days before the steamer left the Bering Sea a black fog closed upon us and shut out from our view the sky and all objects fifty yards distant. Still she pressed on her way toward the Amoukhta [Amukta] Pass, or the 172 meridional passage of the Aleutian Islands.

"When the dead reckoning gave the steamer a position near the Amoukhta Pass, through which I intended she should enter the North Pacific, the fog continued thick and gloomy, but she dashed along on her course, trusting to accuracy of judgment and a hope that the fog would lift so that the land could be seen four to five miles distant should she fail to strike the center of the passage.

"It would have been a culpable mistake to stop steaming or run on a circle because the weather was foggy, in a sea and near islands where currents are irregular in direction and force, for the drift of the ship would perhaps prove more fatal than running on a direct course from last observations. I preferred to run the ship for the passage, assuming that three sights taken from noon the previous day, when the fog cleared for a moment, gave an approximate position to the ship which partially corroborated the dead reckoning (although no two of them agreed), and by taking a middle course for the center of the pass that it would be more prudent to go ahead than to wait for clear weather. It only required a little nerve.

"When I expected the ship to be about the center of the pass, much to my relief land was seen off either beam, and the position of the ship was accurately discovered or ascertained from cross bearings taken. That feeling of security against a danger which is overcome is truly delightful to the senses. It was my first great experience, for it involved the safety of the ship and the lives of all on board. The ship was safe."

The weather cleared, and as the *Shenandoah* swung southeast along the Aleutians, the snow mountains stood revealed in incredible beauty – white peaks, black basalt ridges, and the rich green of grass, broken by fields of yellow and purple flowers, all outlined against a blue-black sea. Smoke rose straight and high from one of the white-crested volcanoes. Long after the land had dropped out of sight astern, the Confederates could see the talisman of a fire greater than any they had started.

"It was a relief to feel we were again bound for the general region of the tropics," Hunt admitted. "Our intention was now to cruise on the Pacific Coast in the hope of capturing one or more of the rich steamers that ply between San Francisco and Panama. How others may have felt I know not, but for myself, I am free to confess that I had had enough of Arctic cruising, and if I never look again upon those icy seas and barren shores, fit residences only for Eskimos, seals, and Polar bears, it will not occasion me one moment's regret.

"The principal part of the duty assigned to us had been discharged in the destruction and dispersing of the whaling fleet. It was with feelings of profound relief that we at last saw these frozen seas, with their many perils seen and unseen, where for weeks we had been battling with ice, or groping blindly in impenetrable fog, fade in the distance.

"All were in good spirits, as we had reason to be, after performing well a laborious and in many respects unpleasant duty, and as each day carried us nearer those genial seas where for a time we expected to cruise, the memory of many hardships faded from our minds."

But the greatest trial of all lay ahead.

ALONE, ALL, ALL ALONE

On July 18, the headlines in San Francisco read:

THE PIRATE SHENANDOAH! SHE STEERS IN THE TRACK OF WHALERS!
TERRIBLE HAVOC EXPECTED

The story was based on roundabout reports. A steamer from Oahu had brought the Honolulu *Advertiser* of June 24, in which edition California editors found the following item:

> A Suspicious Vessel – the Hawaiian schooner *Pfiel,* from a cruise to the southward and westward, arrived on Thursday (June 22) and from her captain we have the following:
>
> On the 30th of March, latitude 3° 53′ N, longitude 167° E at 6 P.M. was brought to by a gun from a vessel of war; hove to, and was soon boarded by a boat, the officers and crew of which were heavily armed. One of the officers demanded the papers. After scrutinizing them closely he said they were all right. He then asked me if I had seen any whale ships on the line or left any in port at Ascencion. My mate questioned the other officers as to the ship's name, and was told a very different name, which he does not remember. One of the boat's crew asked one of my hands where Captain Fish was, and also enquired after several vessels in the whaling fleet. I left at Ascencion, 23 days before being spoken, the *Charles W. Morgan, Helen Snow* and bark *Mercury*. They were all ready for sea, and no doubt sailed within a day or two after me. It was quite dark and I could not make

out the ship's armament; saw that she was a propeller under sail, and feel confident that it was not an English ship-of-war.

There is very little doubt but what the ship is the *Shenandoah.*

Charles James, Collector of Customs at San Francisco, passed the word along in a letter to the Secretary of the Treasury, who, three weeks later, notified the Secretary of the Navy that bad tidings might soon be expected from the whaling fleet. They had already arrived.

The day after James dispatched his letter, the *Milo* limped through the Golden Gate, bringing the first load of refugees from the Bering. David McDougal, the commandant of the Mare Island navy yard and a former shipmate of Waddell's, wired the Secretary of the Navy:

SHIP MILO ARRIVED TODAY FROM THE ARCTIC WITH CREWS OF TEN WHALERS DESTROYED BY THE SHENANDOAH. ADMIRAL PEARSON NOTIFIED BY STEAMER AMERICA, WHICH SAILED TODAY FOR PANAMA

The telegram was lost in channels. It was not delivered until August 18. On July 23, having received no reply from his first wire, McDougal tried again:

GREAT APPREHENSIONS FELT BY MERCANTILE COMMUNITY OF SAN FRANCISCO IN CONSEQUENCE OF DEPREDATIONS OF SHENANDOAH. MERCHANT SHIPOWNERS AND UNDERWRITERS HAVE ADDRESSED MEMORIAL REQUESTING ME TO TELEGRAPH DEPARTMENT FOR AUTHORITY TO CHARTER, ARM AND MAN STEAMER COLORADO OF PACIFIC MAIL COMPANY TO PURSUE THAT VESSEL.

This message, too, went astray en route. It reached the Secretary of the Navy an hour and ten minutes after the first message — shortly before midnight on August 18.

In the meantime McDougal was sweating it out at Mare Island. He had no warship to send out after the raider. He could only wait word from Washington, or from Rear Admiral Pearson, who had dropped down to Acapulco to attend a court-martial being held on a warship stationed there.

All San Francisco was stirred by the threat to shipping. On July 25, the daily *Alta California* carried a story under the heading

> THE SHENANDOAH EXCITEMENT
>
> The raid of the *Shenandoah* and the projects for her capture are, for a wonder, still the principal topics for discussion in business circles. Commander McDougal expresses himself as ready and anxious to render every possible assistance in fitting out a steamer at this port, either the *Colorado* or *St.Louis,* as proposed by members of the Board of Underwriters and others. He has at his command improved marine ordinance stores and small arms and ammunition in abundance, and there are plenty of experienced naval officers ready to volunteer to go on the expedition.
>
> There is also nearly a full crew and a number of marines who could be detailed for the purpose by the commandant at the navy yard. The Government has already been apprised by telegraph of the doings of the *Shenandoah,* and the petition will be sent on in full, with Commander McDougal's endorsement, as soon as the line again commences working.
>
> There are many here who look with distrust, not to say contempt, upon this whole project, as they believe, with a show of reason, that Waddell has long ere this left the Arctic regions entirely and made off either for a new scene of plundering operations or for a convenient neutral port into which to run and abandon his vessel.

The excitement hit a new high on August second, when the *General Pike* came in with more prisoners. The next day's headlines:

> THE ENGLISH PIRATE "SHENANDOAH" STILL AT HER INFAMOUS WORK — EIGHT MORE SHIPS CAPTURED — SEVEN BURNED — EIGHTY

MORE VESSELS AT HER MERCY — TWO HUNDRED AND FIFTY-TWO MEN ROBBED OF EVERYTHING, CROWDED ONTO A SMALL WHALING BARK WITH ADVICE TO RESORT TO CANNIBALISM IN CASE THEIR PROVISIONS GAVE OUT — LOG OF THE "GENERAL PIKE" AND STATEMENTS OF THE OFFICERS AND MEN OF THE BURNED SHIPS. THE ROLL OF THE PAROLED PRISONERS, ETC., ETC.

But still no word from Washington. The *Colorado,* instead of being commandeered for pursuit, left port on a commercial voyage around the Horn. The *Alta California* clarioned an appeal to private initiative:

A BURNING SHAME

The people of San Francisco, which is now admitted to be the second city in point of commercial importance in the U.S. and the great commercial emporium of the Pacific Coast, have recently learned of the most extensive depredations and the most flagrant outrages ever perpetrated on commerce, and this in the confines of our territory in times of peace.

The question is naturally asked: what steps have our government taken to stop the career of this infamous pirate, the *Shenandoah?* Unfortunately we are obliged to answer, none. In the first place there is no U.S. war vessel here capable of capturing the outlaw. The local authorities, although the whole shipping of this port were destroyed, would take weeks to awaken to a proper sense of the fact.

What then remains to be done? Our citizens must move in the matter. Let this scourge of the seas be taken by private enterprise. There are vessels obtainable here that could soon be fitted out with an armament equal to the task of taking the *Shenandoah,* and perhaps would not have to go further than the Farallon Islands to meet "Captain" Waddell, than whom no more accomplished villain ever "cut a man's throat or scuttled a ship."

We are a people perhaps the most liberal of any community in the world. No call for charity, or any good work that appeals to the judgment of our folks, goes unanswered. Circumstances

> at present call for action on our part to suppress this wholesale robbery and wanton destruction. Let private enterprise with whatever government aid may be obtained send out an expedition to put a "quietus" to this marauder.
>
> If this is done – and it can be done – promptly, Waddell might soon be added to the collection of beasts in the Willows Museum, and thus gratify many residents of the Pacific.

But it was not done. The same day the editorial appeared, the Navy Department in Washington learned, from the Treasury, of the *Pfiel's* report. The Secretary of the Navy wired the commander of the Pacific squadron, who was still out of town:

> SHENANDOAH MAKING DEPREDATIONS IN PACIFIC. DEPARTMENT RELIES UPON YOU TO EFFECT HER CAPTURE.

Also on that day, Admiral Pearson, who was at Acapulco enjoying the court-martial and the beach, received McDougal's earlier message about the arrival of the *Milo*. He immediately ordered the U.S.S. *Saranac*, which Waddell had once commanded, to put to sea in search of the raider. On August 18, McDougal's telegrams finally reached Washington. The Navy wired back:

> DISPATCHES 20TH AND 23RD JULY RECEIVED TODAY. DELAY EMBARRASSES THE DEPARTMENT IN ADVISING RELATIVE SHENANDOAH. IF PEARSON LEFT BEFORE RECEIPT OF NEWS, CHARTER AND ARM COLORADO FOR PURSUIT, IF ADVISABLE AT THIS LATE DAY. IF PEARSON IS AT SAN FRANCISCO HE WILL ACT AT DISCRETION, SENDING HIM THIS DISPATCH.

McDougal replied that the *Saranac* was moving north after the raider. The Union warship had reached Vancouver Island on her way to the Bering Sea.

A second ship, the *Suwannee*, had been put to sea and would soon enter the chase. The departure of the *Suwannee* restored the *Alta California's* faith in co-operative initiative. On August 21, the paper said:

THE SUWANNEE AND THE PIRATES

The U. S. double-ender iron war steamer *Suwannee,* having been up to Mare Island, repaired, coaled, and provisioned for a cruise in search of the pirate *Shenandoah,* came down to the city at noon yesterday.

She was under full steam but did not show a particle of smoke, and as the 'long, low rakish-looking black hull' plowed through the sparkling waters of the bay at such a rate of speed which showed she would be able in a very short time to run down any propeller-built steamer ever launched, the spectacle presented was one which will not soon be forgotten by the beholders.

The *Suwannee* is similar in construction to the *Wateree,* but appears larger. Her hull is built on the model of the fish called the barracouta – long, sharp, and narrow, and lies so low in the water, when coaled for a voyage, as to present but a poor mark for an enemy's guns, while her immense battery of ten heavy guns would enable her to sink such a vessel as the *Shenandoah* in less time than the *Kearsarge* consumed in sending the twin English pirate *Alabama* to the bottom.

Should she ever get within reach of the *Shenandoah,* it is to be hoped that she will not take unnecessary trouble about picking up prisoners, and that any skulking tender, like that English yacht which stole off the Captain of the *Alabama,* may get a settler on the spot.

2

Meanwhile the source of confusion and object of search was bearing down toward San Francisco from the north.

She jogged along with light air and dashed before occasional gales until she reached the meridian of 129° W. "There," wrote Waddell, "she took the north wind which sweeps down the California coast. Her course was given parallel with the land,

and a sharp lookout was kept. She was in waters frequented by the enemy's cruisers as well as a large merchant marine.

"The ship had by that time lost the cold, cheerless aspect which circumstances had imposed upon her in high latitudes. Her decks were once more the places of resort where Jack took shelter from a scorching tropical sun under the bulwarks and where thirty-seven head of live hogs sunned themselves. The connection is singular, but I have seen Jack use a hog for his pillow, by scratching a hog to sleep in order to use him as a pillow afterwards. A sailor bathes all over every morning, and that is cleanliness; but he is nevertheless a dirty fellow."

Besides musing on the habits of men who had to share their quarters with hogs, the captain was working out the details of an audacious plan. He intended to capture San Francisco and hold it for ransom.

From the papers captured aboard the *Susan Abigail,* Waddell had learned that McDougal was in command at Mare Island. He had little respect for the man. "We had been together in the *Saginaw*. McDougal was fond of his ease. I did not feel that he would be in our way. Any officer of the *Shenandoah* was more than a match for McDougal in activity and will."

Another report indicated that the only ship in the harbor was an old ironclad, too slow to catch the *Shenandoah* but ideal for the defense of a port. Waddell guessed that with easy-going McDougal in command, the ironclad would be poorly guarded.

Waddell knew the harbor well. He had served seven months aboard vessels stationed there. To enter port and collide with the iron ram would be easy, he thought. With the Confederate marines thrown upon the ironclad's deck, possession of her hatches could be quickly gained. No lives need be lost. Then, with McDougal and his officers captured, when daylight came, the batteries of the ironclad and the *Shenandoah* could be turned on the city. San Francisco would be held for tribute.

He confided the plan to no one. It was so daring it might breed dissension. For a time he let his officers speculate on their destination.

"Where will we go to?" Lining mused. "Straight to Europe, or will we stop to cruise? I rather think the Shenanigan is like a dog which has stolen a bone and goes off, its tail between its legs, or better still, like one which having gotten a bone, goes off growling head and tail up to keep off the other dogs. Will we ever reach Europe? For we have a heavy gauntlet to run and 'Murdock of Alpine will have to try his speed.' "

After a time Waddell told his lieutenants that they were after the gold ships which ran between Panama and San Francisco. The word was welcomed. And, indeed, Waddell did want to capture such a ship. "Prudence indicated communication with a vessel recently from San Francisco before attempting the ransom enterprise."

At high noon on August 2, while the *Shenandoah* lazed in a light breeze west of the tip of Lower California, on the track of south-bound merchantmen, the cry of "Sail Ho!" sounded from the masthead.

Steam was raised. The raider sped away on her last chase. At four o'clock the engine was cut. A shot arched across the bark's bow. She ran up the British flag. Waddell dispatched Bulloch, the sailing master, to board her, inspect her register, and bring back any newspapers she might have.

The bark was the *Barracouta* of Liverpool, thirteen days out of San Francisco. After making sure of her nationality, Bulloch asked the captain for news about the war.

"What war?"

"The War between the United States and Confederate States," said Bulloch.

"Why, the war has been over since April. What ship is that?"

"The Confederate steamer *Shenandoah*."

"Good God almighty. Every navy in the world is after you."

The Captain brought out the San Francisco papers and gave them to Bulloch. He assured the Confederate that there was no doubt about the stories being true. In silence, the boarding party rowed back to the raider.

An hour later, Dabney Scales, the lieutenant of the watch, wrote in the ship's log:

> Having received by the bark *Barracouta* the sad intelligence of the overthrow of the Confederate Government, all attempts to destroy the shipping or property of the United States will cease from this date, in accordance with which the first lieutenant, William C. Whittle, Jr., received the order from the commander to strike below the battery and disarm the ship and crew.

After ten months the raid was over. The hunter had become the hunted.

The news seemed too bad to be true. Yet, as Whittle wrote in his journal, "coming as it did from an Englishman, we could not doubt its accuracy. We were bereft of country, bereft of Government, bereft of ground for hope or aspiration, bereft of a cause for which to struggle and suffer."

Cornelius Hunt wrote, "It was as though every man had just learned of the death of a near and dear relative."

Dr. Lining said, "This is doomed to be one of the blackest of all the black days of my life, for from today I must look forward to begin life over again, starting where I cannot tell, how I cannot say — but I have learned for a certainty that I have no country."

For Waddell it was worst of all. The responsibility for having continued the raid after the end of the war rested on him. So did the awful task of getting his ship and men to safety.

"My life had been checked, and I was tutored to disappointment," he wrote of that moment. "The intelligence of the issue of the fearful struggle cast a deep stillness over the ship's company and would have occupied all my reflection had not a responsibility of the highest order rested upon me in the course

I should pursue, which involved not only my personal honor, but the honor of that flag entrusted to me, which had been thus far triumphant."

Some of the officers feared the men. It was suggested that, with a crew of so many nationalities, mutiny would result if the men learned the captain's authority was no longer backed by a government. A proposal was advanced to keep the news a secret. But it could not be done. The crewmen who had rowed Bulloch to the *Barracouta* also had picked up papers. They knew. And, like the officers, they saw the significance of the word repeated over and over in the San Francisco papers – "Pirates"!

"It required no prophet to foretell what construction the people of the North would put upon our actions," Hunt reasoned. "We well knew the inveterate hatred with which they regarded the people of the seceded States. From the first they had stigmatized our cruisers as pirates, even when they were recognized as belligerents by the leading powers of the world, and they would not be likely to let slip such an opportunity as our last escapade had furnished them to glut their vengeance with our blood should we fall into their hands."

Whittle, reflecting on their predicament, declared "it was a situation desperate to a degree to which history furnishes no parallel. Piracy is a crime not against one nation but against all. A pirate is an enemy to mankind, and as such amenable to trial and punishment under the laws of nations, by the courts of the country into whose hands he may fall."

Sadly, Waddell and his officers discussed the problems confronting them. "It is strange," Mason remarked, "how much difference of opinion there is about the course which we should pursue. Two important questions arise. First, are we bound to give up the ship, or would Captain Waddell be justified in destroying her? Second, if we must give up the *Shenandoah,* into what port would it be most advisable to do so.

"Let us take question Number One. One fellow says, 'We know the war is over, of course there is nothing more to be done, therefore let us blow up our ship and go ashore in a foreign land. Why should we give her up? From all we can learn there has been no formal treaty of peace, but an annihilation of our government simply. Now here is the *Shenandoah,* the last remnant of the old Confederacy. Why can we not destroy her?'

"Another says, 'Our government is destroyed. All the property belonging to it is now the lawful prize of the enemy. We should therefore go into the nearest United States port and deliver up our ship and our persons, biding the consequences.'

"Again, a third advocates a medium course. Take the ship into an English or French port, give up our vessel, which is public property, but our persons, not belonging to government, we are not bound to surrender them. This last is the course we will pursue.

"As for question Two, many officers think it would be much better to go into Sydney, where we would meet with a much warmer reception and be less liable to capture en route. I for my part am a Liverpool man, thinking the chances of capture small.

"Our Captain's position is indeed a most difficult and embarrassing one. I do not envy him. He has decided this matter on his own responsibility without calling any regular council. I am sorry to be obliged to confess it, but is is a melancholy fact that our captain is not the firmest or most decided man alive, for as I have just shown he vacillates, never being positive about anything, always afraid of doing either too much or too little. This morning when he spoke to several of us on the poop, his voice was thick and tears stood in his eyes. I was truly sorry for the poor man."

Waddell's officers persuaded him to go to Australia. For one day he sailed on that course. But on the morning of August 3, he changed again, saying it was nonsense to think of going to Sydney and turning loose officers and men penniless in a strange continent.

"But does he think that the same thing must not occur at Liverpool," Lining asked his journal. "Besides there is the risk of getting there. Smith went and asked him to go to Sydney. Bulloch begged him to go there. But to no use, he had made up his mind to go to Liverpool, and he said he would be damned if he did not take her there."

The next morning the crew presented a petition to Waddell, asking to be informed of the exact state of affairs. At 1 P.M. he called all hands aft.

"My men," he began, "I have received your communication, which is a very proper one. The spirit in which it is written is a subordinate one. A commanding officer can ask for nothing more. What you say here is true. The South has been subdued. At the same time you must know that the position of myself and of all my officers is far worse than that of any of you.

"You ask where we shall go. I tell you this. I shall take the ship into the nearest English port. All I have to ask of you men is to stand by me to the last. As for our cruise, it is a record which stands for itself. All you have to do is to be proud of it."

There were cries of "We are! We are!" "We will! We will!"

"No man among you has any reason to blush for the service in which he has been engaged," Waddell continued, his voice breaking. "Our cruise was projected and prosecuted in good faith. It has inflicted heavy blows upon the commerce of our late enemies which will not soon be forgotten. But now there is nothing more to be done but to secure our personal safety by the readiest and most efficacious means at hand. You must trust in me."

"We do," shouted the men. "We do."

The speech moved officers as well as men. Mason was moved to tears and, that night, in his room, confided to his diary, "I am afraid I did the Captain injustice in my last remarks about him. I am sure of it. I was too hard on the old gent."

It was not for some time that the men realized Waddell had not explained which port he considered to be "the nearest English port."

He meant Liverpool. But he told no one. "I first thought that a port in the South Atlantic would answer all my purposes," he said in his notes, "but upon reflection I saw the propriety of avoiding those ports and determined to run the ship for a European port, which involved a distance of 17,000 miles – a long gantlet to run and escape.

"But why should I not succeed in baffling observation or pursuit? There was everything to gain and only imaginary dangers. The ship had up to that time traversed over 40,000 miles without accident. I felt assured a search would be made for her in the Pacific, and that to run the ship south was of importance to all concerned. Some nervous persons expressed a desire that the steamer should be taken to Australia or New Zealand, or any near port, rather than attempt to reach Europe. I could not see what was to be gained by going in any other direction than to Europe. I considered it due the honor of all concerned that to avoid everything like a show of dread under the severe trial imposed upon me was my duty as a man and an officer in whose hands was placed the honor of my country's flag and the welfare of 132 men."

3

The work done joyfully by few hands on leaving Madeira was now sadly undone by many: the *Shenandoah* was reconverted from cruiser to merchantman.

The same tackles that had hoisted the guns aboard from the *Laurel* were rigged. The guns were lowered into the forward hold. The ports were boarded over. The red funnel was whitewashed and run down. No one felt much confidence in the disguise.

"The hilarity which had so long been observable through the ship was now gone," Hunt observed, "and there were only anxious faces to be seen in cabin, wardroom, and forecastle. The lookouts, it was true, still mounted aloft, but it was not to scan the seas for ships that might be captured, but to maintain a faithful watch and ward over any suspicious sail that might make its appearance above the horizon.

"While rolling down toward the Cape with the brave westerlies astern, the lookout one day reported a vessel with all sail set, to fore-topmast studding sail, standing very nearly on the same course as ourselves. Our glasses soon revealed the fact that she was English, and not a man-of-war, and consequently there was nothing to apprehend from her. As she seemed to bear a singular family likeness to our own good ship, we resolved to have a nearer view of her.

"At the time we were under topgallant sails, but before many minutes the topmen were aloft loosing the royals which were soon sheeted home and hoisted away. The fore-topmast studding sail was also broken out, and swayed aloft, the tack hauled out, the sheet sent down, and away we went to try our speed with the stranger. She seemed to understand that a race was on the tapis, and immediately began to show more canvas.

"For a time it was doubtful how the contest would end. Both had a heavy press of sail, and were dancing along at the rate of twelve or thirteen knots, but the *Shenandoah* was too much by the head and at last it became apparent that the stranger was slowly leaving us.

"Observing this we signaled her to learn who and what she was. The bunting soon informed us that it was the sister ship of our own, built by the same firm on the Clyde and in brief, one was almost a counterpart of the other. It was the first time we had fallen in with a vessel that could outsail us, and had we been in equally good trim with the Englishman, I do not think either would have had an opportunity of claiming a victory."

But the fact that they had been outsailed, and at a time when their speed was their sole protection, weighed heavily on the Confederates.

Tempers grew short. Men quarreled over things which at the start of the voyage would have passed unnoticed. Waddell noticed Bulloch and Lining talking aft of the propeller house and called them "a couple of croakers."

Mason noted in his diary that "I must say that twelve months experience at sea has destroyed all the romance of a sailor's life for me. The constant confinement within the narrow limits of the ship, this total deprivation of the society of females, which has so softening an influence on all men, the many other privations, among which the miserable diet is not the least important, all produce a sum total which can only be properly appreciated by those who had experienced them. What must this life, so unbearable to me, be to a common sailor who has ten times the privations that an officer would have?"

The quarrels grew more bitter. "Our noble captain made a terrible slip a few days ago," Mason wrote in mid-September. "Scales having been guilty of the heinous crime of oversleeping himself one morning and getting up too late for quarters was summoned before his august majesty and accused of willful violation of the rules of the ship, giving the crew an example of insubordination, etc., etc. To all these dreadful charges poor Scales could not but plead guilty in part, at the same time assuring the captain that he turned in at four o'clock that morning without the slightest idea or premeditated intent of oversleeping himself and such other excuses as one would naturally make.

"But the captain's wrath was implacable and Mr. Scales was informed that hereafter he would be a passenger in the ship having no duty to perform whatever. The skipper said that having no longer any military jurisdiction over him or anyone else, he would not punish Mr. Scales but would give him a passage to the nearest port. All this was excessively maladroit to say the least. Mr. Scales thanked the captain for the passage which he had so kindly given him, but told him at the same time that if he thought himself under any obligation to the captain he would go forward with the ship's company and work it out. But as he did not see it in that light, he said, he would remain where he was. Thus they parted company.

"A few hours afterward my noble captain called me aft, told me he had given Mr. Blacker, the captain's clerk, charge of the fourth watch, and that if Mr. Browne and myself had any objections to make he would relieve us from duty.

"I replied that under existing circumstances, so long as Mr. Blacker and myself did not come on the same watch, I would sacrifice my feelings for what he considered the good of the ship and make no objections. He did not seem to think that he was taking advantage of his position to violate all laws and custom of the navy, whilst all of his officers were doing everything possible to maintain the usual discipline and more anxious than ever to conform to all laws and rules.

"Mr. Hunt, master's mate, who had the misfortune to be in Mr. Blacker's watch, was guilty of the enormous offense of remonstrating with the captain, whereupon he was immediately relieved from all duty and our magnanimous captain gave him a passage also.

"Blacker was at first unaware of the state of affairs. Getting wind of all this he went to the captain and said in a most respectful manner that the duty assigned to him was a most unpleasant one and that although he would cheerfully obey any order, he begged the captain to reconsider the matter and if possible to excuse him. The captain replied, rather uncivilly, that he did not want him, that he could do without him, he would keep the watch himself.

"The captain's clerk is only a civil officer, not supposed to know anything about seamanship. It was the most preposterous thing to think of giving him the quarter-deck, especially when the first lieutenant, master, and two midshipmen were all able to do the duty. The captain, however, kept his word and kept the dog watch that evening.

"Bulloch then volunteered his services which were accepted. I was sorry to see Bulloch volunteer, for I hoped that after the numerous *bêtises* of which the skipper had been guilty that he might be allowed to keep a few mid-watches as a sort of punishment. *Entre nous, franchement, c'est une vieille bête que celui-la; il n'aurait jamais du quitter le cordon de tablier de sa femme, qui doit porter la culotte par exemple, j'en suis presque certaine.* A few days after the events recorded in the foregoing, Scales was restored to duty and took his watch again as usual. Mr. Hunt was also restored but put on the berth deck."

The next day, Lining reported another squabble. "Old Lee got into trouble this morning for the first time since he has been in the navy. It riles the old fellow a good deal. It seems that this morning in the morning watch he was indulging in a quiet smoke when Whittle came on deck and caught him in the very act. Some words occurred between them. Lee, in a little pet, told Whittle that all hell could not make him leave off his pipe. The fact was reported to the Captain, who sent for Lee and wanted him to make a promise that he would not smoke on watch again. On Lee's refusing to make any promises, he relieved him from duty and put Bulloch on. I think that Lee is perfectly right in not letting any promises be extorted from him."

The next day, Lining picked up the story. "The Captain put his foot in it again. In the afternoon he sent for all the watch officers in his cabin and began by telling them that he was very sorry he would have to put them in three watches but that Mr. Lee had not come forward as he expected he would do to make the promise not to smoke on watch and he therefore could not put him on duty. To keep Mr. Bulloch on watch would be simply to punish Mr. Bulloch.

"Grimball then spoke up and said he thought Mr. Lee was right not to make any promise and that it was a thing he did not think any one had a right to expect from another. He said that he himself had smoked on watches and if he had been caught he expected to have been punished for it, and when the punishment was over to be restored to duty.

"Scales then spoke up and said that he too had smoked on his watches. At which confessions the Captain seemed thunderstruck. He said he had nothing more to say. Afterward he issued a written order against officers smoking on their watches or leaving the deck unless regularly relieved and restored Lee to duty. So ended this '*funcion*' in which like so many others the Captain has come out to leeward."

4

The *Shenandoah* was being sought around the world. President Johnson referred to the chase in a message to Congress. Secretary of the Navy Welles issued special orders for American warships everywhere to be on the lookout for the "corsair." Reports, both official and unofficial, about where the ship was — and wasn't — came in from far and near.

Commander Bankhead of the U.S.S. *Wyoming* reported from Mauritius, in the Indian Ocean, that "I propose leaving here on the second proximo for Batavia, via Singapore and the

Strait of Malacca. I have heard nothing of the *Shenandoah* since the report by H.B.M. frigate *Euryalus* of her having been seen in Bass Strait some time during the month of April."

The San Francisco *Courier* carried a story:

> The terrible corsair, or pirate, whichever it may be called, having need of supplies, sent a ship to San Francisco for them. The undertaking was successful, and the ship, loaded with provisions and everything of which the *Shenandoah* might stand in need then obtained a clearance for Victoria. The whole was done quietly, discreetly, and it appears successfully. It has been stated that the vessel clearing for Victoria has not arrived at that port. These stories appear to be incredible, yet nobody can impugn their correctness.

The Liverpool *Journal of Commerce*, in a dispatch datelined Ceylon, reported the *Shenandoah's* arrival at Shanghai. A few days later the *Journal* admitted its error and said the cruiser was definitely at Manila.

From the Cape Verde Islands came the prediction by a U.S. naval official that the raider might be operating in the Indian Ocean as a freebooter:

> She must return — to England, perhaps, like the *Georgia* — or if she remain, she may turn pirate outright, a not improbable contingency, considering that for the past four years her commander, officers, and crew have been educating themselves as completely as did Captain Kidd when he abandoned the occupation of a pseudo man-of-war in order to reap richer gains of open piracy in those very Indian seas whither the *Shenandoah* has gone. Australian gold ships are more valuable than the tawdry jewels and scanty treasure of a petty Indian prince.

The commander of the *Iroquois* sent a warning from the Strait of Rhio that

> It is still probable that the *Shenandoah* may appear near China or the Bay of Bengal and I shall continue to watch this neigh-

borhood until, from the great mail center at Singapore I can receive advices by which I may determine whether she is intended to operate in the East Indies or in the Pacific.

The Honolulu *Advertiser,* on September 2, speculated that the raider might have gone to Mexico or Japan or China.

A few days later the San Francisco *Alta California* asked

IS THE SHENANDOAH AT OUR DOORS?

The bark *Milan,* eight days from Teekaleet, arrived on Tuesday, and yesterday the bark *Vernon,* ten days from the same port, arrived. Captain Downing of the *Milan* reports seeing on Saturday week a large propeller steamer with three top-royal yards and a short stump of a topgallant mast, lying in the mouth of the Straits of Fuca, in or near Neah Bay. She had no flag flying, and her description does not answer to any vessel known to be in these waters, while it does not answer exactly to that of the *Shenandoah.*

Captain Huckins of the *Vernon* also reports seeing the same steamer and adds that on the night of the Sunday following, the first day out of the Straits of Fuca, a steamer which he supposed to be the same passed him around three times in the darkness but did not hail, and he saw nothing of her at daylight.

Many of the officers of burned whalers agree in the opinion that the *Shenandoah* will soon throw off her disguise of a Confederate cruiser and turn open pirate, preying upon the commerce of all nations alike, and it is not impossible that the scoundrel Waddell may have determined to lay in wait for and capture a steamer from Victoria and Portland, in British waters, or at least within sight of the shores of British territory. These steamers generally carry heavy treasure lists, and are unarmed, so that the attempt to capture would be attended with many inducements, and none of the danger which would be incurred should the thin-shelled pirate come within range of the comparatively heavy guns of one of our Panama steamers.

Shortly after this, the U.S.S. *Saranac* left Honolulu for the Marquesas Islands, northeast of Tahiti, because of a rumor that a large cargo of coal had been landed there for the *Shenandoah.*

And from Pisco, Peru, F. K. Murray, commander of the U.S.S. *Wateree* reported that he had run down a rumor that the *Shenandoah* had been sold to Peruvian revolutionists and found it false.

5

The *Shenandoah* was very short of coal. The scant supply in her hold was needed for ballast – as well as for the emergency of pursuit. Even the small amount used to condense water caused the ship to roll more violently. It was necessary, therefore, to stick to sails for power. After several days in the doldrums, the cruiser caught a strong, favorable wind. Waddell ordered all possible sail unfurled.

For several hours before doubling the Cape under topgallants, the weary ship made fifteen knots in spite of her fouled copper. On Saturday, September 16, she passed to the eastward of the Cape.

"We were just congratulating ourselves upon our fortunate passage round the dreaded Cape," Hunt wrote, "when we encountered a gale which for a few hours was absolutely terrific, and we lay to under close-reefed main topsail, and fore-storm staysail, with a tarpaulin in the fore-rigging to ride it out.

"The sea ran mountains high, dashing its spray far up into the rigging, and more than one huge wave made a clean breach over us, leaving such a quantity of water on our decks as to engender at times grave fears for our safety. The ship tossed about like a cockleshell, but happily we sustained no serious injury and when the tempest had finally blown itself out we got clear of 'old Cape Misery.' "

The storm forced the *Shenandoah* far to the south. This took her safely out of the track of other vessels – but into an area of icebergs, more dangerous than any they had encountered in the Arctic.

"Passed near the Shag Rocks in cold and boisterous weather," Waddell noted in his journal. "Day after day icebergs and savage blocks of ice came near us. We were without a moon to shed her cheerful light upon our desolate path, and the wind was so fierce that the ship's speed could not be reduced below five knots per hour. It was more prudent to go ahead than heave to, for we were without observations for several days and in an easterly current. Some of the icebergs were castellated and resembled fortifications with sentinels on guard, but although the nights were dark we escaped injury."

Hunt described the icebergs as "hundreds of feet in height, slowly drifting as they were influenced by the undercurrents of the ocean, fit representatives of the Antarctic region from whence they came. One day we passed no less than fourteen of them. I obtained the altitude of the largest by means of the sextant, and found that from its visible base to the pinnacle it measured no less than 320 feet. When first discovered it bore a striking resemblance, in form, to a church with a lofty, pointed spire, but as we neared it and it gradually turned, it assumed the appearance of a merely shapeless block of polar ice, in parts white and sparkling in the sun's rays like crystal and in others deep blue and seemingly as imperishable as solid rock."

The ship was a cheerless place. They had seen no land since the Aleutians three months before. It was six months since the men had last been ashore. Depression over the Southern fate, uncertainty over the future, distaste for the present were every man's companions.

"The struggles of our ship were but typical of the struggles that filled our breasts upon learning that we were alone on that friendless deep without a home or country, our little crew all that were left of the thousands who had sworn to defend that country or die with her," Waddell declared. "There were moments when we would have deemed that a friendly gale which would have buried our sorrowful hearts and the beautiful *Shenandoah* in these dark waters. The very ship seemed to have partaken our feelings and no longer moved with her accustomed swiftness."

Gradually the *Shenandoah* worked northward. As the danger from bergs subsided, the men began to speculate again on their destination. Wardroom and forecastle were divided into two camps, the "Longitudes" rooting for Waddell to take the ship to Cape Town, the "Latitudes" for Liverpool. The ship was still in a position where it could make for either port. Daily the tension between the parties grew.

On Tuesday, September 26, the ship reached a point where another day's run would reveal Waddell's intention. If he continued north it was England; if he turned west it was Africa.

Conversation at the mess was tightly worded. Emotions were coiled like springs. The officers tried to keep from debating their destination – but failed. In the midst of a casual conversation about an albatross that had been following the ship, Grimball burst out, "By God, I'd rather be captured and kept in prison twenty years than go sneaking into Cape Town."

Engineer O'Brien leaped to his feet and shouted, "And if we go into the North Atlantic, I hope we are captured."

That night the ship made a long run northward. Everyone knew. The destination was England.

The showdown had come. Breedlove Smith, the paymaster, an advocate of going to Africa, drew up a petition which he circulated among the senior officers. Signed by six officers, it was presented to Waddell on Thursday, September 28:

> In considering the present unparalleled state of affairs, we have taken the liberty of respectfully laying this communication before you, to convey to yourself the anxiety and regret with which we regard the prospect of a passage in this ship, under the altered circumstances in which she is placed, to a country so distant as England. We desire before proceeding further to remind you that it is only this very alteration of our condition which has influenced us in forming these our opinions.
>
> So long as we had a country and a Government to support and sustain it was done cheerfully and with alacrity; so long as there was an object to be gained that object was sought for by none more eagerly than ourselves; so long even as this ship herself was engaged in cruising none co-operated with her more zealously than ourselves. Now we respectfully submit, all these motives for exertion are gone. Our country and Government have by the sad fortunes of war ceased to exist; our cruise, as such, has long since come to a conclusion; our battery and small arms struck below; we are entirely without means of defense – in point of fact, without even the right to defend ourselves if attacked – and are consequently at the mercy of any passing cruiser.
>
> Under these circumstances, an idea that it would be for the best interests of all parties concerned to land at the nearest and most convenient port, and thus relieve us from our anomalous position, has forced itself upon us with such force and convincing power that we have deemed it a duty to ourselves as being parties interested to the last degree in this question to lay before you, not for your guidance but for your impartial consideration, the reasons which have appeared to us so cogent.
>
> We regard with a proper horror any prospect of capture or imprisonment at this late day, with no Government where would be any show of authority sufficiently great to secure for us any of the amenities usually granted to prisoners of war. It is a well-known fact that during the war, and with threats of retaliation sounding in their ears, the United States authorities frequently, almost generally, treated our prisoners with great rigor and severity. How much more will such be the case now that the

war has concluded in the present manner. Our risks of capture in going from our present position to Cape Town would be comparatively small. At best we would have to run the gantlet some 2,000 miles, whereas in going to England we would be exposed to the risk almost certainly doubled for about three times that distance. This appears so clear and to us so forcible it were needless to dwell upon it.

Next we respectfully urge that if the welfare of officers and men is to be consulted, no more certain manner of ascertaining what would be the general welfare or the good of the whole can be found than to take each individual wish or desire and by combining them to sum up and find the aggregate. In a matter so entirely personal as the welfare of either officers or men we respectfully submit that the person himself is the best judge of what is most to his advantage, and a sufficient number of individual advantages will compose the general advantage of the ship.

As to the disposition of the ship herself, that is a subject entirely distinct, and one which we are far less concerned with, from the fact that we consider it out of our province; but where our persons are concerned, when capture and imprisonment are a possible alternative to their passage to England, then we are indeed nearly concerned, and deem it a duty we owe to ourselves and to those belonging to or dependent on us at least to bring to your notice these, our ideas and opinions as to our individual interests and advantage, and to request your consideration thereof.

What do we gain by proceeding with this ship to England that we would not gain by proceeding there in some neutral vessel from a neutral port? What do we avoid by going to Cape Town with this ship? All risks of capture, be they great or small. In a word, we have, in our humble judgment, everything to gain by the latter course and nothing to lose, and just the contrary by the former.

We leave entirely to yourself all questions as to the condition and ability of the ship herself to accomplish the voyage and contend against the terrible weather we must expect in the North Atlantic and off the English coast. We see that she is already quite light and would, if chased by a United States cruiser, hardly be able to carry on the requisite amount of canvas to enable us to escape, etc. Still we leave all that with perfect confidence entirely to your judgment.

In conclusion we feel that you will do us the justice to attribute this letter to its proper motive, viz., a sense of duty, and not an intention of casting any disrespect upon yourself. We distinctly disclaim any intention or desire to trammel your judgment or interfere with your functions.

We have the honor to be, very respectfully, your obedient servants

F. T. Chew
Irvine S. Bulloch
Charles E. Lining
Matthew O'Brien
W. Breedlove Smith
O. A. Browne

The petition was presented to Waddell in the morning. He made no comment.

A second petition was drawn. It was written by the captain's clerk, James Blacker, and circulated among the steerage officers. Far more than the first, it was challenging in tone. Every junior officer except Cornelius Hunt signed it:

Steamship *Shenandoah*
At sea, September 28, 1865

Sir: We the undersigned officers of the steamship *Shenandoah*, under your command, most respectfully submit this letter for your consideration, and trust that it may be met in the same spirit which dictates it.

The ship has now arrived at a position where we feel the urgent necessity of impressing you with our feelings as to the destination. On a previous occasion you declared your intention of proceeding to the nearest English port. We are now near one, viz., Cape Town, which for many reasons holds out more inducements than any other port to make us wish to be taken there.

It is right that we should here state our reasons for preferring this port to the chances of proceeding to Europe. Cape Town is a harbor of constant resort by the homeward-bound Indiamen, and other means of prosecuting our journey to Europe are afforded by the mail steamers and the Calcutta steamers. From the universal sympathy that has always been showed to all engaged in our cause during the late war, we entertain no doubt that passage would be allowed or offered us in these vessels, and even were the reverse the case, we could always work our passages in the aforesaid ships.

Again, Cape Town is now so near that the passage there would only occupy ten or fourteen days, whereas to go to England would take fully forty days at least. Our chances of capture are also lessened, for even were an American ship-of-war lying in port the English authorities would never give up our persons, whatever they might do with the ship.

Now on the other hand, proceeding through the North Atlantic we run two risks, both of them very grave indeed in their nature. The first is capture, and as this ship has gained for herself great notoriety, we may very readily conclude that ships are already on the lookout for us on the usual route, and no other one can we adopt in consequence of the scarcity of our fuel. We can not reasonably expect any good treatment if we fall into the hands of the U.S. government. Their treatment of prisoners already has sufficiently shown how we will be dealt with, and as there are several paroled prisoners on board it will go doubly hard with them.

The next risk lies in the state of the ship herself. She is already so light that even the small quantity of fuel consumed during the last few days in condensing has made a most perceptible difference in her stability. Now, to enable us to shorten our voyage or avoid capture by taking an unusual route, recourse must be had to steam, thereby placing the ship in a most dangerous condition, which can not be remedied, and which will render the ship totally unfit and unable to contend with the furious weather that constantly prevails on the British coasts from November to April. Here the lives of all on board will be placed in more jeopardy than their liberties and we entreat you to seriously weigh over these considerations.

In conclusion we would request that should you determine not to enter either of the harbors at the Cape you would give us an opportunity of landing at some one of the bays to the northward, which we would infinitely prefer to the chances of capture, or shipwreck.

We have the honor to remain, sir, your most obedient servants,

WM. H. CODD
JOHN HUTCHINSON
ERNEST MUGGUFFENEY
J. F. MINOR
LODGE COLTON
THOMAS MANNING
J. C. BLACKER
HENRY ALCOTT
G. P. CANNING
J. C. LYNCH

Blacker handed the petition to Waddell, who read it in his presence. The captain was furious. He noted, especially, the threat of secession and the fact that the signers had laid aside all grade and titles, addressing him merely as "Captain, Steamship *Shenandoah*," and signing themselves simply as individuals. Trembling with anger, he turned on Blacker and replied, "I will be captain, sir, or die on this deck."

But the situation was clearly out of hand. Only six of the officers had not signed one or the other of the petitions. After deliberation, Waddell summoned a council of the watch officers – Chew, Grimball, Scales, Lee, and Whittle. He showed them the petitions, explained that it had been his original intention to go to Cape Town but that he now thought it best to go to a European port. The petitions, however, put a new light on matters. Since there was such a difference of opinion, he would leave the decision to his watch officers.

Whittle, who was a Cape Town man, declined to vote, on the ground that as executive officer he should not be on record as opposing the captain. The other four voted three to one in favor of Liverpool.

"I consider this the smartest thing the Captain has ever

done on board this ship," Lining observed bitterly. "He knew before he called them into the cabin the opinion of every officer, because this thing had been openly and loudly and angrily discussed, time and time again, in the wardroom, where every word could be heard in the cabin. He knew that he would have a majority on his side. He left out of the Council, Bulloch, who had always heretofore been called in – not to mention other officers who were present at important consultations. . . . In this way, certain that it would be decided as he wished, he threw all the responsibility on the shoulders of the Council, and said goodly, 'Gentlemen, I will be guided by you.' "

Before the decision to proceed to Liverpool was made known, two more petitions were presented to Waddell. The first came from Grimball, Lee, Scales, McNulty, and Mason:

> SIR: It was not our original intention to address you on the subject of the future destination of the *Shenandoah*, but since you have received two communications, signed by most of the officers of the ship, expressing views and opinions in direct opposition to those entertained by yourself, viz., your intention to take the ship to some port in England or France, it will be a source of gratification for us to know that in connection with those documents you have also this one which expresses our unqualified approbation of the course you have determined upon.
>
> Be the fortunes of war or shipwreck in our passage (which appears to excite so much uneasiness in some) what they may, we consider either England or France the only proper destination for the *Shenandoah*.

And from the petty officers and men, most of whom, being British, wanted to be taken home, came the final word:

> We, the undersigned, take the liberty of writing this petition in consequence of a certain paper purporting to be the petition of the crew having been formerly laid before you.

Sir, in complete denial of this paper and its object, and of petitioning you on such a subject whatsoever, and to show our complete reliance and trust in whatever it should please you to do under any circumstances is the earnest and sincere feeling which has caused us to lay this before you.

Trusting our intention will be our excuse, we remain, sir, your most humble servants.

(70 SIGNATURES)

The debate left much bitterness. "This morning at breakfast everyone looked as black as midnight," Mason remarked the day after the council. "I scarcely dared speak to anyone of the Cape Town crowd, even Smith, who is always so cool and hard to ruffle could not conceal his disappointment. He has been a sort of oracle amongst a certain crowd, his opinion has been often asked by the Captain in points of law; on the whole he has an exalted opinion of Smith, and when he took this matter in hand I am sure he was perfectly confident of success, having used all his plausible arguments to bring over those who were wavering or who had not decision of character enough to form an opinion of their own. After all his pains to fail totally was not only a disappointment but a wound to his pride that touched him to the quick. Being a Liverpool-ite to the backbone, I was of course pleased with the decision. Although it is anything but a Christian spirit I must acknowledge that I cannot help feeling immense satisfaction at their signal defeat. As Grimball says, 'We hogged them after all.' "

The next day the *Shenandoah* crossed the path of her outbound voyage. In celebration, Waddell sent a bottle of champagne to the wardroom with a note congratulating the officers on being aboard the only Confederate ship to circle the globe. Three of the Cape Town advocates arose and walked out. "I thought this public display was in exceedingly bad taste and showed a rather contemptible spirit," said Mason. And Lining, who had not left, remarked, "Whether they left because they did not wish to drink at such an unseasonable hour or that they did not wish to drink to the event when so set out, I know not; but I do think a point might have been strained under the circumstance. I think it was kindly and politely meant."

Ill-feeling remained. But new feuds distracted the "Longitudes" and "Latitudes," channeling their anxiety and frustration into other patterns.

A rumor sped through the ship that Cornelius Hunt had failed to turn in several hundred dollars he found aboard a Yankee whaler. Joshua Minor seemed to be the originator. Hunt heard of the story and rushed to Waddell, begging him to investigate. Waddell did, and cleared Hunt of the charge. But a new hate had been added. The list was long.

6

The *Shenandoah* crossed the Equator for the fourth time of the voyage on Wednesday, October 11. There was no formal celebration. King Neptune ignored his nephews. But Dr. McNulty, who had been relieved from duty because of chronic drunkenness, went on a one-man binge. Loaded with alcohol, he started discussing politics with Blacker. The Irishmen argued with increasing heat. Finally McNulty screamed, "Shut up, you damned English-Irish Orangeman."

Blacker, in a rage, rushed off to Whittle and reported that McNulty was drunk and insulting. Whittle ordered the assistant surgeon to go to his quarters and stay there. McNulty staggered below and began rummaging in his bag for a gun. Whittle, coming down to check whether the drunken officer was obeying orders, saw the pistol.

"Give me that gun, sir," he ordered.

"Stand back," said McNulty, raising the pistol. Whittle leaped forward and took it away from him. McNulty collapsed on his bunk and began to cry. Whittle walked out with the gun.

The next morning, McNulty complained to Waddell. He said that his quarrel with Blacker had not started over politics or religion but over an insulting remark Blacker had made about Waddell. He denied being drunk. He said he had taken out the pistol to show Whittle.

Waddell called in the executive officer to hear his version. Whittle blew up. He told the captain that McNulty was a drunk, a liar, and a sycophant. Then Whittle stalked off to his own room, called in McNulty, and with Scales and Lee as witnesses, bluntly insulted him.

"Sir," he began, "the captain tells me that you told him you had not been drinking last night. I do not believe it, but I will let that pass. But he also says you told him that you took out the pistol only to show it to me. What do you mean by that?"

"I mean to say that I only did take it out for that purpose."

"I don't believe that you did any such thing," snapped Whittle. "Nor do I believe that you thought so when you reported it to the captain."

"Well, sir," said McNulty, turning brick-red, "when we get on shore there is a way of settling all these things."

"Very well," said Whittle. "I am willing at any time and place to settle this."

"Do you waive all rank?"

"Yes, I waive all rank and will give you any satisfaction you want."

"Very well. You will hear from me." McNulty left the room.

The next morning, Lee called on Whittle. He brought a letter from McNulty demanding an apology "or the satisfaction that one gentleman may expect from another."

Whittle called on Dr. Lining to serve as his second. He explained to Lining that he was willing to fight McNulty as soon as they reached port, but that from Lee's conversation he believed that McNulty wanted satisfaction immediately. At Lining's suggestion, Whittle wrote a letter to McNulty saying that his language explained itself and that on reaching port he would give him full satisfaction.

Lining took the letter to Lee. He asked the Virginian to read it at once, and then explained to Lee why he felt the fight should not be held on the ship. "It would be a bad example for the men," Lining argued. "The executive officer could never again punish a man for a like offense without having to fight him. Further, there is the matter of weapons. I have not spoken to Whittle as to how he would give satisfaction, but I assume that it would be with pistols as it is not usual for gentlemen to settle such matters by fisticuffs."

Lee agreed. "It would have to be with pistols."

"Now, then. Where could such a fight be held."

"On the poop," said Lee, promptly.

"That would not be a fit place for such an affair. It would be in the presence of the officer of the deck. Further, the helmsman would see it, and officers should not settle their differences before sailors."

"What about the wardroom?"

"I had thought of that, but it would be too dangerous. If either should miss, he might hurt someone. But beyond all this, it seems to me that we cannot be too careful not to offend against the laws in any way at this time, and especially, since England is our destination, we should not break the laws of England. If any unfortunate accident should happen in this duel, we would lay ourselves liable to be apprehended for murder, for dueling is looked on as such by English law."

Lee thought it over. He agreed to ask McNulty. Later he came to Whittle. "It is agreeable," he reported. "But it must be understood that we expect satisfaction as soon as we get into port."

"It is understood," said Whittle.

The matter never came up again. Not everyone was satisfied with the peaceful ending. "I am by no means a bloodthirsty man," Mason told his diary, "indeed, I am opposed to dueling most emphatically. But these things are sometimes unavoidable; civilized nations have by usage made it the only gentlemanly way of settling such disputes as the present, and if these fellows must fight it out, let them do it now when there is no danger. Certainly this is better than running the risk of being hung or imprisoned in England."

7

Two weeks after crossing the Line, the *Shenandoah* was fanning along in slight breezes when a masthead lookout cried, "Sail ho!"

The cry no longer sent men joyfully into the rigging. Now, sailing between the bulges where Union cruisers might be expected, the Confederates wanted to see sails less than ever before.

"Glasses swept the northern horizon in search of the stranger," Waddell said, "but she was visible only from aloft. I sent a quartermaster up with orders to communicate to me only what he could ascertain from the appearance of the sail. He reported her under short sail with her mainsail up or furled, and that from the spread of her masts she seemed to be a steamer.

"She was standing a little more to the east of north than the *Shenandoah* was heading. The sun was thirty minutes high and the sky was cloudless. I could make no change in the course of the ship or the quantity of sail she was carrying because such an evolution would have aroused the stranger's suspicion, expose the *Shenandoah* to investigation, and whatever she might be, she had seen the *Shenandoah* and might be waiting to speak her.

"I sent the quartermaster aloft again with orders similar to those he had previously received. He reported her to be a cruiser, and he believed her waiting in order to speak.

"The *Shenandoah* had come up rapidly with the sail, and there seemed little chance of escaping communication. A danger was that she would approach too near during light. She could already be seen from deck, and darkness came on more slowly than I had ever observed it.

"The situation was one of anxious suspense; our security, if any remained, depended on a strict adherence to the course; deviation would be fatal. Boldness must accomplish deception. Still she forged toward the sail and it would be madness to stop her."

For the first time the men aboard cursed the *Shenandoah's* speed. She was moving forward too fast. The propeller was lowered so that the drag would slow her. Buckets were hung over the stern for the same purpose. Orders were given to prepare to raise steam in case it came to a chase. But at last darkness cut off sight of the stranger.

"What a relief," exclaimed Waddell. "She could not have been four miles off. The *Shenandoah's* head was turned south and steam was raised. The sails were furled so that they would not stand out against the tropical moon which was to rise at nine o'clock. The coal was Cardiff and the smoke was a white vapor which could not be seen two hundred yards. Now that the engine was working the steamer headed east and we had at least all the advantage to be expected. It was the first time she had been under steam since crossing the Line on the Pacific side. Indeed, the fires were not lighted for a distance of over 13,000 miles."

The *Shenandoah* ran east for fifteen miles, then turned

north. When the sun rose the mysterious stranger was no longer in sight.

8

During a year at sea, in which she had circled the globe and captured thirty-eight ships and nearly a thousand prisoners, the *Shenandoah* had neither taken nor lost a life. But during the final days of her voyage, while running the gantlet along the European coast, two of her men died.

The first was Bill Sailor, a Hawaiian from Maui, who had joined from the *Abigail* in the Okhotsk Sea. "He died so easily and suddenly that they who were with him thought that he was asleep, so that I was not called until after he was dead," Lining wrote. "Poor fellow. He had been suffering from venereal for a long time and was covered with ulcers. He is the first of our ship's company whom death has carried off and I can only hope it will be the last, though I hardly can expect it to be."

The Hawaiian was buried off the poop deck, so that the sight of the funeral would not disturb the ship's other invalid, Sgt. George Canning of the marines. Canning was a mystery man. He had appeared on the deck of the *Shenandoah* outside of Melbourne, accompanied by his Negro servant, Weeks. He represented himself as a former aide-de-camp to the Right Reverend Major General Leonidas Polk, the South's least victorious general, and said he had been invalided out of service after receiving a shot through the lung at Shiloh.

Shipboard life had not helped his wounded lung. He had been sick for almost the entire voyage. While in the Okhotsk Sea he had asked to be put ashore on Kamchatka; he thought he had a better chance of surviving a trans-Siberian trip than the rest of the ocean voyage. Since crossing the Equator he had been kept in a cot on deck. On Monday, October 30, he suddenly turned to his Negro servant, who was sitting by his side, and said, "Good-bye, Weeks, I am going. Take care of yourself, old fellow."

Weeks called Lining. "He died very easily," the doctor wrote, "had been conscious but a few moments earlier, and even recognized and attempted to speak to me after I came down. He only gave four or five gasps and all was over. His disease was phthisis brought on by a gunshot wound through the right lung.

"There is something in the history of this man that none of us know. His being on General Polk's staff, his coming over to Europe with a wife – a Southerner by birth, whom no one has ever seen since, nor has anyone ever heard him speak of her; his going out to Australia and not having her with him; his great reticence on all subjects that related to his past life, not even mentioning any of his family or whom they were or where they lived. In fact, we know nothing about him."

Hunt described his burial. "The body was draped for its ocean grave in sailor fashion by being sewn up in his own hammock, to the foot of which were securely fastened two thirty-two pound shots, and the next day the boatswain's whistle summoned All Hands to Bury the Dead.

"A more solemnly impressive scene than a burial at sea can scarcely be imagined. At the well-known signal the whole ship's company assembled on the deck, not with the gay alacrity that characterizes their movements when responding to any other summons but with slow steps and serious faces that were in keeping with the occasion.

"Upon a smooth plank, one end of which rested on the taffrail, while the other was supported by two seamen, lay the enshrouded form of our late comrade, while near by stood the ship's surgeon with open prayer book in hand to read the solemn burial service of the Roman Catholic church to which the deceased had been attached.

"All remained uncovered while the surgeon with impassive voice and manner recited the solemn formula and as he repeated the words, 'We therefore commit his body to the deep, looking for the general resurrection in the last day, when the earth and sea shall give up their dead,' the inner end of the plank was lifted, and with a sullen plunge the body disappeared from our view."

9

Riding the southwest trades, the *Shenandoah* pushed up to within 700 miles of Liverpool. Then the wind died out one night. Morning found the ship becalmed. Eleven sails were in sight, all unwelcome to the worried Confederates.

All through the day the *Shenandoah* lay in the midst of her enemies, her sails sagging in the cool, still air. At night the canvas was quickly furled. With almost the last of her coal, the ship steamed away. "Discretion," said Waddell, "is always the better part of valor. I considered it prudent to avail of darkness."

Three more days of steaming by night and sailing by day brought the ship almost within sight of Ireland. Gulls were wheeling overhead and resting in the rigging. Old sailors claimed they could smell the bogs. Everyone counted hours.

"On the fourth of November," wrote Hunt, "our reckoning showed us to be near land, and all eyes were anxiously scanning the horizon for a glimpse of old England. We knew not what reception was in store for us, for momentous changes had taken place since we set forth on that adventurous pilgrimage around the world, but we were weary of suspense and all were desirous of making port and learning the worst as soon as possible.

"Night, however, closed round us with nothing but the heaving sea with which we had been so long familiar in sight.

The following morning a dense fog was hanging over the water, effectually concealing everything from view at a ship's length distance. Extreme caution was now necessary as we had only our chronometers and the patent log towing astern to rely upon for showing us our position, but we steamed slowly ahead with all sails furled, laying our course for St. George's Channel.

"Soon the fog lifted, revealed to our view the green shores of Ireland on our port beam, the first land we had seen since we lost sight of the snow-clad bluffs of Northern America."

Since leaving the Aleutians, the *Shenandoah* had been at sea 122 days without sighting land. She had covered 23,000 miles. "Mr. Bulloch," said Waddell, "made an excellent landfall. The navigation was very beautiful."

Through the day the ship continued northeast under steam, toward Holyhead. The crew was paid off. "None seemed dissatisfied except a few who were drunk," said Lining. "This evening I heard that there is a report that they intend to come aft tonight and see if they cannot get some of ours to make up their own. But all this is bosh! The men are too near England to attempt such a thing. Besides they know the officers too well to try it."

Around midnight the lights of a pilot boat were seen. Very early in the morning the pilot came aboard. Whittle met him at the rail and wished him good morning.

"Good morning. What ship is this?"

"The late Confederate steamer *Shenandoah*."

"The hell you say. Where have you fellows come from last?"

"From the Arctic Ocean."

"And you haven't stopped at any port since you left there?"

"No, nor been in sight of land, either. What news from the war in America?"

The officers, who had crowded around the pilot, waited

hopefully for the answer. Always, for some of them, there had been a belief that the *Barracouta's* officers were wrong, that the San Francisco papers were lying, that the news was not as bad as it seemed.

"Why, the war has been over so long people have got through talking about it. Jeff Davis is in Fortress Monroe, and the Yankees have a lot of cruisers out looking for you. Haven't you seen any of them?"

"Not unless a suspicious looking craft we sighted off the Western Islands was one."

The pilot was taken to Waddell's cabin. The captain quizzed him more about the war but found him to be "a king of know-nothing." He asked the pilot to guide the ship up the Mersey. As the *Shenandoah* moved into fresh water for the first time in thirteen months, Waddell bent over his desk putting the finishing touches on a letter to the British Government.

Shenandoah
November 6, 1865

My Lord [Earl Russel]:

I have the honor to announce to your lordship my arrival in the waters of the Mersey with this vessel, late a ship of war under my command, belonging to the Confederate States of America.

The singular position in which I find myself placed and the absence of all precedents on the subject will, I trust, induce your lordship to pardon my hasty reference to a few facts connected with the cruise lately made by this ship.

I commissioned the ship in October, 1864, under orders from the naval department of the Confederate States, and in pursuance of the same commenced actively raiding the enemy's commerce. My orders directed me to visit certain seas in preference to others. In obedience thereto I found myself in May, June, and July of this year in the Okhotsk Sea and Arctic Ocean. Both places, if not quite isolated, are still so far removed from the ordinary channels of commerce that months would elapse before any news could reach there as to the progress or termination

THE OLD *RIP* OF THE "SHENANDOAH."

CAPTAIN WADDELL (AS RIP VAN WINKLE). "Law! Mr. Pilot, you don't say so! The war in America over these Eight Months? Dear! dear! who'd ever a' thought it!"

of the American war. In consequence of this awkward circumstance I was engaged in the Arctic Ocean in acts of war as late as the 28th of June, in ignorance of the serious reverses sustained by our arms in the field and the obliteration of the Government under which authority I had been acting.

This intelligence I received for the first time on communication at sea, on the 2d of August, with the British bark *Barracouta* of Liverpool, fourteen days from San Francisco. Your lordship can imagine my surprise at the receipt of such intelligence, and I would have given to it little consideration if an Englishman's opinion did not confirm the war news, though from an enemy's port.

I desisted instantly from further acts of war, and determined to suspend further action until I had communication with a European port, where I would learn if that intelligence were true. It would not have been intelligent in me to convey this vessel to an American port for surrender simply because the master of the *Barracouta* had said the war was ended. I was in an embarrassing position; I diligently examined all the law writers at my command, searching a precedent for my guidance in the future control, management, and final disposal of the vessel. I could find none. History is, I believe, without a parallel.

Finding the authority questionable under which I considered this vessel a ship of war, I immediately discontinued cruising, and shaped my course for the Atlantic Ocean.

As to the ship's disposal, I do not consider that I have any right to destroy her or any further right to command her. On the contrary I think that as all the property of the Government has reverted by the fortune of war to the Government of the United States of North America, therefore this vessel, inasmuch as it was the property of the Confederate States, should accompany the other property already reverted.

I therefore sought this port as a suitable one wherein to 'learn the news' and, if I am without a government, to surrender the ship with her battery, small arms, machinery, stores, tackle and apparel complete, to Her Majesty's Government for such disposition as in its wisdom should be deemed proper.

I have, etc. JAMES I. WADDELL

As Waddell wrote he was interrupted by a sudden, sickening, scraping crunch. The ship had gone aground. Whittle ran in with word that she was fast on a bar but that the pilot thought high tide would float her free before dawn. Wearily the captain gave orders for a doubled watch to be kept that night.

Soon Whittle was back with more bad news. He had overheard the rumor that Lining had reported earlier – the crewmen were about to mutiny. "The fear that the rest of their wages would not be forthcoming had suggested to some this desperate expedient," said Hunt. "It must be confessed that their prospects for payment were not brilliant. At least none but a very credulous man would feel much confidence in the feasibility of collecting a debt due him from a defunct government."

With the ship stuck on a bar, Whittle feared it would be easy for the crew to overpower the officers, load the small boats with valuables, row to shore, and disappear. Waddell agreed. He sent his lieutenant around to warn all officers to sleep with their revolvers at their sides. But morning came without trouble.

The tide raised the *Shenandoah* off the spit. In a thick fog she steamed up the Mersey. "The fog shut out the town from our view," said Hunt, "and we were not sorry for it, for we did not care about the gaping crowd on shore witnessing the humiliation that was soon to befall our ship."

The Confederate was maneuvered into position alongside H.B.M. ship-of-the-line *Donegal*. At 8 A.M. the anchors, which had been tight on her bows for seven months, were run down. A few minutes later an officer from the *Donegal* came aboard. He officially informed Waddell of the end of the war.

At 10 A.M. all hands were called aft. Waddell appeared in full uniform. He made a short speech, thanking the men for their loyalty, assuring them they had nothing to be ashamed of, and promising that he would do all in his power to look after their interests.

Men and officers stood at quiet attention. Sorrow and uncertainty diluted their relief at reaching port. On the poop deck Whittle stood erect, his arms folded across his chest, tears streaming down his cheeks.

At a signal from Waddell, the quartermaster stepped forward and slowly, in dead silence, ran down the last flag of the Confederacy. Carefully he rolled up the ensign. With the slowness of a funeral march he carried it to the captain.

The cruise was over. The last Confederate had surrendered. The *Shenandoah* was again in British hands.

CRUISERS, LIKE CHICKENS . . .

THE RETURN of the prodigal cruiser aroused much comment but little enthusiasm in England. To the Foreign Office, especially, the sudden arrival of the raider in a British port seemed like having the family skeleton come clattering out of the closet during a formal dinner: Her Majesty's Government had just handed the American Minister a note formally denying British responsibility for the damages done by the *Alabama* and other English-built raiders.

Having reversed her informal policy of naval aid to the Confederacy, the British wanted only to forget the past and to establish a rule which would prohibit neutrals building navies for warring powers. But with the *Shenandoah* floating in the Mersey and the American minister demanding that its crew be turned over to the United States authorities for trial, the past was uncomfortably present.

The British press unhappily editorialized over what to do. The *Times* sniffed haughtily on the morning after the *Shenandoah's* arrival:

> The reappearance of the *Shenandoah* in British waters at the present juncture is an untoward and unwelcome event. . . . It would have been a great relief to ourselves though little to the advantage of the United States had the *Shenandoah* been simply excluded from the Mersey and left to rove the seas till she should fall into the hands of her pursuers.

The *Star* angrily announced its hope that:

. . . if the commander of the *Shenandoah* imagines that in England he is to escape with impunity, the action of her Majesty's government will promptly undeceive him. Waddell and his crew are not belligerents in any proper acceptation of the term. If the professions of Earl Russell of his readiness to enforce the law are not mere words, of course these men must not be permitted to walk abroad unchallenged as if they had been engaged in a meritorious enterprise. . . . It is disheartening to reflect how much the cause of maritime rights has been prejudiced by the fatal apathy we exhibited toward these Confederate cruisers.

The *Pall Mall Gazette* sighed:

Small thanks are due to the commander of the *Shenandoah* for the preference which he has given to Liverpool for the purpose of bringing his cruising to an end. It is some satisfaction to know that he is under the charge of an English officer, but it is most unsatisfactory to remember that we shall now have to say what is to be done with him. . . .

The Tory *Herald* held that:

Even if, for the sake of vengeance on the destroyers of his country, Captain Waddell had gone on burning their ships after he knew that they had accomplished their work, his crime would have been essentially a political one; and Englishmen will never consent to give up political offenders.

The *Telegraph* reasoned hopefully:

The inability of the United States navy to catch this light-heeled enemy is an apt commentary on the pending claims for compensation on account of damages inflicted by Confederate vessels. The claim which the American Government now urges is almost as extravagant as if London policemen were expected to aid those of Paris and New York in repressing crime in those cities.

The *News* managed to get on nearly every side of the question:

The *Shenandoah* has arrived in a British port and surrendered to a British officer. The Americans may be inclined to say that this is as it should be, that it was only fitting her end should be as British as her origin; but we cannot help asking how it is that this cruiser has been able to pursue her course without the least interruption from the navy of the United States. We have heard of her in various parts of the world dealing destruction and scattering dismay among merchantmen, whalers, and other unarmed vessels, but no war-vessel of the United States appears to have molested her. It is possible that the expectation of recovering from this country compensation for the losses resulting from her depredations has made the Government and people of the United States less eager for her capture than they otherwise would have been. If the world generally should come to that conclusion, from observing the impunity which Captain Waddell has so long enjoyed, it would be one of the strongest practical arguments against the admission of such liability as Mr. Seward is just now endeavoring to establish against this country. It is stated that Captain Waddell has forwarded a letter to Lord Russell, the contents of which are at present unknown. . . .

2

While Waddell's letter to Russell moved slowly through channels, the officers and crew were confined to the ship, feeling, in young Mason's words, "every feather like a Christmas goose."

A British gunboat was lashed alongside the raider to prevent her returning to sea. Waddell, who took this precaution as an insult, blamed it on the American Minister. "It was intended to be an offense offered to a defeated but unconquered enemy, to men who had succeeded in disposing of the *Shenandoah* in a way not congenial to the Yankee nation."

Hunt observed that "there was enough uncertainty involving our fate to depress the most buoyant spirits. But sailors seldom quite despond. They generally discover some bright spot in the darkest horizon and are prompt to take courage if their situation is anything short of desperate. As night closed round us, one of the passed midshipmen, with half a dozen of the junior officers at his heels, made his appearance in the steerage and having taken the general ground that so far from having done anything to be ashamed of, we had every reason to be proud of our exploits, he proposed that care be kicked to the wall and all apprehension drowned in a general jubilee.

"It was just the kind of proposition to strike favorably a sailor's ear. Ere long a frolic was inaugurated that gradually extended through almost the entire ship's company. A stranger dropping down among them would have been entirely justified in thinking, from the boisterous hilarity everywhere observable, that we had returned in triumph from some grand expedition, and were celebrating our victories; and had he been told that that noisy, rollicking company were waiting to be handed over to implacable enemies to be tried for their lives, he would have considered the informer either insane or endeavoring to practice upon his credulity."

Captain Paynter, who had taken charge of the *Shenandoah* for the British Government, issued orders that nobody was to leave the ship. Waddell, though no longer with official authority, repeated them to his men. Paynter several times invited Waddell to come on board a British ship for a visit. Waddell refused, explaining that he would not leave the ship until at liberty to go where he pleased, adding, "otherwise, I must be taken out of her as a prisoner."

After the first night at anchor, the ship's company appeared somewhat reduced. Captain Paynter came to Waddell and reported that several men had been seen leaving the vessel. "But," he added pleasantly, "I don't care if the lads do take a run on shore after night as long as I do not know it."

Waddell expressed his regret that anyone had left the ship.

"Oh," said Paynter, "you won't leave the vessel, I know, so it don't matter about the others going on a bit of a lark."

Waddell said he was sure that those who left the ship had no intention of deserting. Waddell was wrong. Desertion was exactly what was contemplated.

"Among the thinking," said Hunt, "the gravest apprehension began to be entertained. There was little else talked of among the officers, and the opinion prevailed that the British authorities, fearing that they would be held responsible for the depredations we had committed, would turn us over as a sort of peace offering to appease the wrath of the United States and it was tacitly understood among us that the time had arrived when each man must look out for himself.

"About nine o'clock in the evening I went on deck, feeling more wretchedly depressed in spirits than I ever remember to have been before or since. A miserable, drizzly rain was falling; in brief, it was the kind of night to make one melancholy under any circumstances. I had firmly resolved that the *Shenandoah* and I should part company that night at all hazards. I had a constitutional objection to ornamenting the yardarm of a Yankee man-of-war, but by the appearance of things I stood a remarkably fair chance of obtaining that elevated position. How was I to effect my escape? We were at anchor in the stream, our decks were closely guarded by the marines and sailors from the *Donegal*, and no boat was allowed to approach us, under severe penalties.

"But the attempt had to be made — at the worst I could but fail. Approaching a marine who was pacing backward and forward near where the accommodation ladder was suspended over the side, I opened a careless conversation with him, and watching my opportunity, slipped into his hands a bottle of the veritable old whiskey we had captured in the Okhotsk Sea.

"The fellow gave me an intelligent glance, pocketed his Bourbon, and marched sedately forward, while I dove down to the wardroom and in a few moments metamorphosed into as genuine an old shellback as ever broke biscuit in a forecastle. As I made my appearance on deck again, the sentry glanced with a half-amused expression at the immense sea boots, oilskin coat, and sou'wester hat which decorated my person; but his attention was conveniently called to something on the opposite side of the deck, and the next moment I was over the side and standing on the lower step of the accommodation ladder, effectually concealed from anyone on board, unless they were looking for me at that particular place.

"A number of small boats were plying in various directions, and one of these passed so near that I was able to speak her without unduly elevating my voice. The man hesitated for some moments, but good nature, with perhaps the hope of a fitting pecuniary reward, finally overcame his prudence. He shot his little craft alongside. I sprang in, and in an instant was gliding shoreward.

"The voyage was accomplished without accident, and ere long I set foot on the landing stage at Liverpool. I gave the boatman two pounds, which left me with eight, the sole proceeds of my thirteen months cruise in the *Shenandoah.* With such feelings of relief and thankfulness as I am unable to describe, I strode up Lime Street in the direction of the Washington Hotel, an inn much frequented by my countrymen.

"As I approached it I saw Mr. Adger, a cotton speculator from Charleston, with whom I had been well acquainted, standing on the steps. I went up to him and extended my hand. He glanced curiously at my outlandish costume, but evidently did not recognize me, which was encouraging, considering the possible necessity of resuming a similar disguise at some future occasion. When I told him my name he grasped my hand with such genuine warmth and gave me such a cordial welcome that I felt I had indeed met a countryman.

"Mr. Adger insisted upon my accompanying him to his hotel, the Adelphi, and I complied without much persuasion. The clerks and attachés of that rather elegant establishment stared in blank amazement when they saw Mr. Adger, whom they well knew, enter the office, yardarm and yardarm with what seemed to be an old salt, fresh from the forecastle, and their astonishment was in no wise abated when he demanded to have me established in the room adjoining his own.

"My friend in the kindness and generosity of his heart would have at once supplied all my needs from his own purse, but I could not bring myself to trespass farther on his bounty than to accept a hat, which I substituted for my sou'wester, and a pair of shoes to replace my sea boots. Under my oilskin, I wore a suit of citizen's clothes, so for the time being I felt under no particular apprehension of drawing upon myself unwelcome scrutiny.

"The next day I began to feel some compunctions of conscience at the way I had left the ship. It was true I had neither flag nor country to claim my service, but it seemed to me on reflection that it would have been more manly to have remained with my brother officers and shared their fate whatever it might be. The more I thought of it the stronger became my conviction, and about ten o'clock I sallied forth from the Adelphi, firmly resolved to go on board again and take my chances with the rest.

"At the landing stage, I encountered Captain North, late of the Confederate Navy, and Mr. Robinson, formerly one of our agents. On learning of my escape and intended return, both gentlemen joined in urging me to desist from my purpose. They argued, and truly, that I could do nothing to aid my companions, many of whom had doubtless ere this adopted similar means of getting out of harm's way. Both were impressed with the notion that the ship's company would be transferred to U.S. Authorities, which simply meant resigning them to summary execution. They recommended me instead of going on board to make a straight wake for Paris.

"It required but a few moments' consideration to see that this was the counsel of wisdom, and there did seem to be a question whether any code of honor would require me to sacrifice myself with my comrades, when all of us were powerless to aid each other.

"Moodily I walked back to the hotel, revolving these things in my mind. Sometimes momentarily congratulating myself that I had acted the part of a sensible man, and again falling back upon my former opinion that it was an act of poltroonery to leave my friends in the hour of danger whether I could render them assistance or not. On gaining the hotel, however, the gratifying rumor reached me that our troubles were soon to be over."

3

Earl Russell, the Foreign Secretary, on receiving Waddell's letter, turned it over to the Crown Law officers. Those worthies wrestled forty-eight hours with the problem, then sent back a decision which, in the words of an American diplomat, "smacked more of convenience than conscience."

Neatly sidestepping the problem of English responsibility for the escape, outfitting, and repair of the raider, the law officers held that as a cruiser she had a right to raid, that as a Confederate vessel the ship should be turned over to

American authorities; but the crew, except British subjects who had violated the Foreign Enlistment Act, would have to be released. If the American Minister believed that acts of piracy had been committed, he would have to bring charges in a British court.

The decision was telegraphed to Liverpool. Captain Paynter chartered a ferry and went at once to the *Shenandoah*. He told Waddell that "only British subjects will be held."

The crew were summoned to the deck. Word of the decision had reached them; they were smiling. Paynter asked Waddell to point out which men were English. Waddell said that he had paid no attention to nationalities but that he assumed that with the exception of the Hawaiians and Swedes, all were American.

Whittle came out with the roll. Paynter and Waddell stood on the poop watching. Whittle called off the names. As each man's name was shouted, the sailor stepped forward. A British officer (named Cheek) asked him his nationality. One after another they answered Virginia, or Louisiana, or Texas, or Georgia, or Alabama. When the roll call was complete not one had boasted of British antecedents. Paynter shrugged. "Everyone can go," he said.

Waddell asked, "We are released unconditionally?"

"Without conditions."

The men scurried below to pick up their belongings. Customs authorities went through the baggage "more for tobacco than treasure." They received from Waddell a bag containing the ship's remaining money – $820.38 in mixed gold and silver.

Waddell gave his tumblers, decanters, bedding, and a few trophies from Ponape and St. Lawrence Island to Captain Paynter for his wife. ("He was a good fellow and faithful to the discharge of his duty.")

Then Waddell, the faithful Paynter, and the crew went aboard the Ferry *Bee*. As they steamed toward Prince George

Landing, Waddell made his last speech. He told the men he "hoped they would always behave as good sailors should."

They responded with three cheers.

Reporters from the Liverpool papers were waiting at the landing. The man from the *Mercury* wrote:

Some of the seamen appeared to have retained a few articles produced during the cruise among the American whaling fleet. Telescopes, looking glasses, pictures, and odd-looking pieces of furniture, resembling cabin fixtures, were rather plentiful. The weight of some of the boxes brought ashore caused a good deal of surprise — for in some instances comparatively small boxes, such as are generally used by sailors, appeared to be so heavy as to require three or four men to carry them.

The sailors seem to be quite in ignorance as to what will be done in regard to paying them, or who are to be their paymasters. We were informed by one of the crew that as yet none of the men have been paid, although some of those who have wives have been drawing their half-pay during the cruise. The man to whom we spoke — an intelligent young fellow belonging to London — said he did not care much for the money as he had friends, but that it would be very hard upon some who "had not a center," and who had wives and families, if they were to go unpaid, after the great risks they had run. He also remarked that he was sure as soon as Captain Waddell heard of the termination of the war he at once ceased his hostile operations in regard to American merchant ships, as he was too much a gentleman to do anything so nefarious as to attack these vessels after having had unmistakable testimony that the Confederacy had been defeated.

The whalers for the most part were not valuable prizes, as they had little money on board; but if they had succeeded in capturing the American mail steamer in the Pacific, which had a large quantity of specie on board, the booty would have been immense. Our informant calculates that each of the crew of the *Shenandoah* would have had something like three thousand dollars. On a doubt being expressed as to the intention of those on board the *Shenandoah* to capture the steamer, the person referred to said there was no question about the matter; that they had positive information as to the course the mail steamer would take; and that it was only the receipt of the news of the close of the war that prevented her capture.

Everything seems to have been conducted on board in an orderly manner, the same discipline being maintained as is observed on board a man-of-war. The vessel on her arrival was a model of cleanliness and order. Her rigging is taut, trim and man-of-war like; every rope and spar is in its proper place and in working order, and from her appearance altogether one would more readily believe she was about to proceed on a voyage than that she had been buffeting about for many months in the Pacific. The seamen speak in terms of admiration of her sailing qualities, asserting that she could sail at the speed of sixteen knots an hour, and that the vessels which were in pursuit of her would have had some difficulty in effecting her capture. The tars were evidently proud of the craft, and when the last batch left one said, "I am sorry to leave the ship, especially as the Confederate flag is not at the gaff, where it has been so long."

The correspondents for the Liverpool *Post* found some less satisfied sailors:

During the last seven months, some of the crew said, the men were particularly anxious to get ashore, as they had become tired of their wild life; and from some of the conversations, it seems pretty certain that aboard the *Shenandoah* the news of the cessation of the late war was believed, however lacking positive information may have been. One unfortunate, who had been taken from a whaler sunk by the *Shenandoah,* seemed glad enough to be quit of her."

Once ashore, the officers went to hotels. Seamen who had friends or families in the vicinity, hurried off to them. The others, accompanied by Southern sympathizers who sang "Dixie" and "The Bonnie Blue Flag" went to the Sailors Home.

The celebration ended at the door. Once inside, the raiders registered as common seamen from a British merchantman. There were Yankee seamen at the home, and though free, the Confederates did not care to call attention to themselves.

The next day the officers gathered in Waddell's suite in George's Hotel. The Captain had received some money from the Confederate Naval Fund set aside by Bulloch for just such an emergency. Each officer was given from fifty to a hundred pounds. Lewis Wiggins, the quartermaster, went to the Sailor's Home and paid off the crew. They received about one shilling in three on their claims.

Men and officers hurriedly left town. Though the British would press no charges, there was a strong possibility that the American Minister would present the Government with complaints strong enough to warrant piracy trials. Charles Dudley, the American Consul in Liverpool, already had detectives following the Liverpool men who had been in the crew.

On Saturday, November 11, 1865, the British Government turned the *Shenandoah* over to the American Consul. That same afternoon, Waddell presented a formal summary of the *Shenandoah's* accomplishments to Bulloch, the chop-whiskered, Confederate agent who had planned the raid. The document ended with a proud recapitulation:

> The *Shenandoah* was actually cruising but eight months after the enemy's property, during which time she made thirty-eight captures, an average of a fraction over four per month. She released six on bond and destroyed thirty-two. She visited every ocean except the Antarctic. She was the only vessel that carried the flag around the world, and she flew it six months after the overthrow of the South. She was surrendered to the British on the 6th November, 1865. The last gun in the defense of the South was fired from her deck on the 28th of June, Arctic Ocean. She ran a distance of 58,000 statute miles and met with no

serious injury during a cruise of thirteen months. Her anchors were on her bows for eight months. She never lost a chase, and was second only to the celebrated *Alabama*. I claim for her officers and men a triumph over their enemies and over every obstacle, and for myself I claim having done my duty.

THERE OUGHT TO BE A LAW

THE release of the *Shenandoah's* crew infuriated Americans. As reported to the public by angry newspaper correspondents, the action seemed to be nothing more than a final act of an enormous British-Confederate conspiracy. The Liverpool representative of Horace Greeley's *Tribune,* writing of the roll call preceding the release of the crew, exclaimed:

> The rogues, how they must have enjoyed it. Fancy Jack Junk shifting his quid to his sinister cheek and responding, 'Wirginia, damn my eyes!' Sawney Bean's 'Soothron citizen — dunna exawcly remember whar.' and Teague O'Gallowglass's, 'Shure, and I'm from New Orleans.' This unsuspecting British government! . . .
>
> The Anglo-Rebels and Tories morally clap the late commander of the *Shenandoah* on the back as 'a hero' and 'a gallant fellow!' and decide 'We are not in any way responsible.'. . .
>
> I am not a bloodthirsty person, but somehow it provokes me to hear it everywhere taken for granted that the United States government oughtn't to arrogate to itself the privilege of capital punishment for treason 'because it's a republic, you know, and not a regular government.'

The crotchety Greeley himself, discounting war talk, scratched out an editorial which went no further than the remark, "If Britain is willing to abide by the precedents she has established, we can bide our time; but it certainly will be unsafe for her to embark in another war."

The New York *Herald,* most widely circulated American paper, with the nationalist truculence which marks mass publications, roared:

> This is an outrage that this country cannot stand from such a source; and unless England repudiates and in the most unqualified way, the act of her pigmy Minister it will so complicate the present disturbed relations of the two countries that their peaceful settlement will not be possible. If we have got to fight, we had better do it right here.

On the opposite coast, where seamen who had been left at Ponape were still being brought back, the San Francisco *Alta California* declared:

> The frozen regions of the Arctic seas are illumined by the bright lights of British neutrality, and covered with the charred remains of American whalers, the unresisting victims of British perfidy.
>
> It is the duty of the Government of the U. S. to its injured citizens to represent their claims, duly authenticated, to the Government of Great Britain. If Britain refuses, the laws of nations and indeed of common sense, point out the remedy which our Government would have the right to adopt: the issuance of letters of marque and reprisal upon British commerce, or an open declaration of war. Let no sickly sentimentality as to the kindred relationship of the people of Great Britain to those of the United States deter our insistence upon national rights.
>
> Our government has long enough borne with insult from some European nations, amongst them England. Now that its hands are free, let it assume some of the dignity and fearlessness which "in days of yore" caused it to be loved, feared, and respected, alternately.

The British Government was neatly spitted by a dilemma: it wanted an international law established which would prevent United States shipyards from equipping a hundred *Shenandoahs* to prey on British commerce when England next went to war, but it also felt it could not admit having done wrong in supplying the South with raiders.

Charles Francis Adams wrote in his diary:

> The original blunder, inspired by the overeagerness to see us divided, has impelled a neutral policy carried to such extremes of encouragement to one belligerent as seemingly to hazard the security of British commerce whenever the country shall become involved in a war. The sense of this inspires the powers of eastern Europe with vastly increased confidence in pursuing their particular objects. It is not difficult to see that whatever views Russia may ultimately have on Constantinople will be much fortified by a consciousness of the diversion which might be made through the neutral ports of the United States against the British commerce to one half of the globe. We lose nothing by the passage of time; Great Britain does.

When Lord Clarendon called on Adams and insisted that during the war Britain had observed a strict neutrality, the American observed sharply that "a similar observation of it, as between two countries so closely adjacent as Great Britain and France, would lead to a declaration of war by the injured party in twenty-four hours." Adams wrote his government advising that nothing be done "to help Britain out of the mess it had got itself in."

At first the Americans asked only that Britain pay for the damage done by the ships built in her yards. But as time passed without settlement, resentment against Britain crystallized. Anglophobia became a political fact exerting its influence over parties, policies, and, naturally, politicians.

From being held responsible only for the damage inflicted

upon individual citizens, Britain came to be held liable for the cost of pursuing the vessels, then for increased shipping rates paid by Americans, and finally for prolonging the war by recognizing the South's belligerency.

At first, British officials and newspapers ridiculed these expanded claims, arguing – probably sincerely – that they must have been advanced only as bargaining points. But before long the moulders of British opinion were warning the public that America meant it. The *Daily News* cautioned:

> . . . against the flippancy with which this question is being treated in some quarters; against the affectation of believing that there is nothing serious in the remonstrances of the American government and the language of the best representatives of American opinion. The Americans may be altogether mistaken, both as to the law and the facts on which they lay their claims; but that they are in earnest in making their claims, as earnest as any country ever was in requiring satisfaction of another, he would be blind who should deny.
>
> It would be a great mistake to ignore the fact that this dispute has assumed a gravity which has not hitherto belonged to it. At the same time, we do not apprehend war as a consequence of these claims, provided only care be taken to treat them in a spirit conformable to the character of both the parties to the dispute. All that the world knows of the action of the Government of the United States assures it that the policy of that Government is one of peace; and it would be an eternal disgrace to both Governments to confess themselves unable to find any but a violent solution of their difference.

In 1868, Charles Francis Adams stepped down from the post he had so admirably filled. He was succeeded by an amiable congressman, Reverdy Johnson, who with good-natured gusto set about cleaning the Augean stable of Anglo-American relations. By January, 1869, "the junketing Mr. Johnson," as the New York *Herald* unkindly called him, had reached an agreement with Lord Clarendon. The proposal was that all claims which had arisen since 1853 would be submitted to arbitration. Although the agreement made no mention of the national claims advanced as a result of Britain's recognition of Southern belligerency, Secretary of State Seward was pleased with the proposed convention. He was almost alone. When the terms of the proposed arbitration were made public, the press screamed that Johnson had sold out to the Anglo-Rebels. The unhappy Reverdy did his cause no good when he attended a Liverpool banquet and shook hands with Laird, the Confederate ram-builder.

In March, the Grant administration took office. The next month the Johnson-Clarendon convention came up for a vote in the Senate. It received one favorable vote, fifty-four unfavorable.

The one-sided debate on the measure was highlighted by an extreme speech by the Chairman of the Foreign Relations Committee, Charles Sumner, who has been called "probably the most intolerant man that American history has ever known." The Senator from Massachusetts estimated Britain's bill at more than two billion dollars. He estimated that the Confederate "hounds of hell"—cruisers—had done $15,000,000 in direct damages, and $110,000,000 by driving commerce from the seas. But beyond this, he said, there was:

> That other damage, immense and infinite, caused by the prolongation of the war. . . . The rebellion was originally encouraged by hope of support from England; it was strengthened at once by the concession of belligerent rights on the ocean; it was fed to the end by British supplies; it was quickened into frantic life with every report from the British pirates; nor can it be doubted that without British intervention the rebellion would have soon succumbed under the well-directed efforts of the National Government. Not weeks or months but years were added in this way to our war, so full of the most costly sacrifice. . . .
>
> The Rebellion was suppressed at a cost of more than four

> thousand million dollars, a considerable portion of which has already been paid, leaving twenty-five hundred millions as a national debt to burden the people. If, through British intervention, the war was doubled in duration, or in any way extended, as cannot be doubted, then is England justly responsible for the additional expenditure to which our country was doomed.

Sumner did not expect the British to hand over two billion dollars. What he and his supporters wanted was Canada. Joseph Medill, founder of the Chicago *Tribune,* had already written Sumner stating flatly that "the only adequate atonement for the injury she inflicted on us in the hour of our adversity [is] the surrender of her North American colonial possessions to our government."

Britain was seriously alarmed. The press came up with paraphrases of "Millions for defense, not one cent for tribute." The British liberal, John Bright, no advocate of the wartime cruiser policy, said that Sumner was "either a fool himself or else thought the English public and their public men to be fools." Ex-Minister Adams said, "The practical effect of this speech is to raise the scales of our demands of reparation so very high that there is no chance of negotiations left, unless the English have lost all their spirit and character."

The picture was complicated by the change of administration. New actors took over the roles of President, Secretary of State, and Minister to England. No one knew where Grant stood on the Alabama Claims (as all U.S. claims for damages done by the cruisers had come to be called), least of all Grant. But he was quoted as being in no hurry for a cash settlement. Rumor had him saying that if Sheridan couldn't take Canada in six weeks he should be cashiered.

The new Secretary of State was Hamilton Fish, of New York, an able, urbane, conservative lawyer-politician, very wealthy, who wanted Canada — but not as much as he wanted peace.

The new Minister, John Lothrop Motley, was a handsome, hotheaded historian, a friend of Sumner's, and about the last man in America for the job. Adams said of him that he expected to represent two powers abroad – Mr. Sumner and the United States Government.

Britain could not tell which of the men determined U.S. policy; neither could they. It was a free-for-all. Within a year Sumner had called the President "a colossus of ignorance," and the Secretary of State "a gentleman in aspect with the heart of a lackey." Grant was seen to shake his fist at Sumner's house. Fish urbanely remarked of Sumner, "I don't like to think the man a deliberate liar, but he certainly makes extraordinary statements and then denies them." Later, not so urbanely, he declared, "I am convinced that he is crazy; vanity, conceit, ambition have disturbed the equilibrium of his mind."

When Sumner howled that "Mr. Fish has insulted the most illustrious citizen of Massachusetts in my person," the Secretary replied that this raised two questions: had he really insulted any citizen of Massachusetts, and was Sumner the most illustrious of them. "The former I deny, the second I doubt."

Motley failed to follow the policies laid down by Fish. He was first suspended, then removed from his post – which gave new offense to Sumner. By 1870, Fish was in firm control of foreign policy. He had decided it should be a policy of peace and speedy settlement. Britain, too, was anxious for an agreement; the new German Army was racing through France, and Russia had torn up the treaty of 1856 which limited the Czar's Navy to the Black Sea. The British Ambassador in Washington warned his government that "although the better-thinking people in America might have regard for the duty of neutrals, there are multitudes of adventurers in this country who would fit out vessels like the *Alabama*, and no government would be able to prevent them from sailing."

Under this stimulus the governments got together. As the price for starting formal negotiations on all differences, Her Majesty's government agreed to express regret specifically for the damage done by the cruisers. Negotiations were carried on by two five-man teams.

Secretary of State Fish was hopeful but not confident. In a letter to America's diplomatic Don Juan, the amorous Dan Sickles, he said, "What may come of it remains to be seen; they promise far, but we are dealing with perfidious Albion. Old Father Ritchie used to say, '*Nous verrons*,' which according to his Latin meant, 'The best trump will take the trick.' A fair and liberal settlement is more to their interest just now than to ours."

Negotiations began on February 24, 1871, in the old Orphan Asylum building where the State Department was housed. They continued two months. On April 23, an agreement was reached. To celebrate, the diplomats ate ice cream and strawberries.

The treaty contained an expression of "the regret felt by Her Majesty's government for the escape, under whatever circumstances, of the *Alabama* and other vessels from British ports, and for the depredations committed by these vessels." It then stated that during the course of the war a neutral government is bound:

> First, to use due diligence to prevent the fitting out, arming or equipping, within its jurisdiction, of any vessel which it has reasonable ground to believe is intended to cruise or to carry on war against a Power with which it is at peace; and also to use like diligence to prevent the departure from its jurisdiction of any vessel intended to cruise or carry on war as above, such vessel having been specially adapted, in whole or in part, within such jurisdiction to warlike use.
>
> Second, not to permit or suffer either belligerent to make use of its ports or waters as the base of naval operations against the

other, or for the purpose of the renewal or augmentation of military supplies or arms, or the recruitment of men.

Thirdly, to exercise due diligence in its own ports and waters, and as to all persons within its jurisdiction to prevent any violation of the foregoing obligations and duties.

The governments agreed to arbitrate the claims on the cruisers on the basis of these three points. Decision was to rest with a five-man tribunal to be selected by the President of the United States, the Queen of England, the King of Italy, the Emperor of Brazil, and the President of the Swiss Confederation.

Grant, who rather liked the idea of what American-built *Shenandoahs* could do to British commerce, expressed an opinion in a cabinet meeting that the neutrality requirements in the treaty might prove a little too stringent. He was not supported and did not press the point. Even Sumner favored the treaty and it was ratified by the Senate, 54 to 12.

Grant appointed Charles Francis Adams as the American member of the tribunal. Bancroft Davis was named manager of the American case; he selected Caleb Cushing, William Evarts, and Morrison Waite as counsels. (Evarts, who was forced on Grant by his friend Fish, distinguished himself by losing his copy of the American case by leaving it in a carriage. The finder sold it to the British Legation. Evarts was for a time known as "the first man to lose a case before opening it.")

The printed cases were presented to the Geneva Tribunal in mid-December, 1871. When the American brief was made public, the national claims for indirect damages were included. Britain was accused of having prolonged the war and was asked to pay for the cost of the struggle after Gettysburg, at seven per cent interest.

Fish intimated that the claims would not be pressed seriously, that they had been inserted "as bars on which the spread eagle might perch." But the British had interpreted the treaty as an American promise not to present the indirect claims. The commissioners who had negotiated the treaty claimed a double cross. Queen Victoria privately told the commissioners that she did not blame them for developments since they had "thought they were treating with gentlemen actuated by honorable feelings and did not suspect a trap." Prime Minister Gladstone told the House of Commons that Britain would not put in arbitration a claim for a sum which only a completely defeated nation would agree to pay.

It was Adams who worked out a compromise. Without actually taking up the matter of indirect claims, the Tribunal announced that such claims were not within its jurisdiction, but that if they were in its jurisdiction the American claims would be rejected. Both sides were satisfied. The Tribunal then began to study claims for actual damage done by the British-built raiders.

During the six months between the presentation of the printed cases and the opening verbal arguments, Bancroft Davis, the American counsel, busied himself buying editors and influencing arbitrators. He paid calls on the neutral members of the Tribunal, flattered them flagrantly, and made certain the American case was translated at once into French so they could all read it.

With the press, he showed a twentieth century talent. Using part of the $250,000 Congress had appropriated for general arbitration expenses, Davis moulded the moulders of opinion. He reported to Fish that:

> I have decided to close an arrangement by which we shut up at least some of the organs which England is trying to control. The list includes all the important political papers except the *Débats* and the *France,* and the *Journal de Paris.* The first two are bought by England; the latter I don't know about. All this costs money but . . . has had a good effect in stiffening public opinion here. The articles which are following are also doing

good. The attacks from England were so steady and so persistent in misrepresentation that public opinion was beginning to set in strongly against us. It is now decidedly turning.

Bancroft bludgeoned all the American consuls to join the publicity campaign. In a highly undiplomatic letter to Fish, he described his efforts:

> I am sorry to say that the Consul General [in Paris] does nothing to help us. He is so overcome with the grandeur of his English friends that he has little heart to say anything against them and for his country. Washburne is outspoken and strong — full of pluck. Jay [at Vienna] is weak as dishwater — needs a strong plaster put to his back every other day. I send with my dispatch today a copy of the last plaster I gave him. It is lamentable to have to use such tools in this work, but I suppose we must take Americans as we find them, and not quarrel with those who love the taste of an English lord's backside.

For ten weeks the arguments went on in a small room in the Geneva City Hall. One after another the Tribunal heard the stories of the British-built cruisers.

Concerning the *Shenandoah,* the British argued that their Government could not have been expected to know she was to be made into a cruiser. They pointed out that she was already at sea when Adams first called attention to her sale to the Confederates. They maintained that when the *Shenandoah* arrived at Melbourne, she could not be confiscated because there was no proof that she was a warship, nor, granted that she was a man-of-war, that she was the *Sea King.* They argued that far from letting her recruit in Australia, the Colonial authorities had overstepped themselves in trying to prevent volunteers from joining her.

The American delegation stuck to its contention that the British were culpable in letting the *Sea King* and the *Laurel* get to sea. Further, they maintained that, once at sea, a ship could not enter a belligerent's navy without first touching at one of the belligerent's ports and that therefore the ship was a pirate and should have been seized at Melbourne. And, under any circumstances, the raider had obviously recruited a large number of men in the Antipodes.

At 12:30 P.M., September 14, 1872, the Tribunal gathered for its final meeting. For a time, only four arbitrators were present – the angry Sir Alexander Cockburn of Britain kept the crowd and his confreres waiting nearly an hour. At last he arrived. The meeting was called to order. The secretary, M. Favrot, stood to read the 2500 words of the report.

By a unanimous vote the five members had held Britain guilty of neglect in the escape of the *Alabama;* by four to one, in the escape of the *Florida,* and:

> . . . whereas, with respect to the vessel called the *Shenandoah,* it results from all the facts relative to the departure from London of the merchant vessel the *Sea King* and to the transformation of that ship into a Confederate cruiser under the name *Shenandoah* near the island of Madeira, that the Government of Her Britannic Majesty is not chargeable with any failure, down to that date, in the use of all diligence to fulfill the duties of neutrality;
>
> But whereas it results from all the facts connected with the stay of the *Shenandoah* at Melbourne, and especially with the augmentation which the British Government itself admits to have been clandestinely effected on her force, by the enlistment of men within that port, that there was negligence on the part of the authorities of that place.
>
> For these reasons,
>
> The tribunal is unanimously of opinion
>
> That Great Britain has not failed by act or omission "to fulfill any of the duties prescribed by the three rules of Article VI in the Treaty of Washington or by the principles of law not inconsistent therewith" in respect to the vessel called the *Shenandoah* during the period of time anterior to her entry into the port of Melbourne;

And by a majority of three to two voices, the tribunal decided that Great Britain has failed, by omission, to fulfill the duties prescribed by the second and third rule aforesaid, in the case of this same vessel, from and after her entry into Hobson's Bay, and is therefore responsible for all acts committed by that vessel after her departure from Melbourne on the 18th day of February 1865.

For damages done by the three cruisers.

. . . The tribunal, making use of the authority conferred upon it by articles VII of the said treaty, by a majority of four voices to one awards to the United States a sum of $15,000,000 in gold as the indemnity to be paid by Great Britain to the United States. . . . And in accordance with the terms of Article XI of the said treaty the tribunal declares that "all the claims referred to in the treaty as submitted to the tribunal are hereby fully, perfectly, and finally settled.

The settlement was neither full, perfect, nor final as far as the British arbiter was concerned. The moment the clerk had closed the reading, the English delegate arose, grabbed his hat, and rushed from the crowded hall out into the sunlit street that was hung with British, American, Swiss, Italian, and Brazilian flags. He did not sign the award. Later he wrote an angry book denouncing the award and his fellow arbitrators. Bancroft Davis replied with a book which outmatched the Briton's in anger and invective.

But the public on both sides of the Atlantic seemed satisfied. The British were glad to remove the threat of American-built commerce raiders, and the Americans were glad to have the British proved guilty.

"We are quite content with the Geneva award," Fish purred. "It decides that 'Great Britain was culpable.' That is the great point on which our people had any feeling. The amount awarded has been of secondary consideration. . . ."

A year later, the British Ambassador, Sir Edward Thornton, visited Fish at the State Department. Taking a seat, he said, "I believe my government owes the United States a sum of money which it is my purpose to pay today." He took two papers from his billfold and, after asking Fish for a pen, said, "I will soon settle this little outstanding indebtedness."

Thornton handed the Secretary a certificate of deposit with the Treasurer of the United States for $15,500,000. Fish signed the receipt.

The cruise of the *Shenandoah* had been paid for.

EPILOGUE

THE bitterness of the final months of the *Shenandoah's* cruise continued to ferment in the memories of her officers.

Waddell learned, soon after his arrival in England, that his wife was under bond not to leave the country. He took a small house in the suburbs of Liverpool and sent her word to come to him regardless of restrictions. In a letter to a friend he explained:

> I am now in exile, but far from being a ruined man. I won't go to sea any more if I can help it. The feeling shown toward me through the restriction placed on my wife is decided. It is just the feeling I like, though the tyranny to her is humiliating to the nature of man. I have written to her to release her bondsmen and inform the government that she owes her allegiance to her husband. As the case now stands, I do not think the bond worth the paper it is written on. In a court of law I know it would fail. . . .
>
> I had, of course, a very anxious time, painfully anxious, because the officers set a bad example to the crew. Their conduct was nothing less than mutiny. I was very decided with some of them; I had to tell one officer I would be captain or die on the deck, and the vessel should go into no other port than Liverpool. So ended my trouble with applications and complaints from the officers. The men behaved nobly, and stood firmly to their decision.

> So ends my naval career, and I am called a 'pirate'! I made New England suffer, and I do not regret it. I cannot be condemned by any honest, thinking man. I surrendered the vessel to the British Government, and all are unconditionally released. My obstinacy made enemies among some of the officers, but now they inwardly regret their action in the Cape Town Affair.

The friend turned the letter over to the Mobile *News*, which published it. Waddell's officers received clippings from their friends. Hunt, who was in Paris, writing an account of the voyage for a British publishing house, saw the letter. He wrote into his final chapter a violent attack on his former commander, accusing him of appropriating half of the money set aside by Bulloch to pay the *Shenandoah's* officers and crew:

> It is exceedingly painful for a sailor to write such things concerning a commander under whom he has served. Had Captain Waddell been content with simply enriching himself at the expense of those who shared the toils and perils of that cruise, which has made his name famous, I should have been silent, for the credit of the service to which I had the honor to belong, but when, after all his officers left England, and he therefore felt secure from all personal chastisement, he ventured to publish that atrocious libel concerning their honor and courage, I could not in justice to myself and my associates do less than exhibit the man to the world in his true colors.

The passage of time and the burgeoning legend of the lost cause threw a softening halo around the *Shenandoah*, its skipper, and its crew. Bulloch, in his memoirs of Confederate activities aboard, made no mention of Hunt's charges. He gave Waddell a clean bill of financial health.

Young Mason, who spent a year in Paris and later tried his hand at farming in the Argentine before returning to America, wrote a brief account of the cruise, in which the captain seems more a model of Annapolis virtue than a man.

Whittle, in a pamphlet published in 1895, said of all the officers:

> These men were not politicians, but when the war clouds gathered felt bound by every sense of duty, love, and devotion, many of them against their judgment as to the judiciousness of disruption, and all of them against their professional hopes, aspirations, and pecuniary interests, when their mother states withdrew, to rally to their standard, resigned and tendered their services. They were accepted, and given commissions properly signed by the Executive, and confirmed by the Congress of the Confederate States. No more loyal men lived on earth. Let no slanderous tongues or libelous pens impugn their motives. Let not their reputation for purity of purpose, as they saw their duty, be handed down to posterity with any stain, but let their children have perpetuated in their minds and hearts the fact that their fathers were neither knaves, fools, cowards, nor traitors.

Dr. McNulty, Whittle's old enemy, describing the cruise in the Atlanta *Constitution*, "indignantly denied as a base lie that Captain Waddell ever put a man in irons because he would not join our ship. James I. Waddell was a gentleman and would never stoop to such conduct." McNulty then dipped his brush in purple and painted a prose picture of the *Shenandoah's* arrival in England:

> Pilot asks us to show our flag. We say we have no flag. Then answers the servant of the nations, "Cannot go on board your ship." Hurried consultation, an anxious exchange of inquiring looks — what shall we do now — we have but one flag — shall we raise it?
>
> It was the flag to which we had sworn allegiance. Shall we lift it once more to the breeze, in defiance of the world — if needs be — and defying all, be constant to that cause which we had sworn to maintain until we knew there was no Con-

federacy, and that ours was in truth a Lost Cause? We will, say all hearts with one acclaim. And let this pilot, or any other, refuse to recognize us if they will.

Then, for the last time, was brought up from its treasured place below the sacred banner of the fair South, to wave its last defiant wave and flap its last ensanguined flap against the winds of fate, before going forever upon the page of history. Out upon the free day it flashed, and the far shores of England seemed to answer its brave appeal — that the banner that had led 1,000,000 men to many victorious battles should now have one more and final recognition, should once more be recognized a flag among the flags of nations. The grim old sea-dog tossing his boat at stern beholds go up the outlawed banner! He sees it floating in the wild, free air and anticipates his England's decision that it shall be recognized for this last time. He calls for a line, swings himself over the old warship's side, and up the noble Mersey, thirteen months after departing from the Thames and just six months lacking four days after the war ended, sailed the Confederate ship of war *Shenandoah.*

And during the seventies, Waddell concluded his commentary on the voyage, "The Last to Surrender," with a passage which added to the legend and was, in addition, an apology to his subordinates:

One word of the noble men who were officers under my command. The circumstance of age and rank alone, not superior merit in devotion to our cause, made me their commander. . . .

To each and all of them I shall ever feel bound by the strongest ties of personal and professional attachment. We received our little vessel with the same high hopes; we encountered in our cruise the same dangers; and we were finally overwhelmed in the same great sorrow at the loss of our country. Gentlemen by family and cultivation, naval officers by education and preference, happily at a period of life when they can without difficulty leave off old and adopt new habits of life, which men of riper years never overcome, they found themselves exiles in a foreign land without a home or government, and by the persevering malevolence of the U. S. authorities excluded from all avenues of professional advance in foreign lands. Some of them have sought to establish themselves in South America and others in Mexico, but wherever they may be or in whatever pursuit engaged, I desire them to feel that although their names may not be preserved by the naval records of a Government, that their late commander in the Confederate service, whose duty it was made by position and circumstance to judge, has borne testimony to their having merited by their devotion and conduct, the grateful regard and remembrance of the people it was their pride to serve.

2

In 1870 Waddell was back in Annapolis with his wife, Ann. (Two years before, the Bulloch brothers, Irvine and James, had returned in disguise to visit their sister and her son, little Theodore Roosevelt, who wrote of the rebels in his autobiography.)

Waddell did not remain landbound. In 1875 he became captain on the Pacific Mail Line, largely British owned, which operated ships running from San Francisco to Japan and Australia. In 1877, while steaming north along the Mexican coast, in waters the *Shenandoah* had cruised, he ran the *San Francisco* onto a rock. A fifty-foot hole was ripped below the water line. Waddell maneuvered the sinking ship to within three miles of shore, supervised the evacuation of the 420 passengers, and was the last man to leave her. Less than fifty yards from the ship when she went under, he was almost sucked down with her. Ironically, the rock that claimed the *San Francisco* was on no charts. It had been discovered in 1861, but because of the confusion at the start of the war, the report was overlooked.

After the loss of the steamer, Waddell retired from the

Merchant Marine. He was named commander of the state boats policing the Maryland oyster beds. His flagship was an old police boat manned by ten men and armed with two howitzers.

One night the boat surprised a fleet of oyster thieves raiding the beds. Waddell called on the pirates to strike their colors. They laughed at him. The howitzers opened fire. One boat was sunk, three were driven ashore, and three were captured. It was Waddell's last battle.

He died on March 15th, 1886. The Maryland State Legislature adjourned in his honor.

3

After the British turned the *Shenandoah* over to the United States, the American Consul in Liverpool hired a merchant captain, T. F. Freeman, to sail her to New York.

Freeman took on a crew of sailors from the Liverpool waterfront. Again the black-hulled vessel put to sea. But the winter weather in the North Atlantic, which had so worried Waddell's subalterns, caught up with her the first day out of port.

Mason, in London at the time, heard she was in distress and "prayed that she might sink." She did not. Badly battered, she limped back to Liverpool minus most of her canvas.

Freeman refused to have anything more to do with her. Dudley, the Consul, petitioned the Navy to send four officers to command her. The admiral in charge of the European squadron refused to allow his officers to supervise a civilian crew.

For months the ship lay idle in Liverpool Harbor. Then the Consul received permission to sell her at auction. The Sultan of Zanzibar bought her for $108,000 – roughly a fourth the price the Confederates had paid. His original purpose was to use her as a yacht, but for reasons known only to the island monarch and his chancellor of exchequer she was soon returned to the tea trade for which she had been built.

In 1879, the copper-plated teak of her hull was ripped open by a coral reef during a storm in the Indian Ocean. The *Shenandoah* foundered. Five of her crew survived – four lascars and an Englishman.

BIBLIOGRAPHY

STATEMENT OF SOURCES WITH AFTERWORD, WSU PRESS EDITION, 1995

During World War Two, I had what I now consider the good fortune to be stationed in the Aleutian Islands. In a letter to my wife I asked her to send a history of "the chain," as the string of islands separating the North Pacific Ocean from the Bering Sea were called. She replied there was no history of the Aleutians and suggested I write one. When I pointed out the absence of libraries and archives in the Aleutians she deluged me with material she unearthed at the University of Washington. Her research eventually resulted in a book the publishers, rejecting my working title of "Those Goddam Aleutians," called *Bridge to Alaska*.

Rosa's research included references to the C.S.S. *Shenandoah* and its attack on the whaling fleet north of the Aleutians. It was the first I had heard of the voyage. When the war ended, I was by mistake transferred to the Pentagon. The arrival of an unrequested private first class perplexed the Signal Corps staff but, noticing that I had as a civilian been employed as an editor at *Time* and *CBS World News* and had been published in national magazines such as *Esquire* they assigned me to the staff of the Chief Signal Officer and set me to writing citations of merit for people they wished to receive medals. I took this as a scholarship grant and set out to learn more about the cruise of the Confederate raider.

Rosa and I spent six months mining data from old books and unpublished documents. It was good digging: we struck several untapped veins. And never were facts unearthed in more pleasant surroundings: the various reading rooms of the Library of Congress, the deep cushioned library of the National Archives, and Jefferson Davis's fine study in the former White House of the Confederacy.

To the staffs of all the libraries we frequented, I owe more thanks than I can possibly express. And if I single out Miss India Thomas and Miss Eleanor Brockenbrough of the Confederate Memorial Literary Society for especial thanks, it is because the warmth of their feeling for the men of the *Shenandoah*, the depth of their knowledge, and the casualness of their generosity with time and information stood out in a group where such virtues were commonplace.

I wish to express appreciation, too, to Charles Olson for suggesting several profitable lines of research and for his editorial advice; and to Howard and Judith Daniel, who helped in many ways.

In the vast amount of uncataloged material on the *Alabama Claims* cases, stored in the National Archives, my wife found the reports submitted by the masters and men of the ships destroyed and ransomed by the *Shenandoah*. This material, which to our knowledge had not been presented before, included reports on the *Brunswick*, *Catherine*, *Congress*, *Covington*, *Edward Carey*, *Euphrates*, *General Williams*, *Harvest*, *Hector*, *Hillman*, *Isabella*, *James Maury*, *Jireh Swift*, *Lizzie M. Stacey*, *Martha*, *Milo*, *Nassau*, *Nile*, *Nimrod*, *Sophia Thornton*, *Susan Abigail*, *Waverly*, and *William Thompson*.

The reports of American consular officials in major seaports also were freighted with a rich cargo of material about the *Shenandoah*. Among those studied were files from Rio de Janeiro, Bahia and Petropolis, Brazil; Panama City; Santiago de Chile; Callao, Peru; St. Pierre, Martinique; Montevideo, Uruguay; Honolulu, Hawaii; Liverpool and London; Cape Town; Melbourne and Sydney.

The naval records section of the National Archives yielded information on the pursuit of the *Shenandoah*, some Confederate military correspondence, an unpublished autobiography of Captain Waddell, and the military records of the Annapolis men aboard the rebel.

The Library of the Confederacy in Richmond is the repository of the unpublished journal of Charles Edward Lining, the ship's doctor, and the diary of John Thompson Mason, a junior officer. There is also a copy of the ship's log, the original of which has been lost from the Naval Files in Washington. (An abstract of the log is published in the official record of the war.)

BIBLIOGRAPHY

Several of the *Shenandoah*'s officers published accounts of the raider's operations. The first to appear was *The Shenandoah, or the Last Confederate Cruiser*, by Cornelius E. Hunt in 1867; it was reprinted in 1910 as Extra No. 12 of "The Magazine of History with Notes and Queries."

Extracts from Captain Waddell's notes on the voyage are included in Series I, Vol. 3, of *The Official Records of the Union and Confederate Navies in the War of the Rebellion: The Operations of the Cruisers from April 1, 1864 to December 30, 1865*, edited by Lieutenant Commander Richard Rush, U.S.N., and Mr. Robert H. Woods, and published in 1896 by the Government Printing Office.

In 1897, Volume XXV of the Southern Historical Society Papers included an article, "The Career of the *Shenandoah*," by John Grimball, which was largely a reprint of a newspaper story which first appeared in the Charleston, S.C., *Sunday News* on February 3, 1895.

In August, 1898, *Century Magazine* carried John Mason's "The Last of the Confederate Cruisers."

The final account by a former officer to be published was William Whittle's privately printed "Cruises of the Confederate States Steamers *Shenandoah* and *Nashville*" in 1910. All of these books are available at the Library of Congress.

The most fruitful of the newspapers consulted were the San Francisco *Alta California* and the New Bedford *Whalemen's Shipping List and Merchant's Transcript*, both of which devoted much space to the operations of the raider. Other papers studied profitably were the New York *Times*, New York *Herald*, New York *Tribune*, Baltimore *Sun*, London *Times*, London *Illustrated News*, *Pall Mall Gazette*, Liverpool *Post*, and Liverpool *Mercury*. *Harper's Illustrated Weekly* also had some reports on the voyage.

The Secret Service of the Confederate States in Europe, by James D. Bulloch, Naval Representative of the Confederate States during the Civil War, in two volumes (New York: G.P. Putnam's Sons, 1884), gives interesting information on the finances of the voyage.

The other major sources of information about the cruise are the published briefs of the United States and British governments for presentation at the Geneva Tribunal.

Since the original publication of my book in 1948, several accounts of the voyage have appeared, adding significant details to the story of the cruise and estimates of its importance. Especially valuable are John R. Bockstoce, *Whales, Ice, and Men: The History of Whaling in the Western Arctic* (Seattle: University of Washington Press, 1986), and Chester G. Hearn, *Gray Raiders of the Sea: How Eight Confederate Warships Destroyed the Union's High Seas Commerce* (Camden, Maine: International Marine Publishing, 1992).

Hearn's book contains much fresh information about the *Shenandoah's* early captures in the Atlantic and her stay in Australia. As to impact of destruction wrought by the Confederate raiders, he concludes:

"Although the payments of indemnity helped individual cases in some small way, they failed to revive the moribund American carrying trade. The United States won the Civil War but Great Britain won undisputed dominance of maritime commerce—for a very small sum, and without a shot fired. Her Majesty's victory was won by her civilian shipyards, aided by James Dunwoody Bulloch.

"The victory lasted nearly 80 years."

John Bockstoce's chapter titled "Civil War in Bering Straits" adds much to my account of the outfitting of the *Shenandoah*. He concludes that "The *Shenandoah* had no effect on the outcome of the war. Even if she had been successful in 'utterly destroying' the Arctic fleet . . . it is unlikely that the act would have caused more than hardship. By that time, the whaling industry was not vital to the North's existence."

Bockstoce ends his account with a moving quotation from Captain Waddell. This excerpt puts in perspective Waddell's distaste for the work patriotism compelled him to do (I present the full account on page 63):

"When we see a great vessel rolling lonely at sea, her masts gone, her gear loose and adrift, and sheets of foaming sea pouring in and out of her helpless sides . . . [p]ractical and unimaginative people may say, what difference does it make to the ship? but no sailor will listen to that . . . There is life in the craft from the time she leaves the ways into the tide until the hour when her timbers are laid on the sand or rocks, or, the saddest of all, in the ship-broker's yard."